Books That Heal

SO-ABA-855

DATE DUE

FEB 0 7 2005		
JAN 1 0 2005		

Demco, Inc. 38-293

Books That Heal
A Whole Language Approach

Carolyn Mohr, Dorothy Nixon, Shirley Vickers

Illustrated
by
Linda East

1991
TEACHER IDEAS PRESS
A Division of
Libraries Unlimited, Inc.
Englewood, Colorado

TEACHER IDEAS PRESS
A Division of Libraries Unlimited, Inc.
P.O. Box 3988
Englewood, Colorado 80155-3988

Library of Congress Cataloging-in-Publication Data

Mohr, Carolyn
   Books that heal : a whole language approach / Carolyn Mohr,
Dorothy Nixon, Shirley Vickers.
   xiv, 283 p. 22x28 cm.
   Includes indexes.
   ISBN 0-87287-829-5
   1. Bibliotherapy for children. I. Nixon, Dorothy. II. Vickers,
Shirley. III. Title.
RJ505.B5M64 1991
618.92'89166--dc20   90-20784
                                    CIP

Contents

Island of the Blue Dolphins — Continued

DEATH

DIFFERENCES

DIVORCE

POVERTY

RELATIONSHIPS

SELF-CONCEPT

STORYTELLING AND READING ALOUD

Preface

Bibliotherapy is a sensitive method of guiding children toward problem solving and coping in their personal lives. In a comfortable setting and in an objective climate, helpful discussions occur. The use of fiction is encouraged because the group can maintain an emotional distance by discussing characters' problems instead of personal problems. The use of role-play and creative dramatics are approaches to this integration of personal and fictional problem solving and modeling. The basic components of bibliotherapy are use of many different media including literature, increasing self-esteem, a synthesis of societal values into the behavior of the group, and a careful choice of literature with active listeners.

Instructors have an advantage due to the large variety of fiction and nonfiction works that deal with personal problems. The majority of these books offer models of coping insights and methods of adjustment to the developmental stages in a child's life. Discussing the outcomes of strategies that are presented aids in appropriate action and discernment of other people's problems.

Whole language emphasizes *real* reading and writing. What better focus than to experience purposeful reading and writing on the *real* problems of children? Thus, the books the authors have chosen address the following problem areas of today's students: coping, death, differences, divorce, poverty, relationships, self-concept, and storytelling and reading aloud.

Introduction

The literature guides in this publication can be used to promote self-understanding through bibliotherapy. Through the methods of bibliotherapy, children can identify with others who have coped with similar situations.

By using all types of materials and approaches, students have more opportunity to interact with the literature. Each literature guide in this book is divided into questions and activities using the following format.

Literal Thinking. Questions and activities that encourage recall of specific facts.

Interpretive Thinking. Questions and activities that encourage inferences about the literature and application to life experiences.

Creative Thinking. Questions and activities that encourage higher levels of creativity through drama, storytelling, poetry, and discussion. Students plan, develop, produce, organize, and originate responses.

Critical Thinking. Questions and activities that encourage students to make judgments and evaluate what they have read.

The additional activities section includes a multidimensional array of activities based upon the reading selections. Areas included are visual art, creative writing, drama, music, social studies, and science. The activities may be used as models for original activities developed by the teacher or facilitator or may be selected as appropriate for group or individual needs. A variety of instructional method examples are given below.

Working with Groups. The story summary at the beginning of each unit provides an aid to deciding on the topic or theme in which to consolidate cooperative teams. Both webbing formats may be utilized for vocabulary study along with the search-a-word and crossword puzzle exercises and in creative writing sessions. The examples provided can be used as models for student creations.

Working with Resource People. Professional storytellers, counselors, and professionals in a specific area can be a great benefit to the teacher and the librarian. An additional written resource guide is the annotated bibliography found at the end of each section.

Contracts. Interaction with bibliotherapeutic literature through independent or partner reading approaches promotes self-motivated learning while providing feedback for the instructors. Bulletin boards can be assembled either by the teacher or facilitator or included in individual and group contracts.

Facilitators. This work is designed to be used by people such as counselors, teachers, librarians and social workers who are knowledgeable and do not address personal problems too deeply, but provide a comfortable climate for discussion. Summaries of the included books are quick references to aid in choosing the most appropriate literature for the facilitators to use for group and individual needs.

For additional information on bibliotherapy, readers may want to contact the following organizations.

The American Library Association Bibliotherapy Forum. This organization publishes a quarterly publication that provides information on bibliotherapy activities. Contact:

Lethene Parks
Bibliotherapy Forum
8520 State Road
302 N.W. Gig Harbor, WA 98335

N.A.P.T. The National Association of Poetry Therapy. This association publishes a newsletter that offers information for people interested in poetry therapy.

N.A.P.T. Newsletter
8839 Tuckerman Lane
Potomac, MD 20854

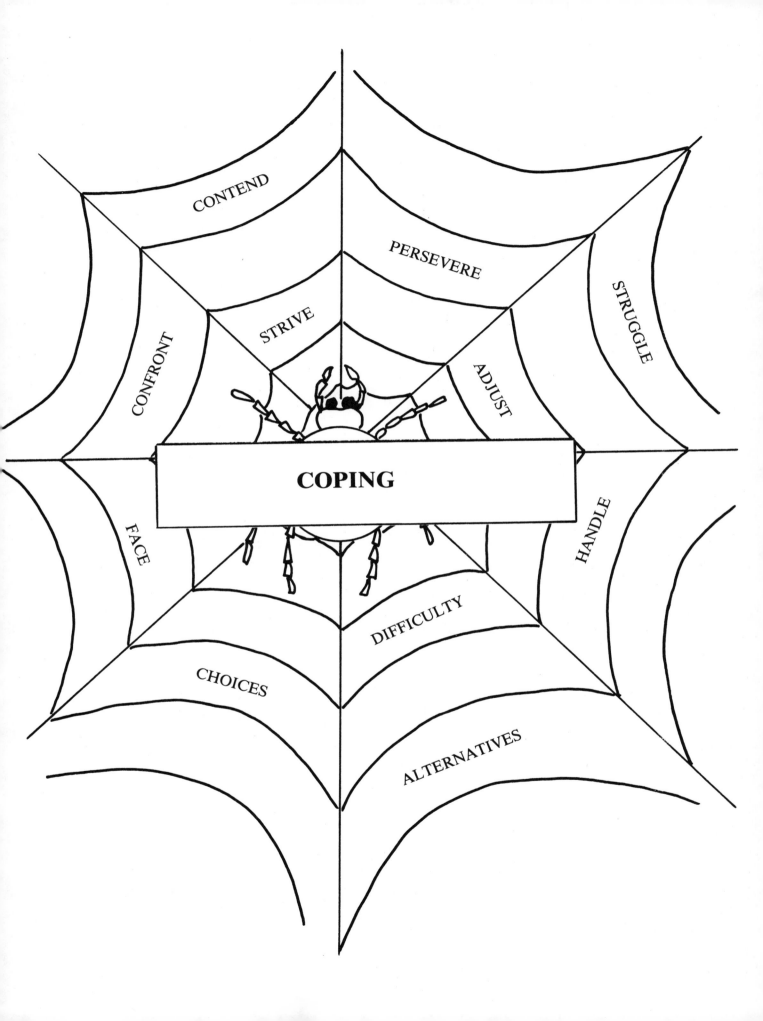

The Silent Storm

Marion Marsh Brown
Ruth Crone

The Silent Storm

by

Marion Marsh Brown and
Ruth Crone

Abingdon Press, 1963

The story of Anne Sullivan is about a skillful, determined, and spirited person. As a child, she felt a burning desire to learn to read. Despite extreme poverty and neglect, through sheer determination and willpower she realized her dream.

Because Anne had experienced emotional and intellectual deprivation, she was particularly empathetic to Helen Keller's problems. Their magic meeting opened the world for Helen and became the prime reason for Anne's existence. The goals and achievements of both women are without parallel in a time when education for the handicapped was in its infancy.

This is an inspiring account of a courageous woman's life of service, and an impressive tribute to the meaning of *teacher*.

DISTRAUGHT

BITTERLY

GLIB

HOPE

DEJECTED

FEAR

RESPONSIBILITY

RELIEF

BATTLE

ARGUMENTS

TENSION

SUCCESS

The Silent Storm

QUALMS

PEACE

FAILURE

DEJECTEDLY

NERVOUSNESS

TEDIOUS

MISFIT

EXPLOIT

PROGRESS

CUM LAUDE

RETICENT

Chapters 1 through 6

Literal Thinking:

1. How did Anne convince the authorities at Tewsbury Almhouse that Jimmy should stay with her?

2. What was the intense desire that Anne had?

3. Who helped Anne get into Perkins?

4. At what age did Helen Keller become blind, deaf, and mute? What was the special significance of this age?

5. What did the children at Perkins buy for Anne to give to Helen?

6. Why did the priest feel Anne's sight might be helped?

Interpretive Thinking:

1. Analyze the statement "Might ... just Might sculpt a soul."

2. How did taking care of Jimmy help Anne handle her own fears?

3. People called Anne Sullivan attractive, but her reaction was always "If it weren't for my eyes." Explain what she meant by the statement.

4. Why did Anne run away from Father Barbara?

5. How could a child with Anne's background have the determination and spirit to pursue her education?

6. There is a saying "Turn lemons into lemonade." How did Anne's positive outlook on life help her to do this?

7. Anne's treasured books opened new worlds for her and brought her into the company of great minds. How has reading done this for you? Explain.

Creative Thinking:

1. Draw an illustration of what Anne's and Jimmy's life at Tewsbury was like, perhaps using charcoal pencil and dark colors. Draw a contrasting illustration with bright colors of Anne's version of her ideal home.

2. Anne wanted desperately to read. Reading was a lifelong joy because it enabled her to pursue subjects of great interest to her. Tell about a subject in which you are vitally interested and about a book that has been a treasure in that area of interest.

3. Describe what it would feel like to never feel so much as a penny in your fist.

4. Role-play Anne telling parts of the story, courtesy of Telly, to the other girls. Improvise the sections she did not hear.

Critical Thinking:

1. What would be the greatest problem if you could not see?

2. Why did Anne not want to leave the poorhouse?

3. What do you think would have happened to Anne had she not met Father Barbara and Tilly?

4. Anne felt her experiences had given her a special kinship with Helen Keller. Relate a time you were most able to help someone because you had experienced a similar situation.

5. Evaluate why the difficulties and problems that hounded Anne through her life affected her personality. Was it a positive or negative influence? Discuss.

Chapters 7 through 12

Literal Thinking:

1. How was Anne honored at Perkins for her high grade average?

2. What were Helen Keller's three handicaps referred to in Mr. Anagnos's letter?

3. Why did Anne choose Mansfield as a middle name?

4. Describe Helen when Anne first arrived.

5. What was the name of the doctor the Keller family consulted?

6. What was the first thing Anne attempted to teach Helen?

7. What proved that Helen was learning to obey Anne?

Interpretive Thinking:

1. Helen's actions showed that her family had trained her very little, which was due to their inability to communicate with her. How would the lack of discipline affect her training with Anne?

2. From James Keller's reactions to the mention of his sister Helen, what can you surmise about his feelings for her?

3. Anne's world had been opened by people who cared. How did the care she had experienced influence her decision to go to Helen?

4. How did Mrs. Hopkins's background influence her rapport with Anne Sullivan?

5. Why did Anne admire the hermit on the path? Discuss.

Creative Thinking:

1. As Helen Keller, give an interview to a reporter about your initial attitude toward your teacher and her methods to teach you.

2. Present Anne's valedictory speech as she would have delivered it.

3. Role-play the scene between Anne and the old hermit.

4. Have you ever felt stage fright like Anne? Brainstorm methods to overcome it.

5. Role-play the scene in which Anne taught Helen not to grab food from plates.

Critical Thinking:

1. How was teaching and living with Helen Keller what Anne termed *real* service as opposed to that of working in an institution?

2. What was the most valuable lesson Mrs. Hopkins taught Anne about channeling her pride and about real happiness?

3. What were the most important elements in Anne's personality that would make a lesson taught by her exciting?

4. Mrs. Keller was concerned for her daughter's happiness and also upset with her behavior. Which of the two feelings should take precedence?

5. Do you agree that "the only real happiness we find in this world is through what we do for others"? Discuss.

6. Why was it so important to gain Helen's trust and love before attempting to teach her?

Chapters 13 through 18

Literal Thinking:

1. What was the form of communication used between Helen and Anne?

2. What was the first word Helen Keller understood?

3. Which person was the slowest to accept Anne and her teaching methods?

4. What was Helen's greatest achievement according to Mrs. Keller?

5. What were the best gifts Anne received for her "first" Christmas?

6. When did Anne feel more like a person than any other time in her life?

Interpretive Thinking:

1. Explain why the change in Helen was good for the whole family.

2. Why did the ability to communicate produce such a difference in Helen? What does this suggest about the reasons behind her previous behavior?

3. What was the one factor that limited Anne's helping Helen?

4. Have you ever felt your destiny was to do a certain thing or be with a certain person, as Anne felt about Helen and her education? Share with a partner.

5. What would you have done if the Perkins Board of Trustee had reprimanded you as it had Anne Sullivan?

Creative Thinking:

1. Design a booklet for Helen of objects she can feel to aid her communication. Use materials that promote the sense of touch, such as fur fabric or sandpaper.

2. Research methods of communication among different cultures: smoke signals, the Cherokee alphabet, and so on. Draw illustrations of the examples.

3. Teach someone a skill such as knitting without speech or sight. Write one word that describes the experience.

4. As Helen, write a letter home to your mother telling about life at the Institute.

5. Create a radio or TV interview with Anne and Helen. Ask each her candid impressions of the teaching and learning process she has experienced.

Critical Thinking:

1. Why did Anne refuse to marry Mr. Anagnos?

2. Why is imitation such a strong method of teaching? Discuss.

3. Compare the technique Anne wanted to use with Helen to that preferred by Captain Keller. Which do you feel would be more successful? Explain your opinion.

4. Once Mr. Anagnos started to talk in a personal way to Anne, she became very uncomfortable. What she thought she wanted was not actually what she wanted when faced with the choice. Relate a time when you thought you knew what you wanted, but once it was within your grasp, you felt differently. Share with a partner.

Chapters 19 through 24

Literal Thinking:

1. Why was Anne's salary discontinued?

2. Explain the discovery Anne made in teaching the deaf.

3. Why was Harvard eliminated as a possible college?

4. How was Helen's tuition fee being paid?

5. Why was Mr. Gilman discouraging Helen from finishing Cambridge too quickly?

6. What did Helen create that gave her great satisfaction?

Interpretive Thinking:

1. Dr. Bell counseled Anne to remember the great service she had done for Helen when charged with plagiarism. Have you ever had difficulty remembering self-worth when criticized? Share with a partner.

2. Why was Anne particularly proud to speak to the Association to Promote the Teaching of Speech to the Deaf?

3. Why did Mrs. Keller give Mr. Gilman complete charge of Helen?

4. Why did Anne want only "oblivion"?

5. Why did the problem over the story *The Frost King* alter Anne's feelings toward Mr. Anagnos?

6. Do you feel Anne should not have been allowed to read the examination questions to Helen? Why or why not?

Creative Thinking:

1. Express what Anne felt when Mr. Gilman told her to leave. Perform your interpretation for the class.

2. Experience conflict in role-play. As cousin Anastasia, admit to recognizing Anne. As Anne, ask why she treated you as she did. Create a resolve for your role-play.

3. What if Helen had not passed her entrance exam? How would this have changed the story?

4. As partners, one blindfolds the other—one leads, the other follows. Go around the classroom, down the hall, and so on. Return and switch roles. Compare feelings and impressions.

5. Create a Braille alphabet. Divide the paper and use a sharp object to make openings necessary to form each letter.

6. There are various forms of sign language. One is the traditional which spells each word, the other involves symbols to represent words. Invite speakers to explain each method. Learn words using both methods.

Critical Thinking:

1. Evaluate the level of Helen's intelligence judging from the way she has reacted to learning. Relate examples from the book.

2. As a class, discuss Mr. Gilman, the telegram, and Anne Sullivan. Predict what will happen.

3. Had the silent story within Anne Sullivan created more positive attitudes such as empathy for others or negative ones such as inadequacy? Debate with supportive opinions.

Chapters 25 through 30

Literal Thinking:

1. Why did Anne Sullivan dread the four years of college for Helen Keller?

2. Why had Helen wanted to go to Radcliffe?

3. Had Mr. Gilman used Mrs. Keller's letter as she intended?

4. Why wasn't Anne happy about the Radcliffe examinations?

5. What did Helen call Anne Sullivan?

6. What improved Helen's composition grade?

Interpretive Thinking:

1. Why did Mr. Gilman dislike Anne so much?

2. Anne had always been a mother figure to Helen. Which incident altered their roles?

3. Tell about the examination ordeal from Mr. Vining's—the examiner's—point of view.

4. Relate a time when, with great determination to reach a goal, you were rewarded. Share with a partner.

Creative Thinking:

1. What if John Macy had wanted to marry Anne Sullivan but not accepted Helen? How would the story have changed?

2. As Mr. Chamberlain, write a *Listener* column about what transpired at Cambridge College.

3. Create Helen's certificate of admission to Radcliffe.

4. What experience has made you feel like "a person in your own right, a person worthy of respect"?

Critical Thinking:

1. Why was the normalcy of the graduation exercises so important to Anne?

2. Why would writing an autobiography teach Helen many things about herself?

3. What were the reasons that Dr. Bell and John Macy saw Anne as a different personality from most people?

4. Mrs. Keller had felt Mr. Gilman would know best how to guide Helen's college work. Debate the wisdom of her opinion.

5. Helen was advised to write from her own life. Relate a time your writing improved because the subject related to your own life.

Additional Activities

Visual Art:

1. Draw a cartoon of Anne as a weather vane in a huge wind.

2. Create a time line of Helen's life from the time she met Anne Sullivan to her graduation day.

3. Did Anne Sullivan and Helen Keller learn profound lessons during their lifetimes? Create pictures for both that illustrate the truths they learned.

4. Create two illustrations representative of Anne Sullivan. Use a medium such as colored chalk, watercolor, or colored markers to create a design of turbulence that was Anne's silent storm. The other design depicts the peace that Anne finally experienced.

Creative Writing:

1. Write about a person who, like Anne Sullivan, helped another reach a goal.

2. Write a message in Braille to a partner. See if he/she can decode your message.

3. Anne Sullivan devoted her life to service. Write a job-wanted column for a class newspaper. Describe a special help or service that you are willing to share.

4. As Helen Keller, write a letter to all students about the joys of learning and why determination to learn must be a lifelong goal.

5. Write a letter to a society created to help the visually and hearing impaired requesting information. Share the information with the class.

Drama:

1. Write and perform a monologue of an older Anne Sullivan recalling important moments in her life story.

2. Create a scene for a play in which no words are spoken.

3. View the movie *The Miracle Worker*. Afterward, mime action-filled scenes. See if your classmates can tell the scene that came before and after the action.

4. Helen Keller, with the help of Anne Sullivan, made her dreams come true. Interview your classmates to find out their goals and dreams and how they plan to make them come true.

Music:

1. Music can be very important to deaf people, for they can sense the vibrations by placing their hands on the sides of instruments. Listen to electronic music to learn how vibrations enrich the musical sounds.

2. Listen to a recording of the song "Wind beneath My Wings." How does this song tell of Anne Sullivan and Helen Keller's relationship?

3. Listen to a lilting piece of music as you write, creatively. Does the music enhance your writing style? Share your experience with a partner.

Social Studies:

1. Research to find out what breeds of dogs are primarily used with blind people. Invite a trainer to your class for an interview. Ask about the courage and intelligence of the dogs in crises.

2. Read excerpts from a biography of Helen Keller. How are current educational practices for the handicapped alike and different from Helen's education?

3. Research the history of the Perkins Institute for the Blind in Boston. Present a report for your class.

Science:

1. Research the studies of Dr. Alexander Graham Bell with deafness. Learn about the earliest hearing aids and up to the new surgical procedures.

2. Find out how the ear is constructed and what safety precautions need to be taken to prevent hearing loss.

3. Research the new surgery for the deaf that implants a sensor to magnify sound vibrations. If possible, contact and interview a physician who has performed the surgery.

4. How does positive immediate reinforcement affect learning? How was Anne Sullivan an expert in using positive reinforcement with Helen Keller?

Bulletin Board

The Silent Storm

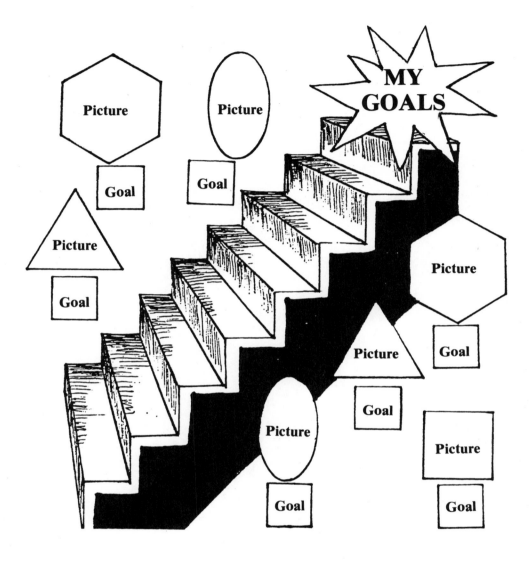

Helen Keller took many steps to reach her goals. Each student writes about his/her career goal with a self-portrait having achieved the goal. Draw a series of steps leading to a goal to emphasize the concept of long-term planning.

A Family Apart

Joan Lowery Nixon

A Family Apart

by

Joan Lowery Nixon
Bantam Books, 1987

This story of the Kelly family begins in New York City in 1860. Mrs. Kelly is a young widow with six children ranging in age from thirteen-year-old Frances Mary to six-year-old Petey.

They live in dire poverty until the oldest boy, Mike, is caught stealing. The courts present a choice between prison and going west on the Orphan Train to relocate with a new family. Mrs. Kelly realizes that she will be unable to give the children all they will need to lead good lives. Her decision is to entrust all of her children to the Children's Aid Society for relocation and adoption in the West. They, in turn, feel rejected and abandoned by the one person who has always shown them love and affection.

They travel on the Orphan Train to Missouri where they are further divided through being adopted by different families. Frances Mary masquerades as Frankie, feeling that if she is a boy she will be able to stay with her youngest brother, Petey. They are placed together, and the remainder of the book tells of her adventures, including involvement with the Underground Railroad.

This is the first book of the Orphan Train quartet. The other three books continue the saga of the remaining Kelly children.

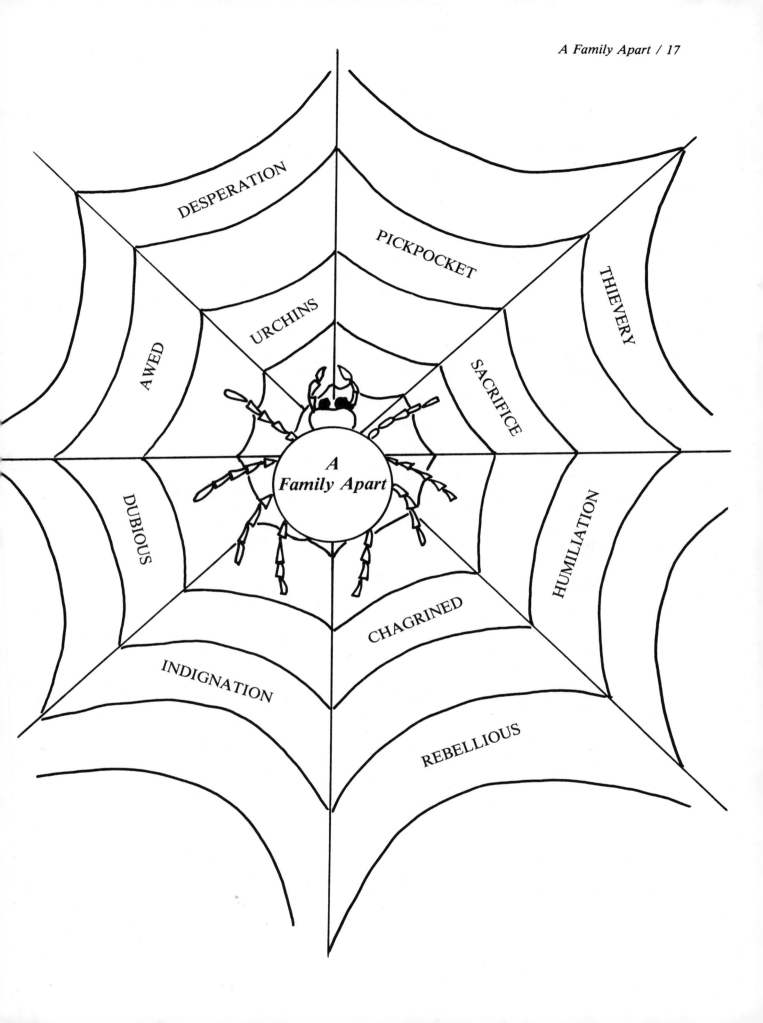

Chapters 1 through 4

Literal Thinking:

1. Why had Frances's parents left Ireland?

2. Tell of the incident that forced Frances Mary into adulthood and the responsibilities it entailed.

3. How did Frances Mary know her brother Mike had been out until just before she and her mother got home?

4. How did Mike make his money? What were people who did this called?

5. What event caused the mother to make the decision to send her children out west?

6. What did Charles Brace do to help orphaned children?

Interpretive Thinking:

1. The family was extremely poor materially but not emotionally. Cite examples of this from the chapters.

2. While Frances Mary was working, she retreated into her imaginary world to help pass the time. Have you ever done the same to get through a tedious activity? Share with a partner.

3. Why did Frances Mary feel that people looked at her as if she had done something wrong?

4. What words show how Frances felt about her family?

5. What did Frances mean when she said that going away was like another death?

Creative Thinking:

1. Compare your day to that of Frances Mary.

2. Which of the children most interests you? Write a telegram from that child to Mrs. Kelly describing the child's new home and parents.

3. Draw a picture of Frances Mary and the little girl in blue velvet with both looking at the china doll.

4. In pencil make a sketch of Mrs. Kelly's face showing her daughter's concept of her at the time she imitated Mrs. Watt.

5. Use potatoes that have been cut in half. Have each student cut the end into a design for a personal and unique potato stamp. Using various tempera colors create a pattern on paper.

6. Children have always created new games to play. The book deals with a time in which they often used everyday items in games. Many of these creations are still popular today, such as Cat's Cradle, Kick the Can, and stilts made out of old wood or cans and string. Have the children make examples of each and go outside so everyone can try them. Also, think of original games using common items.

Critical Thinking:

1. Is this story based on historical fact? Which portions can be researched to find out?

2. Did Mrs. Kelly show a deep love for her children by deciding to send them to new homes? Debate.

3. What is the value of Mama's remark, "The woman sees only the dark side of life and for that we should pity her"?

4. Why did Frances react so bitterly toward her mother?

5. Brainstorm some other possible jobs the family could find to help themselves.

6. If you had been Mrs. Kelly, how would you have reacted to Mike's problem? Compare answers.

Chapters 5 through 8

Literal Thinking:

1. Frances felt she had certain responsibilities as the eldest child. What were they?

2. What was the incident that gave Frances encouragement about the kind of friendships they would find in the West?

3. Explain the meaning of the term *bounty hunters* as it was used in the book.

4. What comforting message did Kathryn Banks have for the children concerning family selection?

5. Why was the last sight of New York City painful for Frances and the children?

6. Describe what Mike did to distract the children and stop them from crying on the train.

Interpretive Thinking:

1. Why does Frances think, "Who would want children whose mother didn't want them?"

2. Why did Frances yearn to be called Frances Mary again?

3. Why did Frances not confront Mike about the part he played in their moving west?

4. How was the West a place of new beginnings for the children?

5. Do you feel the changes in their lives were all Mike's fault?

6. Explain the feelings you believe each of the children had toward their mother. Compare answers.

7. Mike performed a brave act in coming to the aid of Mr. Cranden. Why do you think the man wouldn't acknowledge it?

Creative Thinking:

1. Create either a poster or a logo for the Children's Aid Society. Be inventive so that people will be attracted to it.

2. Research the Overland Stage Line. Present a mini-report to the class along with your illustration of a typical stagecoach.

3. Relate an experience in which you were frightened about being accepted. Imagine the feelings the children had about being adopted.

4. Create a map showing the train ride the children took from New York to Missouri.

5. Write an adventure of the Old West including the outlaw, Frances, Mike, and Bill Cody.

6. How would you have handled the conflict between Mike and Mr. Cranden? Role-play the scene using your new approach.

7. Which of the various people—the outlaw, mail dispatcher, Indian, frontiersman—were the most fascinating? Write an excerpt in a diary for the character you choose. Share the diary with your class.

Critical Thinking:

1. Had Mike learned the right values in putting out the fire for Mr. Cranden? Debate.

2. Why do you think the people have such negative feelings toward the children even after Mike's brave deeds and Frances Mary's explanation?

3. How was the slave Frances saw very much like her? Explain.

4. Evaluate Mrs. Kelly's decision regarding her children. Do you agree or disagree with it?

5. Do you think Mike was justified in breaking his promise to his mother? Discuss your opinions as a class.

Chapters 9 through 13

Literal Thinking:

1. How were the children chosen by the families?

2. Why were the older boys chosen more quickly than the rest of the children?

3. Which Kelly child was the last to be chosen?

4. Describe the family that chose Mike.

5. How did one help influence a state in becoming free or slave?

6. How had Kathryn discovered that Frankie was really Frances Mary?

7. When they talked about the Underground Railroad what was Frances Mary's first mental picture?

Interpretive Thinking:

1. What made Frances finally understand why her mother had sent the children away?

2. Explain how Frances felt when she heard that the two escaped slaves were out of danger.

3. Demonstrate what you would have done had you been Megan and separated from your family.

4. Predict what you feel is in store for each of the children in their new homes. Compare opinions with a partner.

5. Why are memories so important in our lives? Discuss.

Creative Thinking:

1. Draw a paneled picture with the children and their new parents.

2. Set up the scene of the welcome party for Frances and Petey. Role-play the various personalities they encountered.

3. Create a television guide advertisement for *A Family Apart* as if it were a major television production.

Critical Thinking:

1. Was the selection process more emotionally difficult for the adoptive families or the children being adopted? Discuss.

2. Which child was the bravest during the adoption ordeal? Present reasons for your opinion.

3. Compare the children's life in New York to the life of the slaves at that time.

4. Judge how things might have been different if Mr. Cranden hadn't been on that particular train.

5. Predict Mrs. Kelly's life now that her children are gone.

Additional Activities

Visual Art:

1. Draw the actual Orphan Train loaded and traveling out west.

2. Sketch fashions of the 1860s.

3. Create two pictures on folded paper: one depicting Frankie and the other, Frances Mary.

4. Draw *wanted* posters of Odette and James that would have been posted by bounty hunters.

5. Write a rebus story about slaves' escape. For one word in each sentence, draw a picture of the word. See if a partner can decode your story.

6. Create a reminder of the children for their mother. Draw a picture of each child with a caption commenting either on personality or on a particular act. Save for an album.

7. Design a floor plan for a barn with a secret area for hiding runaways. Explain its secret entrance and perhaps an emergency exit.

Creative Writing:

1. As Mike, keep a journal of everything that happened to him from the time Frances Mary discovered him in the alley. Include his feelings and reactions to what is happening to him as well as the repercussions of his actions on his family.

2. Create some form of identification for the children to use in case they are separated.

3. At the end of chapter 11, write a suspenseful new chapter involving the secret meeting with Jake.

4. As an investigative reporter, expose the cruelty of bounty hunters and slave masters.

5. Imagine you are an orphan going west. Write an advertisement for a potential family including your attributes.

Drama:

1. Role-play a conversation between Frances and her mother years later.

2. Set up a mock adoption center. Have a partner and try to convince the audience that you should be adopted.

3. Create a train-of-thought monologue for Frances as she continues to remember her family. Each time she falls into self-pity, a group of students as a chorus says, "Stop it!"

4. Create a dialogue between Frances and the slave. Each expresses how it feels to not have basic rights observed.

5. Use a readers' theatre technique, where everyone is on stage with backs to the audience until an individual's turn to speak. Then he/she turns to the audience to deliver lines and turns back around when finished. Have each of the principals including the children, Andrew, Kathryn, and Mr. Cranden represented. All the characters create their own scripts about their feelings and attitudes from the time they discovered they were leaving to go west until they either are chosen by their family or complete their involvement with the Kelly family. Once each person has a script, meld them into one.

Music:

1. Research some of the tunes Mike sang during the train trip as listed on pages 74 and 75 of *A Family Apart*. Learn some of them and use them for a class sing-along.

2. Research music of this time. Bring some examples and play them for the class and compare to currently popular songs.

3. Research to find how slaves celebrated with music at their funerals. See if their songs had a connection with jazz.

Social Studies:

1. Create a time capsule of this period.

2. Read a biography about Abraham Lincoln. What in his background made him an able leader for a country in conflict?

3. Locate a map of the routes and stop areas of the Underground Railroad. Draw a map of the route for your class.

4. During the latter part of the 1800s and the early 1900s when immigration was at its peak, people organized into national groups. Research such areas as Little Italy and Ireland in New York City, as well as Chinatown in San Francisco; Little Tokyo in Los Angeles; and some of the German and Dutch communities in both Oklahoma and Pennsylvania. Check your local area for towns with similar origins and follow them from their founding through to their current status.

Science:

1. Get information about the potato famine in Ireland. Compare its effects on the population to what occurred in Oklahoma during the time of the Dust Bowl.

2. Research the statistics of the number of children who were on the Orphan Trains. Compare that to runaways today.

Math:

1. Figure out in miles how far the children traveled.

Bulletin Board

A Family Apart

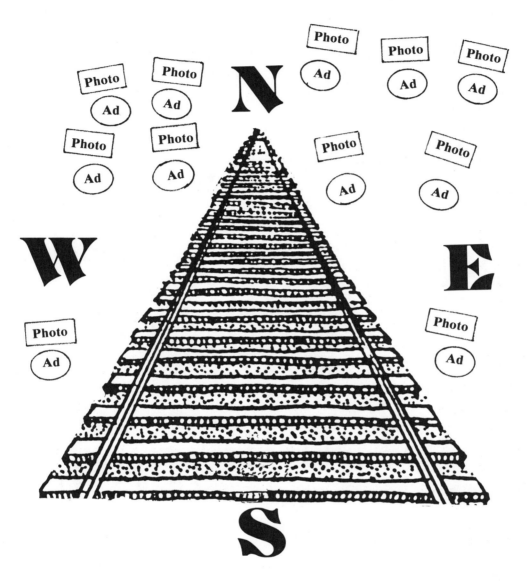

Students write advertisements with their attributes for adoption. These advertisements are mounted along with photographs or self-portraits.

Search-a-Word

A Family Apart

```
U Q N S A X R V A F B O S R E K A U Q Z N K J H A G W J D U
J L D H E Z B H F J L K L X T C N D Y D B T B P I U E Q Z W
D X O M I M J T J S H B U I A I S V W F Z H J O O N N P B S
B C L D Q X Q L C Q Q W E C F H Q W C U R C G D A Y L J X R
W F Y B E K E R V S L D I C F C H O R N C A E C U S Q L M R
S T Y Z K L M S V J I U A H Q H B K Q O Z T M T X R I H T K
J A Y H A W K E R S L L A H S R A M P J T N E R D L I H C X
E M Q L N Z P W Y C U F C L A W P P K E Z P Y U N T G H A K
W I Z I V L Q P R I S O N F J E E P W S E X M N K M Y Y C F
U Y I U R T X K Y X K M I I X R H A V F R E E D O M B O J D
D E L N U S Y T U A F B O G   L G K U A Q K C E C O P K K H
A N M A L A N R U O J W Y S N G O P E T E Y I R E F Q I H T
Q R W G Y N G Q K X M L T R P L N J X V H V F G K M V W L U
A U K E H T U I S O N E P Q R Y O S H S Z M I R I M X D W R
V O D M Y P R G S J A N J I Q X Z C I E H M R O M F N A E J
Q J S S N E O A E L C W X P B Z F Y N V W E C U M I A N G D
H H F E Q M B I E T S E I K N A R F T I B T A N C I H N A B
U Q I V L V S R B C L Y U E R V T B S I L O S D X Y P Y E R
C E Z A N J S E K X H S O X Z I P M R F D Z U R Z I R N C L
G W D L T X N S N D L E Z D X J B O L A B I Z N F L O F U M
F Q M S M A J D W M C F M S H C V Y J H V G F D T H G U E R
M F Y P E D M N U F R A N C E S   M A R Y E E D A Y Y B V K
Q X L Q N A Y A C C U J E P A Y X L P W G T R B J J G C N E
I E V T R J L L N V G C H Z V O K M I C P Y L Y N X U O V F
V G Z Y N U C E L A Q T F A M I L Y W O R W L Z G U H A U X
M W E M E M O R T A E U J C K X J S D S F Z M M R D O A Q A
M X H J X B T I N S L H J R F H T A N I K I Z A R M R W W H
U D C P U W A G O N J U C T I E N I M A F U W Q W X X G O V
H I L X G M T U J O K J V E F Y H J L F M C F I W E H F M E
G C W F D A O R L I A R K I V D Q I X Y Y E U N Z S C H P I
```

Words

ORPHAN
PRISON
BOUNTY
CHILDREN
BRAVERY
SLAVES
FAMILY
LINCOLN
MEGAN
FRANCES MARY

FAMINE
FRANKIE
IRELAND
JAYHAWKERS
MARSHALL
FREEDOM
COPPER STEALER
MIKE
ODETTE
RAILROAD

QUAKERS
WAGON
ADOPTED
SACRIFICE
UNDERGROUND
JOURNAL
JOURNEY
PETEY
DANNY

A Family Apart — Puzzle Answers

```
.  .  .  .  .  .  .  .  .  .  .  .  .  S  R  E  K  A  U  Q  .  .  .  .  .  .  .  .  .  .  .  .
.  .  .  .  .  .  .  .  .  .  .  .  .  .  .  .  .  .  .  .  .  .  .  .  .  .  .  .  .  .  .  .
.  .  .  .  .  '  .  .  .  .  .  .  .  .  .  .  .  .  .  .  .  .  .  .  .  .  O  .  .  .  .  .
.  .  .  .  .  .  .  .  .  .  .  .  .  .  .  .  .  .  .  .  .  .  .  .  D  .  .  .  .  .  .  .
.  .  .  .  .  .  .  .  .  .  .  .  .  .  .  .  .  .  .  C  .  E  .  .  .  .  .  .  .  .  .  .
.  .  .  .  .  .  .  .  .  .  .  .  .  .  .  .  .  O  .  T  .  .  .  .  .  .  .  .  .  .  .  .
J  A  Y  H  A  W  K  E  R  S  L  L  A  H  S  R  A  M  P  .  T  N  E  R  D  L  I  H  C  .
.  .  .  .  .  .  .  .  .  .  .  .  .  .  P  .  E  .  .  U  .  .  .  .  .  .  .
.  .  .  .  .  .  P  R  I  S  O  N  .  .  .  E  .  .  .  .  N  .  .  .  .  .  .
.  Y  .  .  .  .  .  .  .  .  .  R  .  .  .  F  R  E  E  D  O  M  .  .  .  .
.  E  .  N  .  .  .  .  .  .  .  .  .  .  .  .  C  .  E  .  .  .  .  .  .
.  N  .  A  L  A  N  R  U  O  J  .  .  S  N  .  .  P  E  T  E  Y  I  R  E  .  .  .  .
.  R  .  G  .  .  .  .  .  T  .  .  L  .  .  .  .  .  F  G  K  .  .  .
.  U  .  E  .  .  .  .  E  .  .  .  O  .  .  .  .  .  I  R  I  .  .  D  .
.  O  .  M  .  .  .  A  .  .  .  C  .  .  .  R  O  M  .  N  A  .
.  J  .  S  .  .  .  L  .  .  .  .  N  .  .  C  U  .  .  A  N  .
.  .  .  E  .  .  .  E  .  .  E  I  K  N  A  R  F  .  I  B  .  A  N  .  .  H  N  .
.  .  .  V  .  .  R  .  .  .  .  .  .  .  B  .  .  L  O  S  D  .  .  P  Y  .
.  .  .  A  .  .  .  .  .  .  .  .  .  .  .  R  .  .  U  .  .  R  .
.  .  .  L  .  .  .  .  .  .  .  .  .  .  A  .  .  N  .  O  .
.  .  .  S  .  .  D  .  .  .  .  .  .  .  .  V  .  D  T  .  .  .  .
.  .  .  .  .  N  .  F  R  A  N  C  E  S  .  M  A  R  Y  E  E  .  .  Y  .  .  .  .
.  .  .  .  .  A  .  .  .  .  .  .  .  .  .  .  .  T  R  .  .  .  .
.  .  .  .  .  L  .  .  .  .  .  .  .  .  P  .  .  Y  .  .  .  .
.  .  .  .  .  E  .  .  .  .  F  A  M  I  L  Y  .  O  .  .  .  .
.  .  .  .  .  R  .  .  .  .  .  .  .  .  D  .  .  .  .  .
.  .  .  .  .  I  .  .  .  .  .  .  .  A  .  .  .  .  .
.  .  .  .  .  W  A  G  O  N  .  .  .  .  .  E  N  I  M  A  F  .  .  .  .  .
.  .  .  .  .  .  .  .  .  .  .  .  .  .  .  .  .  .  .  .  .  .  .  .
.  .  .  .  .  D  A  O  R  L  I  A  R  .  .  .  .  .  .  .  .  .  .  .  .
```

Island of the Blue Dolphins

Scott O'Dell

Island of the Blue Dolphins

by

Scott O'Dell

Houghton Mifflin Co., 1960

This story is about a tribe that lives on a small island off the coast of southern California. Their peaceful existence is shattered by the arrival of an Aleutian ship hunting otters. The two groups strike a bargain for payment for the skins which is broken by the Aleuts. The resulting battle all but destroys the tribe and drives the Aleuts away for a period of time.

The tribal elders realize that the Aleuts will return for more skins so they prepare an escape route. The new chief delegates himself to travel to the known island to the east for help. Ultimately, a ship arrives, sent by the chief, to move the entire tribe to this new, safe location.

Everyone is on the ship when Karana, a young girl, realizes her younger brother has been left onshore. She jumps overboard to return to the island and her brother.

The remainder of the book consists of Karana's adventures as a child trying to exist alone on an island.

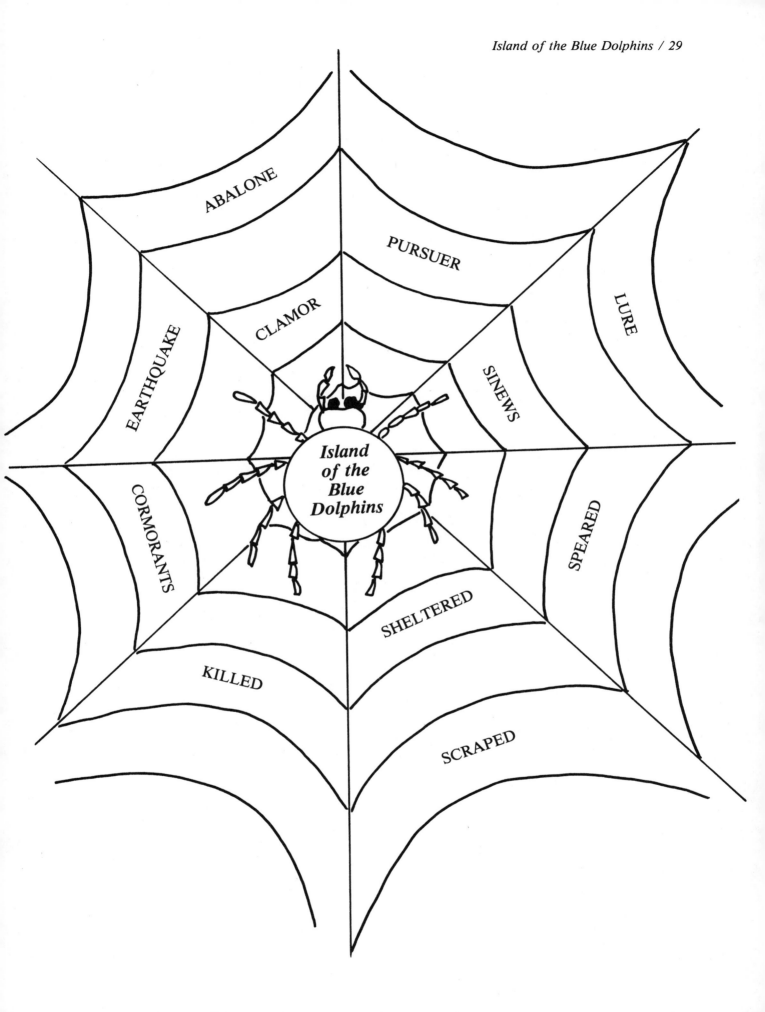

Chapters 1 through 5

Literal Thinking:

1. Why did the Aleuts come to the island?

2. Tell why the warriors in Karana's tribe fought the Aleuts.

3. Why is the early spring a poor time for fishing?

4. Why did Karana feel her father should not have told Captain Orlov his secret name?

5. Explain the need for each tribal member to have two names.

6. Tell how the island got its name.

7. Even without direct communication, how did the tribe know what occurred in the Aleut camp?

8. How did Chowig show refusal of the offered payment?

Interpretive Thinking:

1. Why is the father wary of becoming friends with the Aleuts?

2. Which of the children would more likely have been a poet or an artist?

3. What is your feeling about hunting animals for pelts?

4. Tell why Karana had such a dislike of hearing about the otters killed each day.

5. What tribal rule had Chowig broken which Karana felt had been his downfall?

6. What feelings would you have had toward the Aleuts?

7. The new chief had been a good man and hunter in his youth. Now he was considered to be an elderly man. Discuss why the tribe made this choice with all the turmoil and the unknown they must face.

Creative Thinking:

1. Otters are fun-loving animals. Find photographs of them in comical poses. Draw your versions of the pictures.

2. Make salt-and-flour beads. Paint designs with tempera for an Indian necklace.

3. Imagine you are standing on the cliff overlooking the sea. What sounds and smells are you experiencing? Write a brief descriptive paragraph.

4. Indians often create pots of clay. Invite a potter to your class to demonstrate pottery. Try some of the techniques.

5. Be a topographer and make a detailed drawing of the island and its special features.

6. Research the sea otter and create a papier-mâché head, using pipe cleaners for the distinctive whiskers.

7. Draw an illustration of the Aleut ship in panels. First show a sighting when it resembled a shell until it was anchored.

Critical Thinking:

1. Do you think it was right for the tribe to refuse white bass to the Aleuts?

2. Choose the character you admired the most. Give reasons for your choice.

3. Compare the current disputes about fishing and territorial boundaries. Research the current limits and countries who contest these statutes, such as Japan and Russia. Debate the validity of these restrictions.

4. The bass had beached themselves while fleeing the killer whales. Research other species that have similar traits, such as lemmings, whales, and dolphins.

5. While the tribe discussed the Aleuts, why did Karana's father say nothing and work on a new spear?

6. The new chief immediately encouraged the tribe to work and replenish stores. Why was this important so soon after the Aleut betrayal?

Chapters 6 through 10

Literal Thinking:

1. When was the first time Karana felt afraid?

2. What sea animals were friendly to Karana?

3. Relate the plan of action when the Aleuts returned.

4. What mark did Ulape put on her face before leaving? What did it signify?

5. What was the one thing that angered Karana about returning with Ramo?

6. Explain the tribal "rite of manhood."

7. How did Karana, out at sea, know the night was half over?

Interpretive Thinking:

1. What leads you to think Karana was an inventive girl?

2. Why did the lack of rain cause more concern than it had previously?

3. Why did Karana jump from the ship to find Ramo?

4. Why did they have some confidence in the new visitors?

5. Why did the presence of boys on the ship make a difference to the tribe?

6. Had the Aleuts kept their word about payments for the skins? Refer to chapter 1 if needed.

Creative Thinking:

1. Imagine you are Karana. What feelings would you have as you sat with the body of your brother?

2. The author creates conflict with the threat of the wild dogs. What conflict would you have created if you were the author?

3. Tell of a time you had to cope with a crisis. What did you learn from the experience?

4. Brainstorm ways to eliminate the wild dogs from the cave. Remember that the cave's mouth is too wide to cover with rocks.

5. Design a marker for Ramo's grave depicting various aspects of his personality and self-perceptions.

6. A commonly used phrase is "You can never go back." Evaluate how this applied to Karana and the village. Have you ever encountered a situation when the same expression proved true for you? Share with a friend.

7. Karana had no experience with weapon making because it was forbidden by her tribe. Using rocks, twine, or rope, create a weapon she might have used.

Critical Thinking:

1. Why did Karana burn the huts of the village?

2. Is a story based on fact more interesting? Why or why not?

3. What did Karana do that most expressed her deep loneliness?

4. What were Karana's most important inner qualities for dealing with a crisis? List your ideas and compare with those of classmates.

5. If you had to leave your home quickly and only take five items, what would they be? Explain your choices.

6. Analyze why the tribe was "fearful and yet happy too" concerning their proposed move. Think of a time you felt the same emotions. Share with a partner.

7. Discuss how Ramo's curiosity and enthusiasm could be harmful to him and his sister.

8. Evaluate the importance of the chest left by the Aleuts now that Karana was alone.

9. Evaluate why Karana was fighting herself and her background by ignoring her tribal customs in order to survive.

Chapters 11 through 15

Literal Thinking:

1. What did Karana use to make a fence?

2. When did Karana build her second home?

3. Why didn't Karana choose the stronger sinew to weave through the fence?

4. Why do elephant seal bulls have definite territories they rule?

5. Why was building a fence Karana's highest priority?

6. What did the dead bull elephant provide for Karana?

Interpretive Thinking:

1. Why did Karana have new feelings for the island home?

2. Why was Karana's care of Rontu a surprising turn in the story?

3. Why did Karana feel the leader of the dogs was an Aleut dog?

4. At the time of the fire, how did the leader of the dogs show his bravery?

5. How did Karana know the seal she selected was alone and why this would help her?

6. Explain the importance of the outward rib curve in building the fence.

7. Why did Karana decide not to make another attempt to leave the island?

Creative Thinking:

1. Traditionally, civilizations hand down lessons they have learned to ensure survival. Sometimes the reasons for these lessons are lost. For example, the Indians planted a seed along with a fish. Record such lessons that Karana discovered for herself. Begin with the reason for the location for her home and continue throughout the story.

2. Karana used fish to light and use as a lamp. Given the items she has or can get on the island, create another form of lighting for her.

3. Draw an illustration of the wild dog. Highlight his most expressive feature.

4. Investigate healing herbs. Discover what Karana could use for her injured leg.

5. Tell a new legend of why the island had few trees.

6. Research cave paintings. Wet and crumple a paper bag. While the bag is still wet, straighten and dry it. The result will resemble leather. Draw some of the stone cuttings Karana discovered.

Critical Thinking:

1. Why did Karana have more than one reason to hate the leader of the dog pack?

2. Read *Julie of the Wolves* by Jean Craighead George. How was Julie's relationship with the wolves like Karana's with the wild dogs?

3. Why was Karana surprised that she felt happy to be back at the island?

4. Tribal legend said that two gods fought and therefore the tall trees disappeared. Brainstorm other possible conditions that might have resulted in the loss of the trees.

5. Karana improved on some of the lessons of the tribe; for example, the building of the fire pit. Think of something you learned from another and modified to better fit your needs. Share with your class.

6. How did Karana prove the statement "practice makes perfect"? Do you have a similar example from your life?

Chapters 16 through 20

Literal Thinking:

1. How did Rontu win in his struggle with the dogs?

2. What was in the Black Cave?

3. Why did Karana work on the canoe?

4. What did the dogfight signify?

5. How did Karana know it was spring?

6. Why did Karana feel certain Rontu knew she was watching?

7. Why did Karana decide not to help Rontu?

8. Which abalone variety do seafish prefer?

Interpretive Thinking:

1. Why did Karana show more wisdom than Rontu when the devilfish tried to mislead them?

2. Why is it Karana didn't know how lonely she was until Rontu became her friend?

3. What was Rontu trying to tell Karana when he whined at the wild dogs?

4. How does the author create mystery with the arrival of the ships?

Creative Thinking:

1. Using clay, aluminum foil, and a variety of other materials, create a canoe for Karana. Test in water to see if it is seaworthy.

2. Research the yellow birds with red heads Karana mentions. Their unique sound will aid in their identification. List the most interesting facts about them with an illustration.

3. Read excerpts from *Robinson Crusoe* by Daniel Defoe. Was Robinson Crusoe fearful of being discovered like Karana? Write a short readers' theatre script based on exciting portions of both books.

4. Karana invented many things to cope with her island existence. If you could invent something, what would it be? Draw an illustration, build a model, or write an explanation of your invention.

5. If you were Karana, hiding in a cave, what items would you take with you?

Critical Thinking:

1. When Rontu was the victor in the fight, what did the long howl signify?

2. Analyze if the devilfish was a more worthy opponent than Karana had expected.

3. Evaluate why Rontu reacted as he did after the fight and why the remaining dogs reacted as they did. Discuss your opinions.

4. Discuss what Karana should have done in the deadlock between Rontu and the devilfish. Brainstorm other possible solutions.

5. Karana dealt with immediate fears daily. What permanent fear left her feeling helpless?

6. What action does Karana force Rontu to take that proves she is finally his master?

7. If you had written the book, what episode would you have expanded to add more excitement and drama?

8. Why did Karana not look at the figures on the ledge while she and Rontu were in the Black Cave?

Chapters 21 through 25

Literal Thinking:

1. Why was Karana impressed by the first words of the Aleut girl?

2. Why did Karana change the sea otter's name?

3. What gift did Karana make for Tutok?

4. Why was Karana more afraid of the Aleut girl than of the men?

5. What did Karana find on the flat rock outside the cave?

6. Explain how otters secure themselves against drifting while sleeping.

7. Why didn't Karana attempt to heal the otter's wounds?

8. Why was Karana afraid to reenter the cave?

9. How did Karana mark the passage of time?

Interpretive Thinking:

1. Why did a spoken word mean so much to Karana even though it was spoken by an enemy?

2. Have you ever experienced a friend leaving as Karana did Tutok? Describe your feelings to a partner.

3. What word in the description of the otter reflects Karana's sensitivity?

4. Have you ever lost a pet? How were your feelings similar to Karana's when Rontu died?

5. Why had Tutok left the necklace of black stones at the cave?

Creative Thinking:

1. Role-play the first meeting between the Aleut girl and Karana.

2. Create a circlet, similar to the one Karana made for Tutok, from paper. Decorate it with what Karana might have liked. Explain your choices.

3. Create an epitaph for Karana's faithful friend, Rontu.

4. Illustrate Karana in her cormorant skirt and beads.

5. Write a poem about Mon-a-nee, the sea otter. Create a picture with words about Karana's and the otter's relationship.

6. Find out about island customs of giving decorative necklaces made of flowers to symbolize friendship. Design a necklace of real or fake flowers, shells, or stones from discarded jewelry. Create a necklace for a friend in your class.

7. Have you ever had an invisible companion as the departed Tutok was to Karana? Write a conversation Karana would have had with Tutok about her loneliness, her loss of the sea otter, and her future plans.

Critical Thinking:

1. Why do you think Tutok did not tell the Aleuts that Karana lived on the island?

2. Karana, at first, was like a prisoner in her own cave. How did creativity and problem solving make her life, even here, productive?

3. Read *Where the Red Fern Grows* by Wilson Rawls. How was the main character's need for animals different than Karana's?

4. What is the best way to treat a wounded animal? Invite an animal expert from the Humane Society to give pointers on care of abandoned or wounded animals.

5. Analyze why the cormorant skirt became a bond between the girls. Choose an incident in your life where a common object helped you communicate with a person you have just met.

6. Analyze the Aleut girl's feelings when she saw Karana had not picked up the necklace. Did you agree with the way Karana handled the situation? Explain your feelings.

7. Evaluate the depth of Karana's feelings toward the Aleut girl when she told the girl her secret name.

Chapters 26 through 29

Literal Thinking:

1. How did the three men finally locate her?

2. What did Karana feel was a sound like no other in the world?

3. Who did Karana often think of?

4. Where did Karana climb to escape the enormous wave?

5. What was the greatest loss to the girl that was due to the earthquake?

6. What had happened to the ship that had carried the island people away long ago?

Interpretive Thinking:

1. It is said that truth is stranger than fiction. How does this relate to Karana's life?

2. Why did Karana feel uneasy without a canoe?

3. How did the dolphins say farewell to Karana?

4. Why did Karana want Rontu's son and no other wild dog?

5. Why was it important to the men that Karana have a proper dress?

Creative Thinking:

1. Karana was becoming more anxious to make contact with Tutok and Ulape. Create a distress signal to be seen by air or sea that would alert people to the fact she was stranded on the island.

2. Create a diamante poem about the fight between the two waves.

3. Share an experience when you were happy to move or change, but still had regrets.

4. Write a letter to Tutok from Karana.

5. Karana used a variety of objects in new ways. Think how an ordinary object could be decorated or changed to give it new use or beauty. Draw illustrations.

6. You are a future archeologist surveying the island of San Nicholas. Write a report and draw illustrations of the objects that tell of Karana's survival.

Critical Thinking:

1. Which is more important: what happens to you or what you do about it? Discuss.

2. Who were Anne Frank and Emily Dickinson? Find excerpts from their writings showing how imprisonment and loneliness led to productivity in their lives. Compare with Karana's solitary existence.

3. Did Karana understand what was happening during the earthquake?

4. Explain why it was important to Karana to be wearing her best when meeting strangers on the island.

Additional Activities

Visual Art:

1. Create a wreath design for either Karana or Rontu including items showing their personality traits.

2. Create a picture postcard of the island.

3. Using sponges, cut shapes of various animals and objects in the story. Dip them in tempera paint and use as stamps on paper or fabric. The finished product may be used for pictures, bulletin board backing, or wrapping paper.

4. As a tribute to Karana's brother, create an illustration of him as the mighty hero and leader he wanted to be.

Creative Writing:

1. The Black Cave with its skeleton is the setting for a mystery story. Write a script for your mystery to be performed by classmates.

2. Turn the story into an undersea adventure, a space adventure, or a tale of the Old West. Note how the setting and time will provoke changes in the plot.

3. Create a newspaper article telling of Karana's experiences.

4. Look in your media center for books that describe the mischievous behavior that makes a sea otter so entertaining. Create your own sea otter character. Give him a name, personality, and write about his adventures.

5. As Ulope, create a reward poster for anyone bringing her sister to civilization.

Drama:

1. Role-play Karana seeing the dog ill and dying, her decision to help it, and her attempts to establish a friendship with it.

2. Interview Karana about her adventures.

3. Role-play the actions and reactions of the tribal members on board the ship when they learned two of their members had been left on the island.

4. See the movie version of *Island of the Blue Dolphins*, then pretend you are a movie critic on television. Give reasons why you did or did not like the movie by analyzing the following: casting, music, special effects, adaptation of the book.

5. Organize a roundtable discussion of Karana, Robinson Crusoe, and characters from *The Swiss Family Robinson* by Johann Wyss. Have characters discuss their island adventures.

6. Improvise a scene at the Santa Barbara Mission. Father Gonzales is trying to communicate with Karana and teach her sign language.

Music:

1. Listen to recordings of the natural music produced by whales and dolphins. Brainstorm what you think the repetitive sounds might signify.

2. Design a musical instrument for Karana using things she had on the island.

3. Write lyrics of a song Karana might have created.

4. Sailors have sung sea chanteys through the ages. Find examples. Write a new sea chantey that the Aleut sailors or Karana, when sailing, might have sung.

5. Find mysterious-sounding recordings to play for a mystery play about the Black Cave.

Social Studies:

1. Locate the eight Channel Islands on a map.

2. Investigate stories of others who have survived alone.

3. The Aleut tactics of attack and capture were much like those of the Vikings. Read about the customs of these warlike people and compare them with those of the Aleuts.

4. Learn how Indians used feathers to decorate war bonnets. All the tribe designs had different meanings. Tell your class about them.

5. A true problem is the destruction of the abalone beds by sea otters. Abalone fishermen feel their livelihood is being ruined by these creatures others find adorable. A further complication is that they are an endangered species and protected by the law. Research the problem. Create a class debate between the fishermen and conservationists.

6. Easter Island is another isolated area with a unique, unexplained feature. The statues of Easter Island have long been investigated by scholars. Research and report to your class.

7. Santa Barbara Island is a popular resort area. Be a travel agent and research highlights most attractive to tourists. Include the glass-bottomed boats and buffalo herd.

8. Research the California mission development. Include the reasons for their development, locations, and the people they served.

Science:

1. Research the sai-sai or grunion. Learn about their unusual spawning patterns.

2. Dolphins are researched because of their intelligence and affinity for humans. Report on instances of dolphins helping people in trouble.

3. Investigate sea life and show your discoveries in the form of a collage.

4. The North Star has been a guide throughout history. Research the placement of this star, the constellation it is in, and its importance from ancient to present time. Using dark paper and a pin, create holes to show the star in its natural setting. Project this with an overhead projector while sharing information with your class.

Math:

1. Create a tessellation drawing of dolphins. Tessellations are shapes repeated in a way that no spaces occur. Geometric forms are created so that the student mathematically determines how many shapes will fit in a given area.

Bulletin Board

Island of the Blue Dolphins

A large half-basket can be purchased from a local craft store or woven from colored poster board. Students can also weave individual baskets from construction paper. Attach them to the bulletin board and fill the baskets with items that are important to them. These items may be drawn, cut out, or may be pictures from magazines.

ADDITIONAL BOOKS
ON COPING

1. *Captain Hook, That's Me.* Ada B. Litchfield. Walker, 1982.

   Judy is an active, bright girl who apparently has adjusted well to the hook she wears to replace her hand. Her difficulty arises from news that they may have to move: She is concerned about acceptance in the new situation.

2. *City, Sing for Me: A Country Child Moves to the City.* Jane Jacobson. Human Sciences Press, 1978.

   Jenny finds life very noisy and different when she moves to the city. She meets Ros, a girl who becomes her friend and shows her the other side of living in the city.

3. *The Flunking of Joshua T. Bates.* Susan Shreve. Knopf, 1984.

   Joshua is having a difficult time between what he feels is the unfairness of having to repeat the third grade and the taunts of his classmates. His fantasies go from planning to run away to being special promoted. His existence is helped by a sensitive, caring teacher who helps him be promoted.

4. *I Can't Always Hear You.* Jean Anderson. Dinosaur, 1985.

   Kim switches from a special school for the hearing impaired to a regular one. The teasing of children compounds her existing difficulties and she intends to quit. The school principal shares her affliction and gives her techniques to help.

5. *Jamie's Turn.* Jamie Dewitt. Raintree, 1984.

   Jamie's life runs into a problem when his stepfather is hurt on a tractor when Jamie is eleven. Throughout the next year he has to manage the farm while his Dad undergoes various operations.

6. *Light a Single Candle.* Beverly Butler. Simon & Schuster, 1973.

   Kathy is fourteen when she is blinded. This book deals with her adjustment as well as the adjustment of those involved in her life.

7. *Patrick, Yes You Can.* Patricia D. Frevert. Creative Education, 1983.

   From birth Patrick suffers from glaucoma and at the age of eight he goes completely blind. Whereas sports had been important to him, now without sight he doesn't want to return to school. His father encourages him and he eventually rises to the top through honor roll, through sports, and socially.

8. *The Purple Mouse.* Elisabeth MacIntyre. Nelson, 1975.

   Teenage Hatty is frightened of every magnified sound of the world received by her hearing aid. The unlikely role model of an accidentally dyed mouse, which overcomes all obstacles, gives Hatty the strength to cope with being different.

9. *Ride the Red Cycle.* Harriette G. Robinet. Houghton Mifflin, 1980.

   Jerome's biggest dream is to be able to ride a "cycle." Everyone feels this is virtually impossible as Jerome is physically handicapped and unable to walk. He is extremely stubborn and perseveres which, along with strong love and support, brings success.

10. *The Summer of the Swans.* Betsy Byars. Viking Press, 1970.

    Fourteen-year-old Sara is preoccupied with the uncertainties of her own adolescence—until the night she gets involved with the disappearance of her younger, retarded brother.

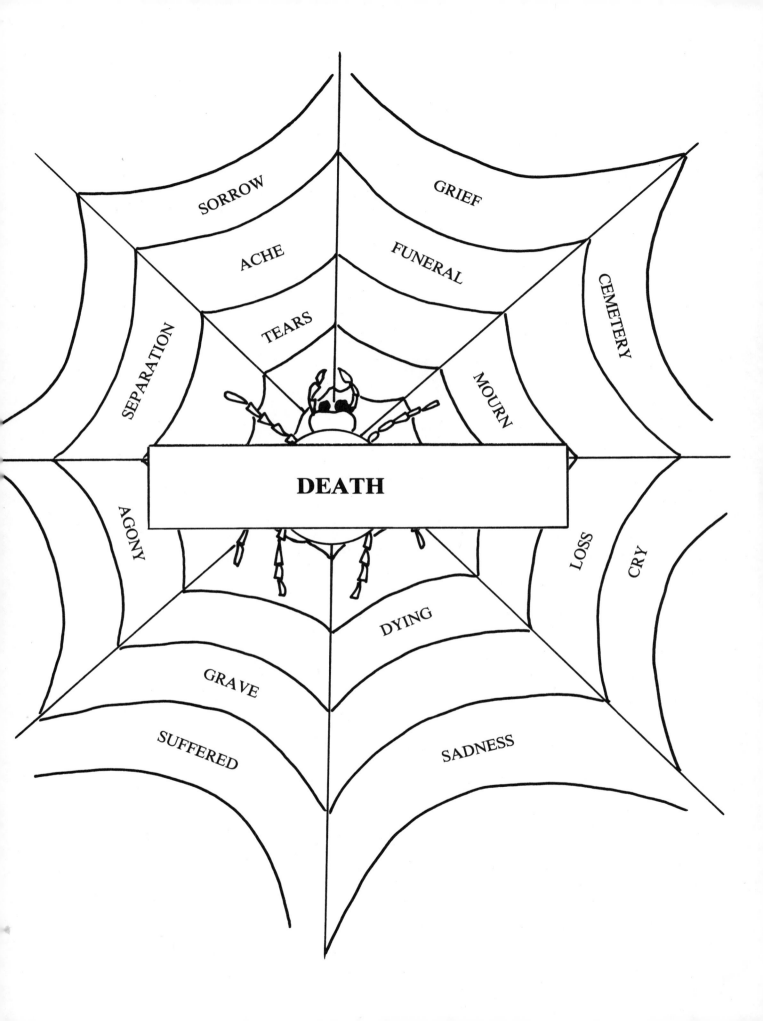

On My Honor

Marion Dane Bauer

On My Honor

by

Marion Dane Bauer
Clarion Books, 1986

Two best friends take off on their bicycles to go to the park. Joel had gotten permission from his father to ride only to the park. He had to say, "On my honor."

Tony, a spirited and reckless boy, talked Joel into going swimming off the bluffs of the treacherous Vermillion River. He teases Joel to the point of anger, so Joel then challenges Tony to swim to the sandbar. Tony is not a good swimmer.

After Joel discovers that Tony has disappeared in the water, he searches frantically for him. In his search, he almost drowns and has the terrible stench of the river on him.

Joel tries to get help from teenagers who are driving by, but they cannot find Tony. Finally, after thinking of hiding or running away, Joel returns home. He denies any knowledge of Tony's whereabouts.

Because of the pain and guilt, plus remorse and fear, Joel finally breaks and tells his story to authorities and parents.

With the help of his father, Joel begins his long journey to the acceptance of Tony's death and to his recovery to fill the emptiness with which the tragedy has left him.

SCORCHER

WATERY

WHINE

MIMICKED

EXUBERANCE

CINCH

THRASHING

ENGROSSED

ERRATIC

WHEELIES

DIBS

On My Honor

CONVULSED

BARRAGE

CURRENT

FRETTING

FISHTAILED

TREADED

JIG

BETRAYED

FLAILING

REVERBERATED

GLOWERING

Chapters 1 through 4

Literal Thinking:

1. What promise had Joel given to his father before he left home?

2. Why was it surprising that Joel and Tony were friends?

3. How did Tony often manage to get out of telling his mother his whereabouts?

4. From where did Joel expect Tony to suddenly appear when he couldn't find him?

5. Give a reason for river bottoms being so dangerous for swimmers.

Interpretive Thinking:

1. How did Joel feel he could maneuver his way around going with Tony without being called a chicken?

2. Give your definition of the phrase "On my honor." What does reciting that vow (promise) mean to you?

3. Compare the given descriptions of both fathers. Why was each upset with the other's perception of his father?

4. Why did Tony never admit that he could not swim?

5. Relate an incident in which peer pressure led you to do something against your better judgment. Share with a partner.

6. Share an experience in which you gave wise advice that saved a friend from a dangerous situation.

7. Do you think Tony had a sense of humor? Explain.

Creative Thinking:

1. How would you have handled Tony's request to go to the park?

2. Demonstrate for the class the different swimming strokes mentioned by the boys.

3. Perform a soliloquy of Joel's feelings and attitude changes while he was swimming out to the sandbar. Continue through his discovery that Tony was no longer behind him.

4. Create an illustration of Tony as a prehistoric monster emerging from the river.

5. Write all the adjectives you can think of that relate to Joel's feelings when he stepped off into the nothingness of the deep water.

6. Create a memorial TV interview about Tony. Interview his father, teachers, and friends for the broadcast.

Critical Thinking:

1. How could Joel have better reached his goal of swimming on the swim team? Make a chart for your classroom outlining the general steps to reaching any goal.

2. What was the most dramatic scene in chapters 1 through 4? Support your opinions by being a drama critic.

3. What do you think Joel really thought of his friend Tony?

4. Give reasons why you think Tony was so insistent on going to the park.

5. Joel felt to "win this argument was to lose." Recount a situation in which you felt the same way. Share it with a partner.

6. Analyze the relationship between the boys. Include such instances as the time Tony had dibs on Joel's bike. Have you ever been involved in a relationship you felt was one-sided? As time passed, what happened to the friendship? Share in a class discussion.

7. A famous fable talks about the *Boy Who Cried Wolf*. Read it to the class and analyze the similarities between that boy and Tony.

Chapters 5 through 8

Literal Thinking:

1. How did Joel know that Tony could not have gotten out of the water?

2. Why did the girl agree with Joel about letting her, alone, go to the police?

3. What did Joel feel was the biggest problem with having two parents?

4. What smell constantly reminded Joel of his harrowing experience?

5. Who did Joel's brother remind him of when he wanted to go with him on the paper route?

6. What did Joel decide to tell his parents about the incident?

7. When did the reality of Tony's death finally hit Joel?

Interpretive Thinking:

1. Why did Tony think that he too was going to die?

2. What incident on page 52 leads you to think Joel knew that Tony was often careless?

3. Why didn't Joel feel the thistle in his foot?

4. Why didn't Joel want to hear what the teenager was saying to him about the possibility of finding Tony?

5. Joel had difficulty admitting his knowledge of Tony's death. How would a history of family sessions with in-depth sharing have helped him at the time of the tragedy?

6. What stopped Joel from calling out to his father?

Creative Thinking:

1. Draw Joel, illustrating his summary of thoughts while he was swimming to the sandbar.

2. Create a distress signal that Joel could have placed on the bridge to attract a passing car while he looked for Tony.

3. Role-play the scene between Joel and his father in the house. Include his father's anger and guilt as well as Joel's.

4. Create a missing-person poster as made by Mrs. Zabrinsky about her son, Tony.

5. Role-play Joel and a counselor talking of how Joel feels about Tony's death. Decide what positive action can be taken.

6. Consider Tony, Joel, and their fathers' points of view. Write short soliloquies from each to express their contributions in the tragedy.

Critical Thinking:

1. Why is telling a lie more emotionally exhausting than telling the truth? How could your energies be more wisely used in any situation in which the truth is especially important?

2. Translate what is meant when Joel was relieved that his mother had not smelled the stench of the river, but—curiously—he was also angry.

3. Two emotions that go hand in hand are fear and anger. Often the first reaction following a fear for someone is anger that the person would be so inconsiderate as to scare you. Describe a time when you or someone you know reacted in this manner.

4. The fact that Joel knew he had broken his promise influenced his thinking about the tragedy. Discuss how personal guilt can color one's responses and attitude to something. Discuss this concept in the class.

5. Determine a better way for Tony to have gained self-esteem than his choice. What would be your best way to increase self-esteem? Explain.

6. Why are realistic adventure stories like *On My Honor* intriguing? Determine the most important elements. Write your own realistic adventure that teaches a lesson. The characters are Joel, Tony, and you.

Chapters 9 through 12

Literal Thinking:

1. What was Joel going to teach Bobby as soon as possible?

2. To whom did Joel finally express his deep sense of loss?

3. What was the one thing Joel wanted his father to take away?

4. At this time, what was the one thing Joel felt was easy? Did he really feel this way?

5. Why did Mrs. Zabrinsky assume Joel knew Tony didn't swim?

6. Who is the only one who ultimately didn't have to live with his choice?

Interpretive Thinking:

1. Why did Joel feel as responsible as if he had pushed Tony into the river?

2. Relate how the discovery that Tony had been afraid of water shocked Joel.

3. "Tears are healing": Do you agree or disagree? Debate your position.

4. Why do you think Joel was taking things out on Bobby?

5. What in Joel's and Tony's past relationship led Joel to feel he should take the responsibility for Tony's irresponsible choice?

6. Read aloud portions of the story that lead you to think Joel's father may be suffering as much as Joel.

7. What is the importance of sharing our troubles and conflicts with a trusted individual?

8. Describe what Joel was feeling when he was in the garage tinkering with his bike and his parents were talking with Mr. and Mrs. Zabrinsky.

9. Analyze what Joel's father meant by "You can't live your life by maybe's."

Creative Thinking:

1. Create a crossword puzzle using words from the vocabulary web.

2. As the river personified, tell your version of what happened on the day of the tragic accident.

3. What if Tony and Joel had had a secret sign language to signal trouble? Develop a sign language between you and a friend to quickly and privately express your feelings.

4. Turn *On My Honor* into a mystery story. Perhaps Tony and Joel discover an abandoned cabin or strange footprints near Starved Rock....

5. Write a newspaper article describing the accident at the lake. Interview witnesses.

6. Draw a picture of Joel and Tony on a happier biking expedition. Use their personalities as guides for details about each picture.

7. Role-play the last scene between Joel and his father. Express the grief they both shared. Include Joel's surprise at his father's feelings.

Critical Thinking:

1. Read *Bridge to Terabithia* by Katherine Paterson. How was Joel's relationship to Bobby like Jesse's to May Belle after their friend's death?

2. Sometimes it is very hard to do what is right. At these times, Tony would call Joel *chicken* or *old grandmother*. In reality he was neither of these, but why are such labels that hurt so much so effective? Discuss the personal opinions of the class and particular incidents if someone wishes to share.

3. "Hindsight is the best teacher" has real meaning in this story. Discuss its application here and to aspects of everyone's life.

4. Do you agree with the statement "It's the not knowing that's the worst"? Defend your opinion.

5. Why hadn't Tony thought about his mother and how she would have worried?

6. Do you think Joel might have felt differently about the incident if his father had not made him give his honor that he would go no further than the park?

7. Do you think that Joel and his father will have a closer relationship?

Additional Activities

Visual Art:

1. With colored markers, colored chalk, or crayons, create two abstract illustrations to represent emotions. The first design depicts Joel's confusion as he struggles with his guilt. Perhaps rapid movement, harsh strokes, or deep colors could be used. The second design illustrates his release after confessing his problem. Soothing colors and movements may be used.

2. Create a board game that teaches your classmates lessons learned in the story.

3. Create bumper stickers or badges to make children more aware of water safety.

4. Use crayon resist to illustrate dramatic scenes. First sketch the scene, then apply a heavy coat of crayon. Paint lightly over the picture with black tempera.

5. Create panels on a poster board showing the sequence of the book with titles and pictures.

6. Design the perfect bike for Tony. Include items that he, with his adventurous streak, would particularly enjoy.

7. Rivers are not the only waterways with particular problems. Design warning signs for major beaches, such as shark warnings and undertow areas. Also create ones that are humorous, such as Beware of Flying Beach Balls.

Creative Writing:

1. Write a story as a young child living along a river waterway during the 1700s or 1800s. Do some research to include incidents that authenticate your story.

2. Write a letter from Joel to Mrs. Zabrinsky relating the events of the accident.

3. Using rhymed or unrhymed poetry, paint a picture in words. Write about a time in your life when you learned the value of not always winning.

4. Write a letter of appreciation to someone who has helped you during a crisis.

5. View a videotape of *Ring of Bright Water* dealing with land otters. Write another ending for it.

Drama:

1. In which stories or books can you find the reoccurring theme of humans versus nature? Use a storytelling session to demonstrate the common theme.

2. Role-play a scene between a city planner, a mayor, and students. Each should present views of unique recreational activities that could prevent accidents such as Tony's.

3. Role-play a conversation between Joel and Mrs. Zabrinsky.

4. Role-play Joel developing a lecture program about water safety and traveling to various schools in the area.

5. Develop a scene between Joel and his mother when she learns the truth about Joel's involvement in Tony's death.

6. Role-play a 100-year-old person who has spent his/her life along a river such as the Mississippi or Missouri. Have the person rocking and telling stories of the river. Research historical occurrences to make the recollections believable. Remember mannerisms associated with advanced age—stooped posture, reedy voice, and so on.

Music:

1. Find appropriate background music for this story during different scenes.

2. Choose music that best describes the personality of each boy. Play each example and have the class use it as background for unrhymed poetry about each.

3. Research and share with the class some music generated by life along rivers. Stephen Foster songs such as "Swanee River" told of a particular culture. Jerome Kern's "Old Man River" is another example of the continuity of this life and the importance of the river.

4. Find recordings that help you "see" water. It has many aspects: bubbling, almost laughing, thundering, powerful and destructive, or silent, still, and moody. Write a poem after listening to the recording about how life is like a river.

5. As Joel, write "Tony's Song"—a tribute to a friend you will miss, but always remember.

Social Studies:

1. Interview a police officer who works on a rescue squad. Share the answers with your class.

2. Collect articles in newspapers and magazines of dramatic rescue attempts. Share with your class.

3. Research how certain animals are used in rescue missions, such as St. Bernards in the Alps.

4. Research the Illinois and Mississippi rivers. Discover how their fast-flowing currents aided the movement of people and supplies during the settlement of that area.

5. Look into past newspaper files and compile human interest stories about flooding rivers.

6. "Shooting the rapids" and rafting are sports many people enjoy. Either show the class a true-action videotape or invite a participant to lecture to the class on these sports.

7. Have a discussion on the importance of honest communication with both friends and parents.

Science:

1. Currents play a major part in river and ocean movement as well as in erosion. Research some of the most treacherous currents in the world. Include the meaning of the term *undertow* and what type of current pattern it represents.

2. Take some soil samples from a bank of a waterway and place them in cups. Plant identical seeds in each container. Water each, follow the growth pattern of the seeds, and record the results.

3. Take water samples from various sources including your kitchen tap, placing them in cups with plastic wrap covering. Let them sit in a secluded place with diffused light and observe the results after three, five, and seven days. Discover the developing colonies and cultures. Examine and compare the results both visually and under a microscope. Record your results on a chart. Discuss your findings and conclusions with classmates.

4. What major waterways will have increased pollution by 2001? Brainstorm ways to halt pollution. Write a persuasive message to alert others.

5. Find out about futuristic underwater cities. In a skit, interview the mayor concerning problems of developing such a colony.

6. Interview scuba divers. Find out how the differing levels of very deep water affect divers.

7. Investigate currents in rivers. Discover why they are so dangerous.

8. Discover how far the average person can swim.

Bulletin Board

On My Honor

Cut a gavel from brown paper with a black marker for details. Students create personal or fictional accounts entitled "To Tell the Truth and Nothing But the Truth." Each relates how telling the truth changed a situation and was the best choice.

Sadako and the
Thousand Paper Cranes

Elenor Coerr

Sadako and the Thousand Paper Cranes

by

Elenor Coerr

Putnam, 1977

Sadako dreams of being the best runner in her school in Hiroshima, Japan. She makes progress toward her goal until dizzy spells occur. She thinks the condition can be kept a secret, until the dizziness causes her to collapse at school.

The girl is diagnosed as having leukemia due to the atomic bomb's radiation. During Sadako's final confinement, her best friend brings a folded paper crane. She tells Sadako that if she folds 1,000 paper cranes, her health will return.

With renewed hope, Sadako diligently folds over 500 cranes. She continues until her strength is gone, and she knows the 644th is her last. Her class continues to fold until 1,000 are folded.

The heroine shows true courage and wisdom in this tale, which is based on a true story of a Japanese girl. A statue of Sadako is in Hiroshima Peace Park to remind the world of the loss and futility of war.

PATIENTS

HOSPITAL

PAIN

LEUKEMIA

EXAMINATION

CHAN

GRIEF

DISEASE

DEATH

MIRACLE

TEARS

Sadako and the Thousand Paper Cranes

HEADACHES

FEAR

SHRINES

KIMONO

PEACE DAY

O'BON

SICKNESS

BLACKNESS

RADIATION

DIZZINESS

KOKESKI

Chapters 1 through 5

Literal Thinking:

1. Why did the golden crane have a place of honor?

2. Give the author's definition of *radiation*.

3. Tell how Sadako explained the feelings she experienced at the time of the destruction of the bomb.

4. Name the two good-luck signs Sadako observed on the morning of memorial day.

5. What made Mr. Sasaki especially proud of Sadako?

Interpretive Thinking:

1. What elements in Sadako's personality aided her in facing her illness?

2. Sadako was helped by listening to a story. Tell a story that has helped you in a difficult situation.

3. Analyze why the author placed the prologue at the beginning of the book.

4. Sadako hurried through the building where the bombing of Hiroshima was displayed. Relate an experience that gave you the same feelings as Sadako.

5. Explain why Sadako felt that the spider had brought her good luck.

6. Explain the meaning of adding *chan* after a person's name. Do we have a similar custom?

Creative Thinking:

1. Create paper cranes with a haiku written on their wings. Each child expresses wishes of hope and health for Sadako. Suspend the cranes from the classroom ceiling.

2. Recreate the hospital dialogue between Sadako and Chizuko.

3. Sadako wished she could magically wish away her dizzy spells. Relate a time when you would have gladly had something removed from your life.

4. Research the traditional Japanese kimono, its history and importance. Design one for yourself or someone you know.

5. Interview someone that was in the Pacific front. Share the information from the interview with classmates.

Critical Thinking:

1. How can Sadako's family best influence her recovery? Explain.

2. Decide on an object you would fold that most reflects your personality.

3. Why was Sadako's reaction of covering her ears so instinctive when she heard the bad news?

4. Why was Sadako immediately taken to the Red Cross hospital for atomic bomb victims?

5. Conclude why Sadako kept the dizziness a secret.

Chapters 6 through 10

Literal Thinking:

1. What was Sadako's last vision before she died?

2. How did the Bamboo class help Sadako live on in the hearts of the Japanese people?

3. How did Sadako attempt to cheer Kenji?

4. Explain the meaning of the celebration of O'Bon.

5. How many cranes had Sadako folded before she died?

Interpretive Thinking:

1. How did Kenji make Sadako more appreciative of her own circumstances?

2. What effect does the wish engraved on Sadako's monument have on you?

3. Explain how Sadako's father thought he had been tricked.

4. The family placed bean and rice cakes on a shelf for "ghostly" visitors. Think of similar examples from other countries.

5. Sadako began to feel well and was allowed to go home for O'Bon. What do you think was happening to the leukemia at that time?

Creative Thinking:

1. Find out about the great Greek warrior Achilles and his final view of war. Design a motto concerning war which illustrates the lesson he learned.

2. Invent an interview with Anne Frank after reading excerpts from *The Diary of Anne Frank*. Did Anne and Sadako have similar messages to tell the world about peace? Explain.

3. Create your own version of the memorial from papier-mâché, clay, or other media.

4. Create a diorama or an illustration of your interpretation of how Sadako's hospital room must have looked.

Critical Thinking:

1. Determine an even more creative method of bringing Sadako's message to the world.

2. Albert Einstein believed imagination was as important as information. How did Sadako prove the truth of this belief?

3. Evaluate why folding the cranes gave Sadako a feeling of some control over her illness.

4. Research some of the decision makers' accounts of the decision to drop the atomic bomb. Organize a debate about the necessity of this action.

Additional Activities

Visual Art:

1. Invite an origami expert to your class to demonstrate paper folding. Create a crane or a tortoise, both symbols, in Japan, of good fortune and a long life.

2. Create Noh masks from poster board or paper plates. The masks represent the emotions of joy, anger, sorrow, and hope that are described in the story.

3. Create a class mural of paper cranes, each with a wish for world peace written on it.

4. As a class, draw and color butterflies of different sizes. Laminate and bend them into various positions. Deliver them to a children's ward in a hospital.

Creative Writing:

1. Write a journal as Sadako. Tell about your feelings regarding yourself, your family, and the disease itself.

2. If you were in charge of a children's hospital how might you make life easier for the children?

3. Write a book review of *Sadako and the Thousand Paper Cranes* by Elenor Coerr for your media center.

4. After reading about the events concerning the bombing of Japan, write a class newspaper. Write an editorial or draw a political cartoon about the events.

5. Write a haiku about one of the turning points in the story. Write only half of the poem. Give the partially written poem to a partner to be completed.

Drama:

1. Create a Noh play based on *Sadako and the Thousand Paper Cranes*. Noh masks you have designed add to the authenticity. Actors, with masks, pantomime the story as a chorus chants the story.

2. Research the importance of the tea ceremony in Japan. Role-play a tea ceremony with rice cakes and green tea.

3. Write a play centering on a meeting of eye witnesses to the aftermath of the bombing in Japan.

4. Paraphrase portions of the story and perform a soliloquy as Sadako. Vocal variations can convey her strength and feelings throughout each selection.

Music:

1. Create a rap song concerning the futility of war and the blessings of peace.

2. Listen to a recording of "We Are the World." Create a similar song emphasizing peace and world understanding.

3. With paper, create costumes for hands, using folded paper cranes. Mime to oriental music in a darkened room.

4. Compare ancient Japanese music to the current music popular in Japan. Discuss the reasons for the differences.

Social Studies:

1. Research the flight of the Enola Gay, not only for its historical impact, but the resulting problems.

2. Many aspects of Japanese life were changed after the war. The Japanese had always revered the emperor, but even that changed. Research the before and after of the war including the role of General Douglas MacArthur.

3. In Japan, cranes are considered good luck. Other countries have other animals and insects that are considered lucky. Research and give a report to your class. Examples include crickets and storks.

4. Research the Japanese factory system. How are the Japanese proving that cooperation is more lucrative than competition? Share your ideas in a class debate: Competition vs. Cooperation. Who is the real winner?

5. Find out about the current trade problems between United States and Japan. Select a pen pal in Japan. Perhaps the two of you can think of peaceful and creative solutions. Share letters concerning the problems with your class.

Science:

1. Research the unusual night fishing bird called the cormorant on the island of Honshu. Demonstrate its fishing prowess in a skit for the class.

2. Learn more about the women oyster divers and oyster farming which produces cultured pearls in Japan.

3. Dolphins, porpoises, and sharks are abundant in Japanese waters. Learn more about the defenses of the porpoises against the sharks. Role-play an interview or news broadcast with a porpoise telling how he confronted the shark.

4. Compare the aftereffects of the bombs on Nagasaki and Hiroshima to the effects of the Chernobyl accident in the Soviet Union. How did the information gained from Japan aid in this accident?

5. The first uses of atomic energy were negative. As a class, brainstorm and research some of the positive uses of the same power.

Math:

1. Study the statistics of those killed in Hiroshima by the bomb. Compare the statistics to an American city.

2. Research to find the current value of the yen. Create problems based on the yen's value to stump a partner.

3. Learn to pronounce Japanese numbers. After learning the pronunciation, create verbal addition and subtraction problems.

Japanese Numbers

1	ichi	5	go	9	ku
2	ni	6	roku	10	ju
3	san	7	shichi	11	juichi
4	shi	8	hachi	12	juni

Bulletin Board

Sadako and the Thousand Paper Cranes

Cut four-leaf clovers and a border from coordinating paper. Cut ovals for a central focus. Each student illustrates something that has proven to be a good luck symbol for him/her.

Bridge to Terabithia

Katherine Paterson

Bridge to Terabithia
by
Katherine Paterson
Scholastic, 1988

Fifth-grader Jesse Aarons, an introspective farm boy, plans to be the fastest runner in his school. On his first day he is bested by his new neighbor, Leslie Burke. Because she is shunned by her classmates, Leslie becomes Jesse's friend.

Several weeks later, the friends decide to stake out a magical kingdom in the woods. They build a castle in their magic kingdom of Terabithia. Here Leslie tells Jesse stories from the many books she has read.

During Easter vacation, the creek bordering Terabithia becomes a swift torrent. Jesse all but decides to abandon the kingdom. Before making the decision, he spends a day touring the National Gallery in Washington, D.C.

Jesse returns to be told that Leslie has drowned in the creek. After many days of mourning, he makes a wreath for his departed queen to be placed in the sacred kingdom.

A few days later, Jesse hears his sister May Belle crying for help. He rescues her before she, too, plunges into the swollen creek. Later, he leads her to his magical kingdom and crowns her his new queen. His recovery from the loss of Leslie shows the legacy of strength Leslie has left him. This moving story won the 1978 Newbery Award.

Spider web word diagram labeled with the following words around the center labeled *Bridge to Terabithia*:

BARIPITY
RELENTLESSLY
CRYING
RUMPLED
DREDGING
LOVED
CREMATION
DOUSED
FOUND
STROKING
FRAGILE
RHYTHMIC
FELL
CARED
SHIVERING
SCARED
DIE
LOPSIDED
PROCESSION
DROWN
THREATENED
ACCUSATION

Chapters 1 through 3

Literal Thinking:

1. Why would Jesse be as hot as "popping grease" even when the morning was chilly?

2. When did Mrs. Myers traditionally smile?

3. What compliment did Leslie pay Jesse after the race?

4. Why did Jesse envy May Belle?

5. What message had Jesse received from his father concerning his talent for drawing?

6. Which teacher appreciated Jesse's talent?

Interpretive Thinking:

1. Explain why being the only kid in school "worth shooting" was such a compliment.

2. Why would new additions to the community such as Leslie and Miss Edmunds ultimately be a positive influence for the students at Lark Creek?

3. Describe three incidents showing that Jesse's friends and family had difficulty with differences. Explain how each incident could have been changed by a more accepting attitude.

4. How did Jesse conclude his new desk must have belonged to Sally Koch?

5. What were Leslie's thoughts as she ran like a flight of ducks in autumn, after her first day of school?

Creative Thinking:

1. Pretend you are Jesse. Have a one-man show in your classroom. Draw animals of your choice: mythical, fantastic, realistic. Combine your animal design with a classmate's and write a story together about your animals.

2. Organize a talent day for your class. Each student shares his/her talent, particularly if it is a "secret" talent like Jesse's.

3. Draw a cartoon of Jesse as he would look if he had swallowed grasshoppers. Show a cutout view of the grasshoppers.

4. Draw a cartoon or caricature of Monster Mouth Myers.

5. Jesse said that one day he would fly instead of run. Draw your illustration of this occurrence.

Critical Thinking:

1. Analyze how drawing creates a peaceful feeling for Jesse. Is there something that gives you such a calm feeling?

2. What incidents in chapters 1 through 3 took the most courage for Jesse to face?

3. What animals would best personify Jesse, Leslie, Miss Edmunds, May Belle, and Fulcher? Share your choices with your class.

4. Analyze the difference in the way the father treated Jesse and his sisters. Explain why this was so bothersome to Jesse. Do you agree or disagree? Explain your feelings.

5. Discuss why Jesse and the other boys felt such depression at being beaten by a girl.

Chapters 4 through 6

Literal Thinking:

1. Why did Leslie's parents move to this area?

2. What did Jesse first think a string quartet was?

3. What song led Jesse to decide to become more like himself?

4. What question did Leslie ask that Jesse wished she hadn't?

5. What was considered to be pure poison at Lark Creek Elementary?

Interpretive Thinking:

1. Explain why Leslie's mode of dress was by choice and not from necessity.

2. Explain why the rope was so important to the magical kingdom.

3. Who was the real giant in their lives?

4. Interpret what Leslie meant by "money is not the problem."

5. What attitude did Leslie's teacher model when she suggested writing a composition?

6. What feeling for Leslie inspired Jesse to confront Janice Avery?

7. What was Jesse referring to when he said he couldn't get the poetry of the trees?

Creative Thinking:

1. Add to the story a favorite character from another book. Develop the changes this personality would manifest in a new chapter.

2. Create a trial scene with attorneys, judge, and jury for Leslie, Jesse, and Janice Avery. Decide on a verdict to rehabilitate Janice in which Jesse and Leslie are involved.

3. Create a written description and drawing of Miss Edmunds.

4. Role-play the scene of Jesse helping Leslie on the bus. Include her frustrations and anger and his embarrassment.

5. Draw a cartoon of Leslie being such an angelic student but with mischievous plans going on in her head.

Critical Thinking:

1. Why would living on an old farm be more conducive to learning what is important than would city living? Can you think of a better place to learn it? Explain.

2. Have you ever felt closer to a friend than someone in your family? Explain.

3. Compare the mythical kingdoms of Terabithia, Narnia, and Camelot. Discuss the similarities and differences.

4. Evaluate the phrase "Even a prince can be a fool."

5. Analyze why it only felt like Christmas when Jesse was with Leslie.

Chapters 7 through 9

Literal Thinking:

1. What did Judy read that enveloped Jesse in warmth?

2. List things that are as delicate as a dandelion.

3. What inner reaction did Jesse most fear about himself?

4. What was Leslie trying to understand more?

5. Who was considered to be the guardian and jester?

6. What caused Janice to lose complete control?

Interpretive Thinking:

1. Contrast the stories of Jesse's mother and Leslie's mother.

2. What incident surprised Jesse that was due to his belief that Leslie was unafraid of anything?

3. Relate how Miss Edmund's sensitivity helped Jesse out of a potentially embarrassing situation.

4. What truth had Leslie discovered when she noted that Jesse hated having to do things?

5. Why was Leslie able to look at the essence of a situation quicker than Jesse? Relate a dialogue from the story that supports this point.

Creative Thinking:

1. Listen to recordings of songs taught by Miss Edmunds. Learn your favorites as a class.

2. With a partner, create a special language or code for Terabithia. Write a message from Jesse to Leslie in your secret language. Thank Leslie for bringing such joy to your life. As Leslie, relate how Jesse is making your life more meaningful.

3. Select objects that remind you of Leslie. Arrange them in an interesting way, then draw a still life in charcoal or colored chalk.

4. Think of an imaginative way to have told Leslie of your fears if you had been in Jesse's situation.

5. Jesse's feelings for Leslie were like a stew. Relate how the progress of their friendship was like a four-course meal. Design a menu showing how each course relates to progress in their friendship.

6. Create a how-to booklet for classmates. Illustrate how friendship is better left to evolve than being forced.

7. Find out what *serendipity* means. Write a fairy tale about Terabithia with serendipity as the theme.

Critical Thinking:

1. Jesse knew he could not force the magic. Relate an experience in which you felt your "magic" was forced. Contrast the result to a time when experience was allowed to flow. What experience was the more creative?

2. Jesse transferred words into action concerning Janice Avery. What incident in your life when philosophy changed to action was more effective?

3. Georgia O'Keeffe, famous American artist, felt that empty walls were refreshing. She thought that the emptiness left space for imagination. How was the Burkes' philosophy about their floor similar to the artist's?

4. Do you agree with the rule that Mr. Turner made of not mixing troubles at home with those at school? Why or why not?

5. Evaluate why Jesse decided to alter his attitude toward Mr. Burke.

6. Jesse used a familiar childhood song to keep from being afraid. Relate a time you used a personal technique to keep yourself from being fearful.

Chapters 10 through 13

Literal Thinking:

1. Explain what sound you associate with the term *baripity*.

2. What did Jesse do with the paints Leslie had given him as a gift?

3. Who told Jesse that Leslie had drowned?

4. What question did Jesse want to ask Bill?

Interpretive Thinking:

1. Why did Jesse not want people to snicker at Leslie's burial attire?

2. Analyze what Terabithia meant to the two children.

3. How did Mrs. Myers help Jesse understand he would never forget Leslie?

4. Relate a situation in which your own fear nearly "squeezed you white?"

5. Describe Jesse's feelings when he went to Leslie's home after her death.

Creative Thinking:

1. Read *Sadako and the Thousand Paper Cranes* by Elenor Coerr. Create an origami symbol that would best celebrate Leslie's life.

2. Jesse was described as "shaking like jello." Think of three additional similes to describe Jesse's reactions.

3. Create a diamante poem. Focus on Jesse's desire to pay back the beauty and caring that Leslie's vision and strength had given him.

4. Create your own Terabithia. Use your imagination to develop a place in which you could create anything. Describe the place and what you would do there.

Critical Thinking:

1. Evaluate why Jesse wondered if there was still a Terabithia.

2. Why did Jesse deny that Leslie had died?

3. Evaluate the phrase "The smarter you are the more things can scare you." Compare this with the phrase "Ignorance is bliss."

4. Why was Jesse's imaginary funeral an important step in his healing?

Additional Activities

Visual Art:

1. Design a magical kingdom like Terabithia using a model or mural. Create the entire environment with lakes, buildings, and so on.

2. Create tennis shoes uniquely symbolic of Leslie and Jesse. Illustrate the shoes with drawings of their likes, dislikes, talents, and so on.

3. Collect materials of your choice and create your own wreath.

4. Transfer the phrase "Like an astronaut wandering about on the moon, alone" to a visual picture illustrating Jesse's feeling.

5. Create a wreath for someone or something that has taught you a lesson in life.

Creative Writing:

1. Write a short epitaph for Leslie. Make it unique to celebrate her life.

2. Write a diary describing the adventures of Leslie and Jesse in a fantastic kingdom much like Terabithia.

3. Rewrite the chapter titles summarizing the feelings of each chapter.

4. Have Jesse write a journal telling excerpts from the story. Include the progression of his feelings toward Leslie through each level.

5. Write a letter to a friend or classmate telling why he/she should read *Bridge to Terabithia* by Katherine Paterson.

Drama:

1. Write a short script of future adventures in Terabithia. The main characters are Jesse and May Belle. Role-play for your class.

2. Summarize dramatic incidents to use in a storytelling session with classmates.

3. Depict Jesse as an elderly man telling his grandchildren the story and feelings about Leslie and Terabithia.

4. Create telephone conversations between any two characters. Tell each other about the lesson you have learned by participating in the story.

Music:

1. Find instrumental recordings that exemplify emotional scenes in the book. See if classmates can determine the portion of the story that you are depicting.

2. Learn lyrics of songs from *Free to Be You and Me* by Marlo Thomas and others. How could the meanings of these songs have helped Jesse? How can they help you?

3. Choose music that you feel would be appropriate to scenes in Terabithia. Play it while you read the excerpts for classmates.

4. What could have been the national anthem for Terabithia? Choose music and create lyrics for the anthem.

5. It is said that the teacher becomes the one who is taught. What lessons in life did Leslie learn as she taught profound lessons to Jesse? Write lyrics for a song expressing Leslie's feelings.

Social Studies:

1. Write letters to the Smithsonian and the National Gallery in Washington, D.C. Collect brochures and share them with your class. Plan an imaginary or real field trip.

2. Read *Wait for Me, Watch for Me, Eula Bee* by Patricia Beatty. Find other accounts of children captured by Indians. Write your own adventure as a captive who survived in a historical short story.

3. Atlantis has been recorded in the writings of Greek philosophers. Research Atlantis, its suspected location, reasons for its disappearance, and so on.

4. Research fairy tales from different lands. Choose one that reminds you of the adventures in Terabithia. Share with your class.

5. Learn about the camouflage methods in hunting buffalo by the Plains Indians. Reenact a scene for your class.

6. Family life was the target in this book. Research your own family. Find out when your family arrived in America and any unusual stories about an ancestor, and create a family tree.

Science:

1. Invite a resource person to your class to discuss the dynamics of death and how a significant person reacts to death.

2. Learn more about the songs of the whales. Listen to a recording to find out if you can decode their messages.

3. Research floods, their causes and prevention. Find newspaper or magazine accounts of major U.S. floods. Share the information by role-playing an interview with survivors.

4. Research clabber and why it was a staple in the past. Explain how it has evolved in current times.

5. Create a booklet of the various trees and plants mentioned in Terabithia. Examples are pine, dogwood, redbud, and oak. Explain why, given the natural vegetation, the general location of a story is easily pinpointed.

6. Terabithia was abundant with vegetation. For plant growth in your classroom, try the following procedure. Cut the top from a potato, spoon out a portion, and place wet cotton with a few grass seeds within. Keep the seeds moist. The result will look like green hair. Cut the potato to create a face.

Bulletin Board

Bridge to Terabithia

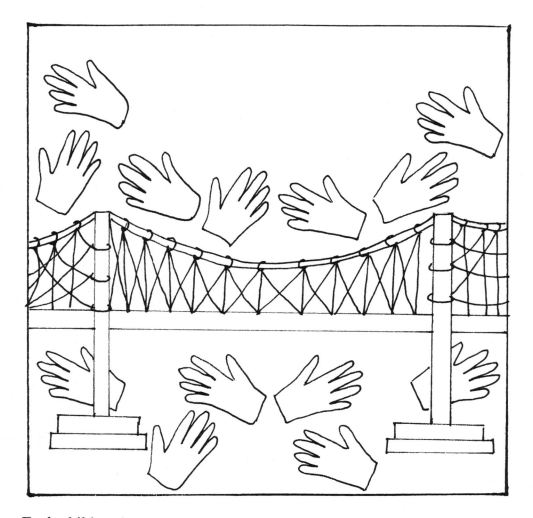

Each child makes an oversized cutout of his/her hand. On the cutout, each student describes how he/she has been a bridge or taken a friend's hand in a situation of need.

ADDITIONAL BOOKS ON DEATH

1. *Allison's Grandfather.* Linda Peavy. Scribner, 1981.

   While visiting her grandparents for the summer, Allison makes friends with Erica. Erica reminisces over pleasant times spent with the grandfather as she tries to deal with his death.

2. *Annie and the Old One.* Miska Miles. Little, Brown, 1971.

   A young Navajo girl attempts to stall the passage of time because she learns her grandmother only has a limited time to live.

3. *Dusty Was My Friend: Coming to Terms with Loss.* Andrea Clardy. Human Sciences Press, 1984.

   Eight-year-old Benjamin tells of his friendship with Dusty after the child's untimely death.

4. *The Empty Window.* Eve Bunting. Warne, 1980.

   C.J. avoids seeing his friend who is dying. Knowing his friend is fascinated with parrots, he resolves to bring one to him. Finding himself with his dying friend, both boys decide to free the parrot. Through their meeting and discussion of the freedom of the bird, C.J. resolves his feelings about his friend's approaching death.

5. *A Gift for Tia Rosa.* Karen T. Taha. Dillon, 1985.

   Carmelda wants to knit a shawl for her dying neighbor, but her neighbor dies before she can complete the shawl. Carmelda's mother helps her realize she can share her love for Tia Rosa with others.

6. *The Magic Moth.* Virginia Moth. Seabury, 1972.

   The story of a young girl who is dying and her special relationship with her younger brother, as well as the effect of her death on her family.

7. *Mustard.* Charlotte Graeber. Macmillan, 1982.

   Mustard, the beloved family cat, has a heart ailment. Alex must learn to bear the grief of having to put his pet to sleep.

8. *The Truth about Mary Rose.* Marilyn Sachs. Doubleday, 1973.

   A little girl who adored her late aunt learns more about herself and this aunt when she accidentally finds a special shoebox belonging to her grandmother.

9. *When Grandpa Journeys into Winter.* Craig K. Strete. Greenwillow, 1979.

   Little Thunder cannot accept his grandfather's impending death. Tayhia, his grandfather, helps him understand that memories live on after death.

10. *Whiskers Once and Always.* Doris Orgel. Viking/Penguin, 1986.

    When Becky's cat, Whiskers, dies, she shows no grief until a careless comment from a classmate results in violence. Becky's punching of Jason shows the emotional upheaval she feels at the loss of her pet.

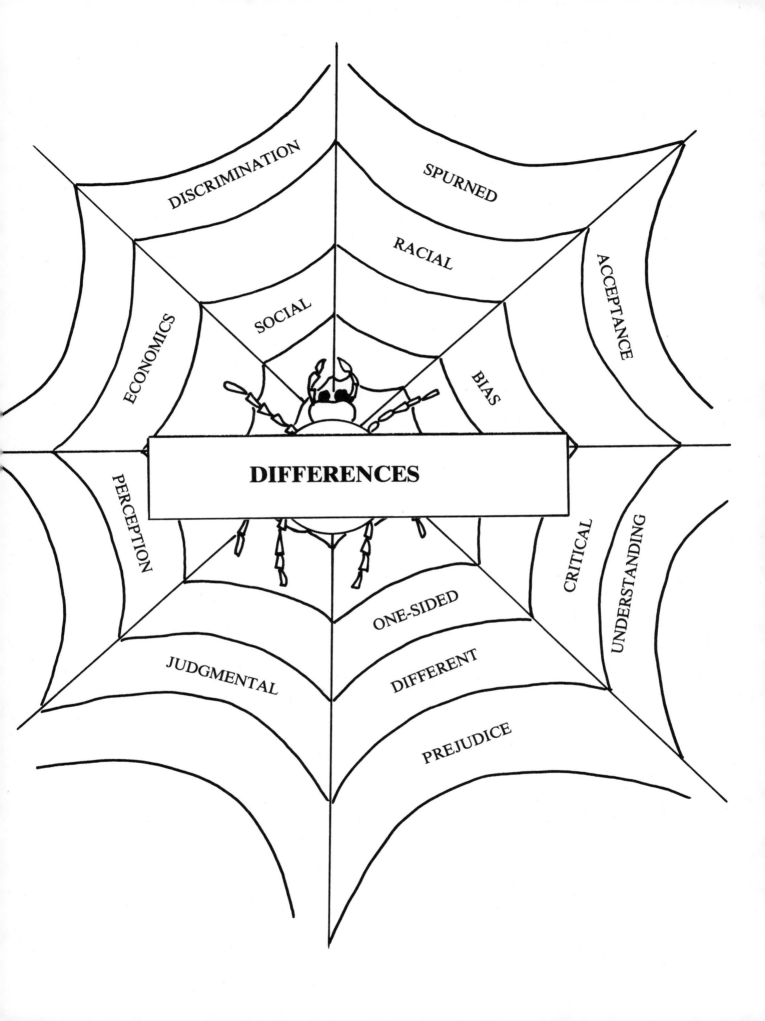

Harriet the Spy

Louise Fitzhugh

Harriet the Spy
by

Louise Fitzhugh
Harper & Row, 1964

Harriet is a gifted child who wants to become a writer. To encourage her, Ole Golly, her governess, suggests she keep all of her observations in a notebook. The notebook becomes Harriet's real world.

Ole Golly and Harriet have a very special understanding of each other. When Ole Golly marries, Harriet's world begins to crumble. She feels deserted except for her notebook.

As Harriet struggles to adjust to Ole Golly's departure, her notebook is filled with candid statements about her classmates. The classmates react with vengeful pranks on Harriet. Feeling rejected, Harriet refuses to go to school.

Harriet's parents contact Ole Golly and a psychiatrist to help them understand their daughter's behavior. Ole Golly's advice is very practical. She tells Harriet to be more kind and to expand her writing. After Harriet directs her writing into a productive venture, which is the school class newspaper, her self-esteem is strengthened.

This book explores the mind of a gifted child, the differences she feels when among peers, and how her talents are wisely channeled by caring adults.

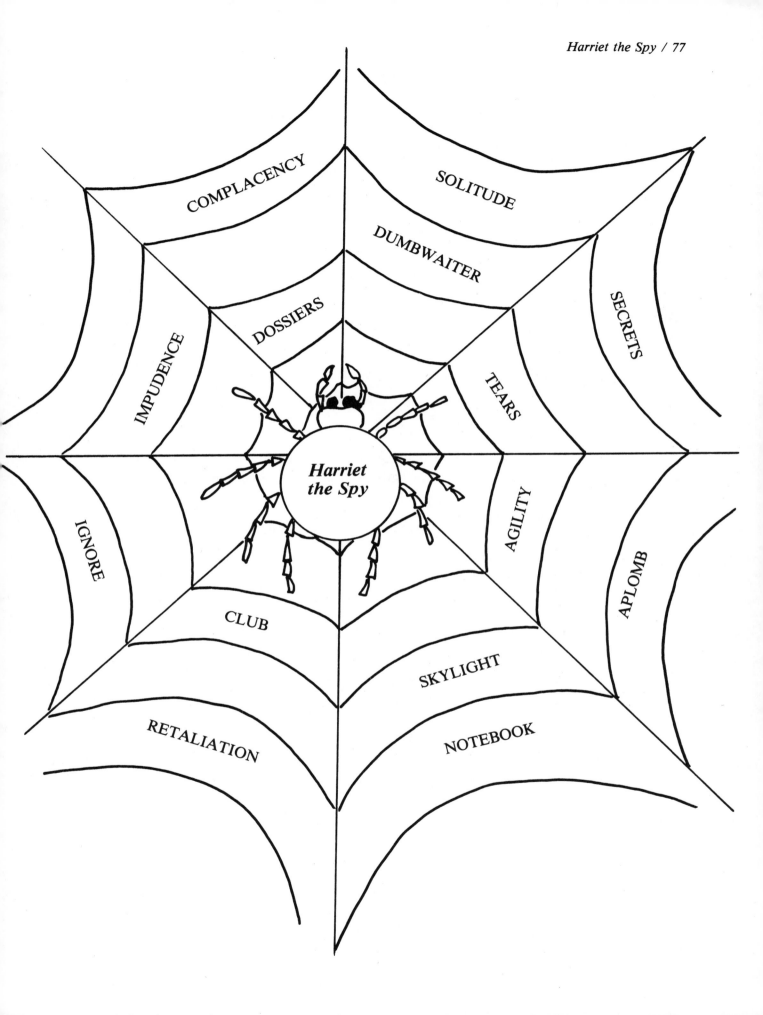

Chapters 1 through 4

Literal Thinking:

1. Why does Harriet write everything down?
2. What lessons were Harriet and Janie determined not to take?
3. Where does Harriet live?
4. What was the name of Harriet's nurse?
5. Why had Harriet christened the boy the "boy with the purple socks"?
6. What was Janie's great plan for the future?

Interpretive Thinking:

1. Why do you feel Ole Golly took the children to meet her mother?
2. What do you think about the patterning of all of Harriet's entries concerning the other students in her notebook?
3. Why do you think there was a need for Ole Golly to take care of Harriet when she had her parents?
4. What in Harriet's home life may have encouraged her to be a spy?
5. What does the silence between the Robinsons tell about their relationship?
6. What do all of Harriet's observations have in common?
7. Why do you think Ole Golly looked sad during the visit with her mother?

Creative Thinking:

1. Create a map of Harriet's spy route.
2. Think of a time of day or night you think is sad and pleasant at the same time. What does this time remind you of?
3. Go to a local shopping mall. Take a notebook and write observations of the people you see. Choose your favorite and write a short story about the character you have described.
4. Which situation was the most mysterious to you and one in which you would have liked to be the spy? Describe the different methods you would use to solve the mystery.
5. As a class, read one of Dostoyevsky's shorter works and analyze its intention and meaning.
6. Harriet had a spy belt with items she felt she might need. With a partner, brainstorm and create a new more complex version.
7. Which character does Harriet feel truly loves his work? Do you know someone like this? Write a short description and sketch a picture of your person doing the job he/she loves.
8. Which character seems the most puzzling to you? Make a list of reasons for a class discussion.
9. Janie walked with her head averted as she was shy and did not want to see anyone. Share with a partner a technique you have used to help overcome shyness at one time or another.
10. Debate the morality of the methods Harriet uses to gather her information.

11.   What do you think is meant by Ole Golly's statement "We would often be sorry if our wishes were gratified"?

12.   Is it a good idea to admit that you do not know something? Why?

Chapters 5 through 8

Literal Thinking:

1.   What was the worst thing Harriet could be told by Ole Golly?

2.   Who helped change Harriet's mind about taking dancing lessons?

3.   What was Mr. Waldenstein's job?

4.   Why was Ole Golly planning to leave before she was dismissed?

5.   List a couple of questions that Harriet felt were unanswerable.

6.   Why had Mr. Waldenstein changed his profession?

7.   Where was Ole Golly going to live?

8.   What was the sixth grade going to be for the Christmas pageant?

9.   What role did Harriet have in the production?

Interpretive Thinking:

1.   Does Mr. Welsch understand the relationship between Ole Golly and Harriet?

2.   One often-repeated phrase is "If you read, you are never alone." Debate the validity of this statement.

3.   What do you think Harriet's father does for a living? Compare answers.

4.   Have you ever been disappointed by someone you trusted? Write about the experience in a make-believe letter to the person who disappointed you.

5.   Mr. Waldenstein said he never knew how to value things. Has there been a turning point in your life that has taught you what you consider the important things in life?

Creative Thinking:

1.   Read Wordsworth's "I Wandered Lonely as a Cloud." Illustrate the phrase "That inward eye/which is the bliss of solitude."

2.   Be an interviewer similar to Harriet. Ask five married people how they were introduced to their spouses. Share results with the class. Which was the most unusual, humorous, embarrassing, and so on?

3.   Ole Golly loved flowers. Draw a floral tribute to her from Harriet. Include a thank-you for all she did for Harriet.

4.   As Harriet, collect objects meaningful to each of the characters; for example, a telephone for Mrs. Plumber, a vase for the Robinsons, and a picture of a cat for Harrison Withers. Tell from your point of view why they are important to the characters.

5.   Create a dance of vegetables. Assume two roles that the children were assigned. Videotape it. As Miss Berry, narrate the story of the vegetables as they dance.

6. Imagine that *Harriet the Spy* is a movie. Write a press release of the movie for a newspaper.

7. Draw a picture of the three going to the movie in Mr. Waldenstein's cart.

Critical Thinking:

1. Analyze the reaction of Mr. and Mrs. Welsch when they came home to find Harriet gone. Relate a time when your parents reacted strongly when you were late or were not where you were supposed to be at a certain time.

2. Analyze why Harriet feels the need to spy on her neighbors even to the point of breaking and entering.

3. Compare the reactions of the Dei Santi family and the auto accident to that of Harriet's parents when they came home and found her gone.

4. Was Mrs. Welsch being fair to Ole Golly when she so quickly dismissed her after the movie accident?

5. Determine what will happen to Harriet now that Ole Golly has gone. Write your opinions in a notebook as if you were Harriet.

6. Debate the question of Ole Golly's guilt in not being more responsible to Harriet. Role-play with judge, attorneys, witnesses, and jury.

Chapters 9 through 12

Literal Thinking:

1. Why did Harriet have to go home for a bath?

2. What was the name of the club in which Harriet was not invited?

3. What happened to Harriet's notebook? Why did it matter so much?

4. Who was reduced to tears over Harriet's notebook?

5. What was the real name of Purple Socks?

6. What entry in her notebook showed that Harriet was beginning to come out of her depression?

Interpretive Thinking:

1. Explain how Harriet had become a Method actor.

2. What difference has Ole Golly's absence made in Harriet's relationship with her parents?

3. Did you agree with the way Mrs. Plumber and her maid handled finding Harriet in the dumbwaiter? Discuss your opinion with a partner.

4. How did the children in class retaliate after the notebook situation?

5. Analyze why Harriet wrote, "Everybody hates me," in big black letters and, "Whatever happens, don't let me cry," in very small letters.

6. Have you ever experienced being left out of a group activity? What did you do about it? What advice could you give to Harriet to do about it? Write about your experience in your journal.

7. Would you want Harriet as a student in your classroom? List reasons why or why not for a class discussion.

8. What would you have done to change the children's attitude toward you had you been Harriet? Make a booklet as Harriet entitled, "What I have learned about making and keeping friends."

Creative Thinking:

1. Using colored markers or pen and ink and large drawing paper, illustrate the incident with the spilled ink.

2. Design a notebook cover that would keep others from reading it.

3. Draw a caricature of students as the different elements of a Christmas dinner.

4. As Harriet, write a note to one of the people upset by her notebook, explaining his/her side of the situation.

Critical Thinking:

1. What were Rachel's real feelings about spilling the ink? Determine them by role-playing Rachel in a discussion at the clubhouse.

2. Do you think Miss Elson could have handled the incident of the spilled ink in a more productive manner? Determine what you think she should have done.

3. Why did the cook's response seem especially insensitive when Harriet was sent home from school?

4. Do you think Harriet intended to hurt her friends? Why or why not?

5. Have each student be something associated with a Christmas dinner. They project what parts they are playing through mannerisms and costumes.

6. Judge Janie's reading Harriet's secret thoughts to everyone. Think about a time when you wrote a note or said something about someone and then the person either read it or was told what you said. Evaluate how you felt. Share with a partner.

Chapters 13 through 16

Literal Thinking:

1. List the ways in which Harriet planned to retaliate against each child.

2. On her first day back at school, why was Harriet purposely late?

3. Why was Sport's father so happy?

4. What plan did Harriet's parents develop to try to help her?

5. Who selected the new editor for the sixth-grade page?

Interpretive Thinking:

1. Since the loss of her notebook, Harriet felt she could no longer think. Why do you think this affected her so strongly?

2. Do you think all of Harriet's problems came from the reading of her notebook? Explain your opinion.

3. By the time of Harriet's return to school, what shows Harriet was accepting herself and others?

4. How would having a classmate like Harriet change activities in your classroom?

5. Harriet did not generally admire the people she wrote about. Take a different approach. Choose a classmate and write about the characteristics you *do* admire. See if your classmates can guess what person you are writing about.

6. Why did Harriet no longer care about signing her name to anything?

Creative Thinking:

1. As a friend of Harriet's, write a letter to her parents giving them some ways to help with the problem.

2. Sometimes working with aspects of a problem helps to solve it. As Harriet, make a collage with pictures and words expressing all of your concerns and worries.

3. Create a three-panel cartoon of the change in Harriet as she listens to her parents' conversation through the library doors.

4. Write a class newspaper for the year 2050. What investigative reports can you create about robots and humanoids and life on a faraway galaxy? Turn the story of *Harriet the Spy* into a fable. What truth does Harriet's story illustrate? Weave this truth into your story.

5. Find out which countries do not observe freedom of the press. Role-play Harriet confronting the officials who enforce censorship.

6. Create club rules for an imaginary club. What do you think is important?

7. Design a pair of glasses for Harriet.

Critical Thinking:

1. In Ole Golly's letter there were two interesting quotations: "Writing is to put love into the world, not to use against your friends," and "I guard my memories and love them, but I don't get them and lie down." Of these, which expresses something you relate to? Explain to a partner.

2. Analyze the phrase "You cannot understand a man until you have walked in his moccasins." How would this help the understanding between people? Debate.

3. Predict what would happen if Harriet carried out her plan of hurting the classmates on her list.

4. What advice would you give a person like Harriet, who struggled to retain her individuality while still part of a group?

Additional Activities

Visual Art:

1. Harrison Withers seemed lonely except for his cats. Can you find a senior citizen or patient in a hospital for whom you can illustrate friendship cards?

2. Design a special clubhouse just for you.

3. Make a spy list or kit for a master spy.

4. Create an official identification card for Harriet the spy.

5. Using a paper-doll concept, with cardboard create the figure of Harriet the spy. Use paper and markers to make various costumes she could use to disguise herself.

Creative Writing:

1. Have students obtain pen pals from another state exchanging observations of their schools and classmates.

2. As Harriet, write an answer to Ole Golly's letter.

3. Have Harriet the spy act as a reporter in an area of the world where there is unrest or a particularly interesting problem occurring. Have her use her unique style to report her news story.

4. Have each student bring in an editorial, either a political or regular cartoon without captions. The students then caption them as Harriet would have done.

5. As Harriet, have students write a recipe for what they consider an interesting life.

6. Realistic fiction such as *Harriet the Spy* is written to seem very real. Write a story about real problems of growth.

7. Design a practical reference book for your classroom. Create a series of realistic fiction summaries of realistic fiction authors such as Robert Burch, Vera and Bill Cleaver, Scott O'Dell, and others.

8. Write a diamante showing how Harriet's feelings toward herself and others changed after she became a writer for the class newspaper.

Drama:

1. Develop a monologue about Harriet and her life, using the theme "The injustice of it all!"

2. Role-play the primary adults in this book discussing this unusual child and her behavior.

3. Be Harriet. Give a three-minute speech on the art of keeping a journal and being a good spy.

4. Role-play a telephone conversation between Ole Golly and Harriet about the rejection of classmates and the final triumph as a newspaper writer.

5. Role-play a scene in which Harriet is explaining her notebook to friends in the clubhouse.

Music:

1. What orchestral instrument would be similar to each of the main characters? For example, Harrison Withers might be an oboe with its haunting tones.

2. Harriet struggled to be an individual. Write lyrics to a song about the different kinds of beauty found in every individual. Use autoharp accompaniment.

3. Listen to a version of the musical show *You're a Good Man, Charlie Brown*. Connect characters in this story to ones in that production.

Social Studies:

1. Interview a writer of espionage or spy stories or write to a famous author for information. Create an outline of interview questions to be used.

2. Nations have carried on cold wars. Research the meaning of this term and apply it to the conflict in this book. What would happen were confrontation to replace this cold war on both fronts?

3. Research famous spies such as Mata Hari, Tokyo Rose, and Anna Rosenberg. Report to the class.

4. Spies may be not only international; there are industrial spies, police informants, and others. Either ask speakers to come to the class to discuss these or research and present mini-reports.

Science:

1. Investigative reporting is much like scientific inquiry in that important questions are raised. List questions concerning science that as a class you wonder about. Look for the answers, and share with the class.

2. Harriet had heard that pigeons make people get cancer. Discover other myths that some people believe about diseases.

3. Create a survey on friendships. As a group, make a list of common questions. Included might be:

   • Do you have a best friend?

   • How long has that person been your best friend?

   • What is the longest amount of time you have been friends with someone?

   • What is the most important quality in a friendship.

4. Investigate a scientific study in which observation was the research method.

Math:

1. The doctor feels that Harriet is intelligent. Investigate the bell curve of intelligence. Where do you think Harriet might fit?

Bulletin Board

Harriet the Spy

Cut a large spyglass from colored paper. Cut out the center and insert cellophane to resemble glass. Surround spyglass with large question marks backed by geometric or striped wallpaper. Each child chooses a subject that is mysterious to him or her. After researching the topic, the student writes an investigative report. Each is arranged on background.

Julie of the Wolves

Jean Craighead George

Julie of the Wolves

by

Jean Craighead George
Harper & Row, 1972

Mijax, or Julie, is trapped in a prearranged marriage. Her husband makes her life so unbearable that she plans to leave the Arctic. Julie's destination is San Francisco.

On the tundra, Julie becomes disoriented and lost. Depending on knowledge of animals she learned from her hunter father, Julie is befriended by a pack of arctic wolves. Progressing on the journey, Julie remembers her life with her father, with her unfeeling aunt, her marriage, and her final escape.

Eventually Julie meets a hunter who tells her that her father is now living in Kangik. She is delighted to see her father again, but her delight turns to amazement when she realizes that he has married a Caucasian woman and has succumbed to society's influence. Julie believes her father has rejected the Eskimo ways. Disillusioned, Julie leaves her father's house to return to the tundra. The reader is left wondering if she will ever adapt to the new customs of encroaching civilization.

WOLVERINES

KAYAK

DESOLUTE

HARPOON

TOTEM

MARRIAGE

LICHEN

SLED

LONELINESS

LARVAE

MUKLUKS

*Julie
of the
Wolves*

GUSSACK

PUFFIN

FUNGI

PACK

SPIRIT

ESKIMO

LONGSPURS

ARCTIC

WATCHFUL

PEAT

TUNDRA

Part 1

Literal Thinking:

1. What gesture signaled respect and leadership among the wolves?

2. What posture did Mijax assume in order to be accepted by the wolves?

3. List the survival skills Mijax possesses.

4. What was the comparison Mijax made between her father and the black wolf?

5. How can many animals tell the difference between hostile and friendly behavior?

6. Explain why damp clothes meant death in the Arctic.

7. How did Mijax finally discover the wolf kill?

8. How did the arctic fox reflect the arctic changes?

Interpretive Thinking:

1. Eating customs differ from culture to culture and with different backgrounds. What things do you eat that Mijax would find strange?

2. Truth is stranger than fiction. Can you think of a true incident in which ingenuity, bravery, and wit turned a negative situation into a positive one? Write a short news story with a headline about your experience.

3. Mijax always remembered to change her course of action when fear gripped her. Recall a time fear seized you and what you did about it. Share with a partner.

4. List adjectives that describe Mijax, Amaroq, Silver, Nails, Kapu, and Jello.

5. Explain how the black wolf's moods and attitude affected the others.

6. Explain the life cycle and patterning of a lemming.

7. Why were the Eskimo nuts and candy and chicken of the north healthy for Mijax?

Creative Thinking:

1. Imagine you are Julie on your way to Pointe Hope and are lost. Write a letter to your pen pal, Amy, about your fears.

2. Tug of War was one of the games the pups played that Mijax recognized. Think of two other children's games that could be adapted for the puppies.

3. Mijax learned many positions and gestures that meant certain things to the wolves. Compile these in a study guide for your class.

4. The wolves followed their leader because he showed himself to be wise and brave. His directions to his pack were clearly expressed. Give a speech for your class with simple directions on how to make pizza, peanut-butter-and-jelly sandwiches, or a simple recipe of your choice.

5. Write a brief description of Jello. Do you find him an appealing character? Explain your answer. If you find him unappealing, create a *wanted* poster illustrating Jello and his characteristics.

6. Develop your own saying for when you are afraid and lonely.

7. Create a stone design as Mijax might have done. Find a stone large enough for painting. Using acrylics or ink, brush on a design suggesting action-filled episodes from part 1.

8. Mijax often used her father's teachings to help her. Recall things you have been told by adults that have helped in a stressful situation. Share with your class.

Critical Thinking:

1. Decide if Mijax should have run away from Barrow, Alaska. What should she have done?

2. The chin pat was a gesture Amaroq could not ignore. Discuss gestures that are universally accepted as nonverbal signs of human friendship.

3. Mijax decided she and Kapu were both joking and serious partners. Do you know someone who would qualify as such a partner?

4. Mijax knew that certain wolf sounds and movements showed goodwill or submission. Discuss which body movements do the same for cats, dogs, and humans.

5. Wealth had an inner meaning for the Eskimo. How would this concept of wealth lead to changes in a person's life? Form a class debate to explore the issue.

6. What elements in Kapu's personality would destine him for leadership in the wolf pack? Contrast his personality with Jello's by writing a diamante poem.

7. What event caused Mijax to be most anxious? Write a short story about the first time you felt most afraid but kept on to overcome your fear.

8. Write an empathetic portrait of Jello. Choose other animals often derided such as snakes or cockroaches. See if you can change opinions of classmates by your persuasive writing.

Part 2

Literal Thinking:

1. What were the English names for Mijax and her father?

2. Give the main reason Kapugen had made arrangements with Nako.

3. Who had helped Mijax escape from Barrow?

4. Explain the ritual of returning the sea bladders to the sea.

5. Why was Julie's harbor sealskin unique?

6. How did Eskimos always know the earth was round?

Interpretive Thinking:

1. How was the reason Julie's father gave for leaving different from the reason for his disappearance?

2. Compare the differences in reasoning and attitudes of Mijax and her aunt Martha concerning Julie's father's move to the seal camp.

3. Julie's father had told her that wolves were brotherly. He taught her to talk to them to win their love. How does this philosophy convert into human relationships?

4. "The old ways are best" was often said by Aunt Martha. What does this statement mean to you?

5. When did Mijax become Julie?

6. What did Julie do that showed how brave she was? Think of a time you were brave but no one knew except you. Share with a partner.

7. Tell why Julie's memories were so avidly associated with color.

8. How did Pearl show her depth of friendship for Julie?

Creative Thinking:

1. Find out the significance of totem poles in Eskimo life. Create totems from poster board and colored markers for your media center or classroom.

2. Beginning with the end of part 2, write an ending for Julie's story. After reading part 3, compare your ending with the author's.

3. Create a wedding invitation for the wedding of Julie and Daniel.

4. Draw an illustration of Amy's house in San Francisco as she described it to Julie.

5. Research the northern lights, or aurora borealis. Find the reason for this occurrence. With watercolors or colored markers, draw your impression of them.

Critical Thinking:

1. What was the worst thing Nako did that Daniel might model?

2. Why had Amy's letters become the most important thing in Julie's life? As Julie, write a letter to Amy telling her of the saddest and most joyous occasions in your new home.

3. What animal would best characterize Julie, Daniel, Aunt Martha, Nako, and Kapugen. Draw an illustration for each. Compare with those of classmates.

4. Analyze your feelings about the Eskimo practice of early arranged marriages. Organize a debate.

5. Explain why the Eskimo felt that one's spirit fled when one was drunk.

6. Judge why Mijax did not question her father's decision to have her live with Aunt Martha.

7. Would you have liked life at the seal camp? Why or why not?

Part 3

Literal Thinking:

1. Describe Mijax's plan after she left Kapugen's home.

2. What is considered to be the "guidepost" of the Eskimo?

3. What single incident made the wolves turn on Jello?

4. How did Kapu help Julie before the storm?

5. What animal did Kapugen teach the Eskimos to raise for profit?

6. After Amaroq was killed, who became the new leader of the pack?

Interpretive Thinking:

1. What did Amaroq do to prove his love for Julie?

2. Why is self-reliance important to a person's concept of himself/herself?

3. List three creative problem-solving techniques Julie used in her fight for survival.

4. Why was Julie so afraid to be seen by the airplane pilots?

5. Share some of the lessons Mijax learned in her ventures.

6. Describe what Mijax sees in her father's house to make her leave.

Creative Thinking:

1. Julie was concerned about the safety of her pack. Create an early warning system for potential trouble such as a fire or tornado.

2. Following Julie's explanation, fashion a cup and dish with turned-up edge. Use materials such as wet paper towels or paper bags. Place in a freezer to harden.

3. Canadian Eskimos often make sealskin stencil prints. You can create a facsimile by cutting a design in paper of an interesting object or character from part 3. Place the stencil on another piece of paper. Brush on color or use colored markers.

4. Self-drying clay can be used to model many of the characters and animals in part 3. Make each look rustic as if Mijax had designed them.

5. Eskimo children often play with wooden or ivory dolls. They enjoy making clothes for their dolls. Using one of your dolls and scrap fabric, feathers, leather, and so on, design and sew clothes to resemble Eskimo clothing. Narrate a fashion show displaying your designs.

6. Research to find illustrations of tribal masks, totems, and ivory carvings. Using the designs as examples, create your own design. Transfer the design to T-shirts using fabric markers.

7. Eskimos danced in huts called dance houses. Here they told the stories of their hunts through dance. Create a dance that tells the story of the hunt and death of Amaroq.

Critical Thinking:

1. Jack London wrote many stories of the North. Read excerpts from one of his stories and compare to *Julie of the Wolves*. How are the stories alike and different?

2. Is the theme of *Julie of the Wolves* a significant one to learn more about? Does the theme relate to a current world problem? Discuss.

3. Why did Julie leave home for the last time? Debate whether you think her reasoning was valid.

4. Read *The Swiss Family Robinson* by Johann Wyss or *Zia* by Scott O'Dell. Were Julie's ordeals like the characters of these books? Discuss.

5. All birds were potential food for Julie. Explain why her feelings were different toward the plover.

6. Discuss why, in a time of deep sadness, Julie could not think of English words to say.

7. How was Amaroq aiding Julie, even after his death?

8. Analyze why Julie felt Kapugen and Amaroq were so alike for her.

9. Julie's tame bird brightened her attitude toward her existence. Discuss how and why pets make a difference in our lives.

Additional Activities

Visual Art:

1. Eskimo women use finger masks designed to fit the first two fingers. They tell a story much as others do with finger puppets. Design your finger masks from paper and feathers to tell an episode from *Julie of the Wolves* for a visiting class.

2. Soapstone is used by Eskimos to make carvings. They believe the image within will emerge as they carve. Using soap, set free a design by carving a character or animal from the story.

3. Research Eskimo mask making. Using paper plates, poster board, feather, and yarn, create full-face masks that resemble those found in your research.

4. Create bookmarks. On one side, depict Julie; on the other, depict Mijax.

5. Using a watercolor background of the northern lights, display an igloo of sugar cubes.

6. Draw each of the wolves in caricature using their unique qualities and personality traits as a guide. For example, Amaroq might be depicted having a scepter, crown, and royal robe.

Creative Writing:

1. As Julie, write a eulogy for Amaroq telling of his personality, strength, and love for his pack.

2. There are many Eskimo stories that explain the nature of life in the North. After listening to one of the stories, write a fable with an arctic animal as the main character. Express a truth you think is important.

3. Julie felt as if she had been left out of the family or group. Have you ever felt like this? Tell about your experience in a journal entry.

4. Learn more about point of view. Write a short script of a telephone conversation Ellen could have had with one of her fellow teachers concerning her new daughter, Julie.

5. Write an epilogue to *Julie of the Wolves*. What happens to Mijax?

Drama:

1. Create a soliloquy by Julie in her tent with Kapu and Tornait. Include her grief, anger, sadness, and plans of reaching her goal.

2. Mime a scene in which Julie, using the wolf language she has learned, warns Amaroq not to follow her anymore.

3. Role-play Julie telling Amy that she would not be coming to San Francisco.

4. Recreate the last scene between Julie and her wolves.

5. Write a short script entirely from the wolves' point of view of Julie's life for parts 1 through 3. Role-play for another class to encourage them to read the book.

6. View the filmstrip of *Julie of the Wolves*. Be a movie critic and determine if the filmstrip gives (1) a realistic portrayal of the book, (2) needs changes and additions, or (3) accurately follows the story line.

7. Mime a scene for each character in the story. See if your class can determine which character and scene you are portraying.

Music:

1. Choose music to depict a night in the Arctic. Write lyrics for it that Julie might sing when alone.

2. Follow Mijax and create a poem about either the tundra or wolves. Perform it for the class, with either a repeating rhythm or song.

3. Listen to a recording of *Peter and the Wolf* by Prokofiev, and especially to the wolf's determined approaches. Relate the portions of musical movement to the movement of the wolves in the book. Read these excerpts while you play the accompanying music.

4. Eskimo men often danced to drums only. Using drums, create rhythms and a dance to tell one of your favorite portions of the story.

5. Julie saw the seasons change year after year. Write joyful words for a rap song that describes an occurrence in your life that is joyously repeated.

6. Although Kapugen had been Julie's hero, she finally realized Amaroq was her real hero. Write a poem to Amaroq that can be read along with softly played music that celebrates Amaroq's life.

Social Studies:

1. Use a map of the Arctic to mark Mijax's trail.

2. Bounties have been offered throughout history. Research some that are offered today. Research fines that are levied against killing certain species. Debate the necessity of each.

3. Scrimshaw is an old Eskimo art form. Research and report it to your class.

4. Investigate the problems of the Eskimo culture and how outside influences such as alcohol have affected the people.

5. Look at a map of Alaska and choose a village or city. Write a letter to the local school system or chamber of commerce asking for information about the area. Share your replies with the class.

6. Learn more about Vitus Bering, William H. Seward, and Captain George Vancouver and their contributions to Alaska. Present the information to your class.

7. Find information about the Iditarod dogsled race. Write a tall tale about the lead dog of the race.

Science:

1. The gland resting on the top of the wolf's tail was very important in signaling the acceptance of Mijax. Research to learn about this form of communication among wolves.

2. Find more about the tundra. Describe the physical characteristics there.

3. Mijax noted that lichens grew heavier on one side of the frost line than on the other. Research reasons for this and what it signifies.

4. Write a letter to the Arctic Research Laboratory in Barrow. Ask for information about their study of wolves.

5. Mijax devised her own compass. Refer to science experiments and create an original one.

6. Eskimos have traditionally been intrigued with superstitions such as releasing seal bladders to the sea. Research and illustrate other examples of their superstitions.

7. Research constellations. Locate the ones Julie would have seen from the top of the world.

Bulletin Board

Julie of the Wolves

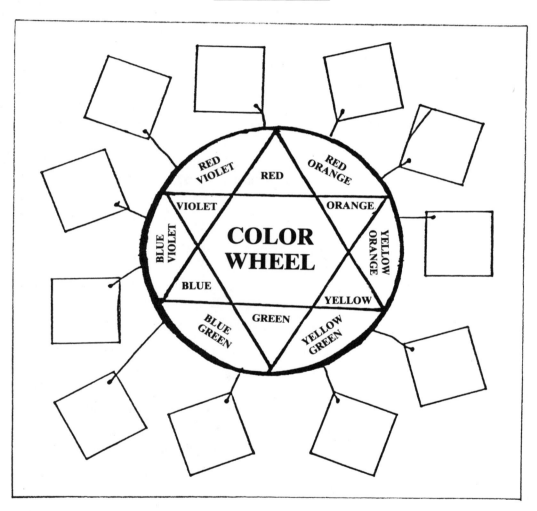

Julie's memories were all touched by color. Create a large color wheel. Using yarn, connect accounts of the most unforgettable memories of the students. At the end of each story, students say why the memory evokes a particular color.

Freedom Train

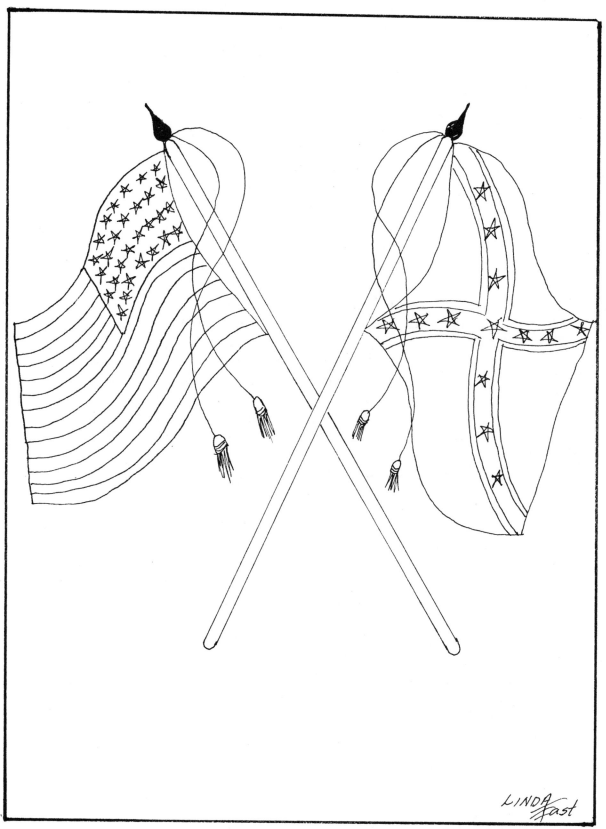

Dorothy Sterling

Freedom Train

by

Dorothy Sterling
Doubleday, 1954

This book relates the life of Harriet Tubman and her ongoing fight against slavery and the unfair treatment of Afro-Americans in the United States.

Harriet was born a slave in the South and lived with constant hunger and unending hard work. Her dream and goal was eventual freedom, that one day she would escape. This she eventually accomplished via the Underground Railroad to the North.

Her life was devoted to freeing her people. She was a wily and inventive conductor on the railroad; ferrying hundreds of people to freedom.

The story follows her life through her job with the Union army and the attempts to educate her people.

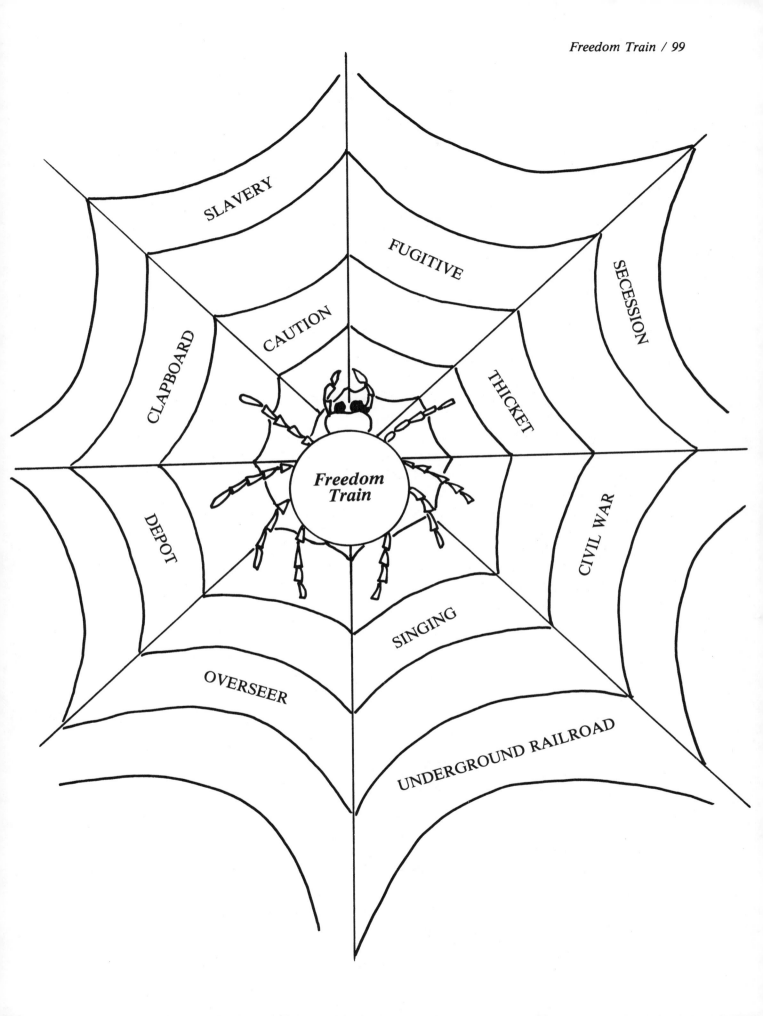

Chapters 1 through 5

Literal Thinking:

1. What time and place is the setting for the book?

2. Where did Harriet hide after she took the lump of sugar?

3. What was the slaves' storybook and guide?

4. What permanent damage did Harriet have after being hit by the weight?

5. Explain the grapevine telegraph.

6. List the boundaries and information Harriet learned from her "schooling."

7. Explain the origin of the term *Underground Railroad*.

Interpretive Thinking:

1. Compare a typical day for the eight-year-old slave Harriet to your day.

2. Why was singing so important to the slaves? Was it more important for the owner to hear them singing?

3. Why do you think Harriet could get away with saying certain things through songs that she would be whipped for if she merely stated them?

4. Why do you feel Cudjoe was so anxious to read the master's newspapers and magazines? Why not books?

5. Why did the Nat Turner incident backfire with most slaves?

6. Why do you think young William Lloyd Garrison was willing to fight for the freedom of black men?

7. Why did Harriet protect Jim?

8. Why did Uncle Cudjoe's preaching make him dangerous to the master and mistress?

Creative Thinking:

1. Make a diorama or model of Harriet's parents home.

2. Using strips of paper about an inch wide, make a weaving and tape it off in the back to form a quilt. With colored markers, draw pictures to create your version of her parents' quilt.

3. The grapevine telegraph is a more involved version of the game Telephone in which something is mentioned to one and it travels to each succeeding person until the last person tells what he/she has heard. Use a line or fact about the story and have it travel this "grapevine" to see what it becomes.

4. Harriet must have felt different from her family and owners. Feel her emotions as you write a story of a kingdom where everyone but you has pink hair and polka-dot bodies, or use other differences of your choice. Share the stories in class.

5. Create a *wanted* poster for Harriet that Miss Sarah might have designed.

6. Rewrite the story of Harriet's childhood with a modern setting and characters as realistic fiction. In the plot, emphasize the theme of necessary risk-taking and courage versus security and boredom.

7. Think of and design words that describe the main characters. For example, Miss Sarah might be described by the word *anxious* written graphically with shaky letters.

8. Imagine you witnessed Harriet staying in the pigpen. Write a brief description of what it was like.

Critical Thinking:

1. Do you think that Harriet's owners felt she was a human being in her own right? Debate.

2. Did Harriet already show spark and individuality at this early age? Cite examples from the book to support your opinion.

3. Explain Cudjoe's part in keeping the slaves' dignity and respect for themselves as human beings.

4. How was Nat Turner a sort of Robin Hood for the slaves? Evaluate the need for a symbolic leader. Compare him to Martin Luther King, Jr.

5. How did the new restrictions after Nat Turner show the slave owners' concern about the potential of the slaves?

6. How did Harriet's injury actually aid her in her fight for freedom? Relate instances in your life when experiences that at first appeared negative were used in a positive way.

7. Why was slavery very damaging to the slave owners' children as well as the slaves' children?

8. Decide if Old Cudjoe had the right to be bitter.

9. Why were the white masters so afraid that the slaves would learn to read?

10. Predict what will happen now that the master is dead.

Chapters 6 through 10

Literal Thinking:

1. Who are the Quakers?

2. What words did Quakers use in place of *you*?

3. How did Harriet let her family and friends know she was leaving?

4. Why did a slave still have to be careful even in a free state?

5. What was the signal of the Railroad?

6. To what two things did Harriet feel she had the unquestioned right?

7. Which of Harriet's family was first to join her in the "promised land"?

8. How many slaves did Harriet help escape in two years?

Interpretive Thinking:

1. What kept Harriet from going into panic when she was lost in the thicket?

2. Why were the Quakers one of the most supportive groups in organizing the Underground Railroad?

3. Harriet felt alone in the strange land of Pennsylvania, where she felt that after such risk she would be welcomed. Relate a time you exerted great effort in reaching a goal but were surprisingly disappointed with the results.

4. Why did the Quakers dislike the common term *Master*? Explain your opinion. Did they feel the same about the word *Mister*?

5. Given "liberty or death," which would you choose?

6. Explain why Harriet's instinctive pattern of distrust helped her during her trips.

7. Tell one of Harriet's ingenious escape plans.

Creative Thinking:

1. Research Quakers and their religious philosophy which forbids them to raise their hands against others. Include how they handled mandatory service during such times as World War II. Was this always an easy or popular path? Discuss your findings and create a scene in which a Quaker explains his/her attitude with a nonbeliever. Remember their use of the word *thee*.

2. Role-play the scene of Harriet being accepted into the Hunn home. Remember, this is a glimpse of life as Harriet has never seen it before.

3. Write a good-bye letter from Harriet to her family.

4. What would you have said to Harriet if you had met her as she stepped into free Pennsylvania?

5. Research to find what mosaic is. Cut large paper shapes that fit together in a mosaic pattern. On each paper, write a statement or draw an object that reflects an important experience in Harriet Tubman's life.

6. How could modern technology have brought a more rapid end to slavery? Write a futuristic story in which all labor is assumed by advanced machines. Share with your class.

7. Harriet "found" many slaves, who, though at first were degraded, later led productive lives. Can you find discarded or ordinary objects and change them into creations of beauty? Display your "found" art creations in your classroom.

Critical Thinking:

1. What types of slavery and oppression are most publicized in current world news? Find newspaper or magazine articles that refer to the issue. You and a partner may write a short script for a news broadcast that describes the events.

2. "Actions speak louder than words" is a famous quote. Which of Harriet's actions in freeing slaves "spoke" the loudest?

3. Why were Harriet's brothers hesitant to take the final step toward leaving? What caused Harriet to feel so differently? Have you immediately felt that something was just "right" to do? Share with a partner.

4. Explain the differences between Mr. Still's concept of family and Harriet's. Which one had a greater grasp of the overall problem of human dignity?

5. Why do you think Harriet could be so open to William Still?

6. Do you think Harriet is wise to return to the plantations to free her people? What would you have done?

Chapters 11 through 15

Literal Thinking:

1. Describe the Fugitive Slave Law.

2. Why could traveling with Harriet be a hindrance for her parents?

3. After 1850, where did the slaves have to go to find true freedom?

4. What continued to be Harriet's biggest problem?

5. What two disguises did Harriet generally use?

6. What name was given to Harriet Tubman because of her numerous rescues of slaves?

Interpretive Thinking:

1. How did the Fugitive Slave Law show that there was increasing fear among slave owners?

2. What observations can one make about Harriet's presence of mind and intelligence?

3. Why was Ben so adamant against looking at any of the fugitives?

4. Why was Harriet impatient with her mother's tears?

5. What does Harriet mean by the statement "I couldn't trust Uncle Sam with my people no longer. They're not safe no more till they're under the paw of the British lion"?

6. Why did the slaves call Harriet "Moses"?

7. Interpret Harriet's analogy to slavery of the man who sowed onions and garlic for his cows.

Creative Thinking:

1. Draw illustrations of disguises Harriet might use.

2. Research the story of the slave Shadrack and his rescue from a Boston jail. Create a factual play.

3. Draw a cartoon illustrating Harriet's belief that her people are no longer safe with Uncle Sam and not until they are under the paw of the British lion. Draw another showing slaves "shaking the lion's paw."

4. Write an editorial and draw a political cartoon supporting or not supporting Harriet Tubman's tactics.

5. The facts about slavery were finally exposed. What subjects would you like to explore as an investigative reporter? Learn the process by inviting an investigative reporter to your class. Make your investigative report to show to the class.

6. Draw a picture album of the events in rescuing Harriet's brothers. Dressed as Harriet, show the album as you tell about the experiences.

7. Learn more about the beliefs of Gandi and Martin Luther King, Jr. Imagine an interview with them to find out why passive resistance is so effective and how it was demonstrated in the anti-slavery society.

Critical Thinking:

1. Judge the fairness of the 1850 Fugitive Law. What status did its enactment give to Afro-Americans?

2. How were the slave owners also slaves?

3. Why is the greater love sometimes letting people go, as Harriet's father poignantly demonstrated?

4. What does the following statement say about importance of freedom? "The two travelers had passed their three score years and ten under the yoke. Nevertheless, they seemed delighted at the idea of going to a free country to enjoy freedom, if only for a short time."

5. Explain what is meant by, "There were no traitors on Harriet's trips."

6. Analyze the difference between "patriarchal" and "peculiar."

Chapters 16 through 20

Literal Thinking:

1. What was Harriet's job in the Union army?

2. What was Harriet's position in the army after the proclamation?

3. What helped Harriet get out of debt?

4. What document written by Abraham Lincoln freed the slaves?

5. List Harriet's achievements throughout her life.

6. What always remained "The War" to Harriet's household?

Interpretive Thinking:

1. Explain how General Hunter managed to circumvent the inability to enlist fugitive slaves.

2. Explain Harriet's continuing use of surveillance techniques for other purposes. Do you feel these talents allowed her to achieve results others could not?

3. How did Harriet's war wound graphically illustrate how much more needed to be done?

4. Do you think her parents really appreciated all Harriet had accomplished for her people? Why or why not?

5. Why was Harriet's age only an estimate?

6. The saying "Truth is stranger than fiction" is proved by Harriet Tubman's life. List the experiences Harriet had that could have been written by a fiction writer. Relate an experience of yours that was stranger than fiction.

7. Where do you find examples of fights for democracy today? Give brief reports to your class.

8. During all the perils and setbacks in her fight for her people, why did Harriet Tubman never give up her cause?

Creative Thinking:

1. Write a proclamation on a current social issue you would like to see changed.

2. Write an epitaph for Harriet Tubman.

3. Harriet Tubman did not consciously set out to be a heroine. Create a story with a main character who becomes a heroine in spite of herself.

4. Learn about other famous Americans who have accomplished goals despite great difficulty, such as Mary Bethune, Abraham Lincoln, and George Washington Carver. Write a short story about a hero or heroine who accomplishes much through great difficulty.

5. John F. Kennedy said, "Ask not what your country can do for you, but what you can do for your country." How did Harriet Tubman exemplify this belief? Make a picture book for younger children expressing this theme.

6. Reenact the reading of the proclamation of 1863.

7. Perform a monologue of the aged Harriet recounting her experiences to her great-grandnieces and nephews.

Critical Thinking:

1. Harriet's feeling was "Our time is coming." Has it completely arrived for Afro-Americans? Debate.

2. Speculate as to what would have happened to this country if the Civil War had had a different conclusion.

3. Evaluate the manner in which Afro-Americans fought for the Union yet did not receive equal pay. Discuss the moral aspect of such a decision.

4. Do you agree with the old man who states that the people are not free, just contraband?

5. Decide why John was a "troublemaker" as a slave and not as a farmer and fisherman.

6. Learn more about John Brown. Organize a class debate about his methods of freeing slaves.

7. Write a script for interviews with John Brown and Martin Luther King, Jr. Each supports his own view: John Brown for uprising and Martin Luther King for organized resistance. As a class, vote on the most effective method for evoking change.

8. How was Harriet Tubman both a visionary and a realist?

Additional Activities

Visual Art:

1. Slavery did not emphasize individual differences, yet each person is unique as proved by his/her fingerprints. Using an ink pad and paper, place fingerprints to create designs. Narrow-line markers can define your design.

2. Create a collage pertaining to slavery.

3. Create a class mural following the history of Afro-Americans from their early abduction by slave ships through modern times.

4. Illustrate some of the folk legends that were attributed to "Moses," such as "Moses is the tallest woman you ever did see," or "like a cat she can see on the darkest night," or "the fiercest dog will lick her hand."

5. Research Victoria's Diamond Jubilee medal and recreate in a drawing the one given to Harriet.

Creative Writing:

1. Make posters that you would have nailed on trees telling the slaves they were free.

2. Write a commendation for Harriet from Abraham Lincoln, citing all her accomplishments during the Civil War and her military service.

3. Write a letter as Harriet to President Lincoln outlining the unequal conditions for black versus white soldiers.

4. Write a letter to Afro-Americans today from Harriet Tubman. Write a letter from Martin Luther King, Jr.

5. Write a TV description for a movie called *Freedom Train*.

Drama:

1. Storytelling is an ancient African tradition. Find examples of African fables for storytelling. Invite a visiting class to hear your stories.

2. Dressed as Uncle Cudjoe, retell the stories that so influenced his people.

3. Create a dialogue between President Lincoln and Harriet.

4. Create a discussion between Jefferson Davis and Abraham Lincoln regarding the necessity of war.

5. Role-play a discussion between Rosa Parks and Harriet over the "No blacks allowed" incidents they both were involved in during the Afro-American struggle.

Music:

1. Afro-Americans have a rich cultural background in music. They used it to express their feelings about themselves, their surroundings, and the conditions of their life. Research old songs dealing with slavery, down through jazz. Report to the class with musical examples of each stage.

2. Create your own song, using either a familiar melody or one of your own, to tell about a portion of this book you especially enjoyed.

3. Create a message to a friend using the song "When That Old Chariot Comes."

4. Explore Afro-American spirituals such as "When the Saints Go Marching In." Learn to sing as a group.

5. Listen to some famous spiritual/gospel songs and evaluate their involvement and source of enthusiasm for faith.

Social Studies:

1. Learn about the current fight for freedom in South Africa. Pretend as a news reporter to interview some of the outstanding civil rights leaders such as Nelson Mandela.

2. Create a time line of famous Afro-American leaders.

3. Do a mini-report on the life of Martin Luther King, Jr., and include his accomplishments.

4. Research abolitionists and their philosophy. Cite examples in which they actively fought for their beliefs.

5. Study the Civil War and afterward. Discover what conditions prevailed in the South.

6. Investigate the education of Afro-Americans from 1827 to the present. Compare and evaluate opportunities for education.

Science:

1. Investigate myths that were believed about Afro-Americans in 1850.

2. Cotton was a major crop in the South during Harriet Tubman's life. Create a series of pictures with explanations that demonstrate the process of growth and harvest of cotton.

3. Research two of the most common diseases of Harriet Tubman's time, malaria and smallpox. Report to the class on their causes, spread, and recovery.

4. Research the contributions of Afro-Americans. Report the findings to the class.

5. Investigate medical discoveries and progress made during the Civil War.

Bulletin Board

Freedom Train

Each student illustrates an important event in Afro-American history or what freedom means to him/her. As a class, determine whether quilt blocks will be created from paper with markers or on fabric with liquid thread. Combine the quilt blocks by stapling or stitching.

ADDITIONAL BOOKS
ON DIFFERENCES

1. *Anna's Silent World.* Bernard Wolf. Lippincott, 1977.

   Through therapy and effort, Anna goes to school with other children. She uses devices such as hearing aids and lip reading to lead an active life.

2. *Captain Hook, That's Me.* Ada B. Litchfield. Walker, 1982.

   Judy, who has a hook for a left hand, is concerned when she learns that she must move away. Despite her worries about being different from other children, she finds acceptance and many new friends.

3. *Cornrows.* Camille Yarbrough. Coward, 1979.

   A sister and brother learn of the origin of a hairstyle that began in Africa and symbolized status. The children are then more proud of their heritage.

4. *Don't Feel Sorry for Paul.* Bernard Wolf. Lippincott, 1974.

   A photo-documentary of a boy born without complete hands and feet. The emotions and determination needed to deal with the handicap are explored.

5. *I Can't Always Hear You.* Joy Zelonsky. Raintree, 1980.

   Kim is hearing impaired and teased at school. She learns valuable coping devices from the school principal.

6. *It's Okay to Look at Jamie.* Patricia D. Frevert. Creative Education, 1983.

   Jamie wears a leg brace because of spina bifida. She runs a race which taxes her determination and body. This is a true story of how a handicapped child struggles to lead a normal life.

7. *Liking Myself.* Pat Palmer. Impact, 1977.

   Themes of feelings, self-esteem, and acceptance of others are explored in this book.

8. *Ride the Red Cycle.* Harriette G. Robinet. Houghton Mifflin, 1980.

   Jerome's dream is to ride a "cycle" even though he can't walk. Through determination and the support of his family, he reaches his goal.

9. *Stay Away from Simon.* Carol Carrick. Clarion, 1985.

   Lucy and a brother lose their way in a snowstorm. A retarded boy who has been shunned rescues them.

10. *The Flunking of Joshua T. Bates.* Susan Shreve. Knopf, 1984.

    Joshua must repeat his grade and is harassed by former students. His new teacher helps him gain self-esteem. Joshua finishes a successful year.

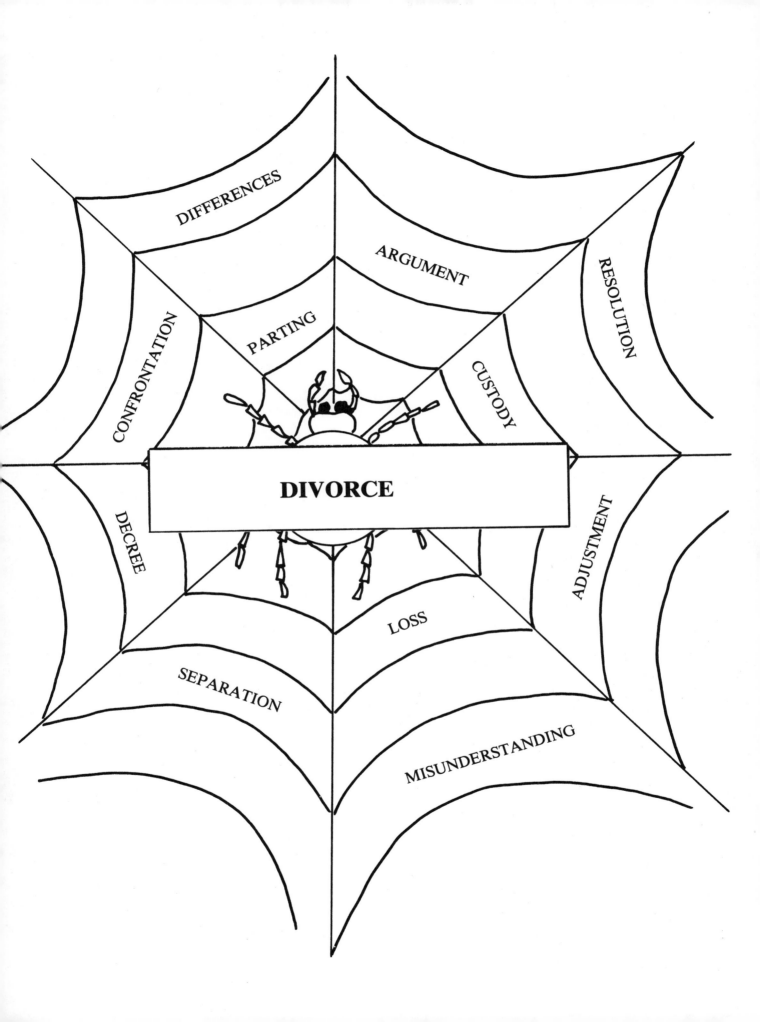

It's Not the End of the World

Judy Blume

It's Not the End of the World

by

Judy Blume
Bradbury Press, 1972

The Newman family was falling apart. Karen's father had moved out a few weeks ago and was now planning to go to Las Vegas for a divorce. Even worse, her mother was actually happy about all of this.

The three children learned about their parents' separation after the fact, at a restaurant during a family dinner with their mother and her ever-present sister and brother-in-law. The three adults attempted to explain the situation, but it was difficult for the children to accept.

At her dad's new apartment Karen meets a new friend, Valerie Lewis, whose mother is also divorced. She goes out a lot with one man, and Valerie is left by herself. She recommends that Karen buy a book called *The Boys and Girls Book about Divorce*, as she feels it was written just for children like them.

Karen doesn't lose hope that her parents will reconcile. She believes that if she can only bring her Viking diorama home early it will be there when her dad comes to pick the children up for dinner. Since it is fragile, he would have to come into the house to see it and she would have both parents in the same room. She learns some things aren't meant to be, as much as we may want them.

Her brother goes through his adjustment to the divorce by running away. Their mother finally turns her life into something she wants, and her new-found security helps the children adjust better.

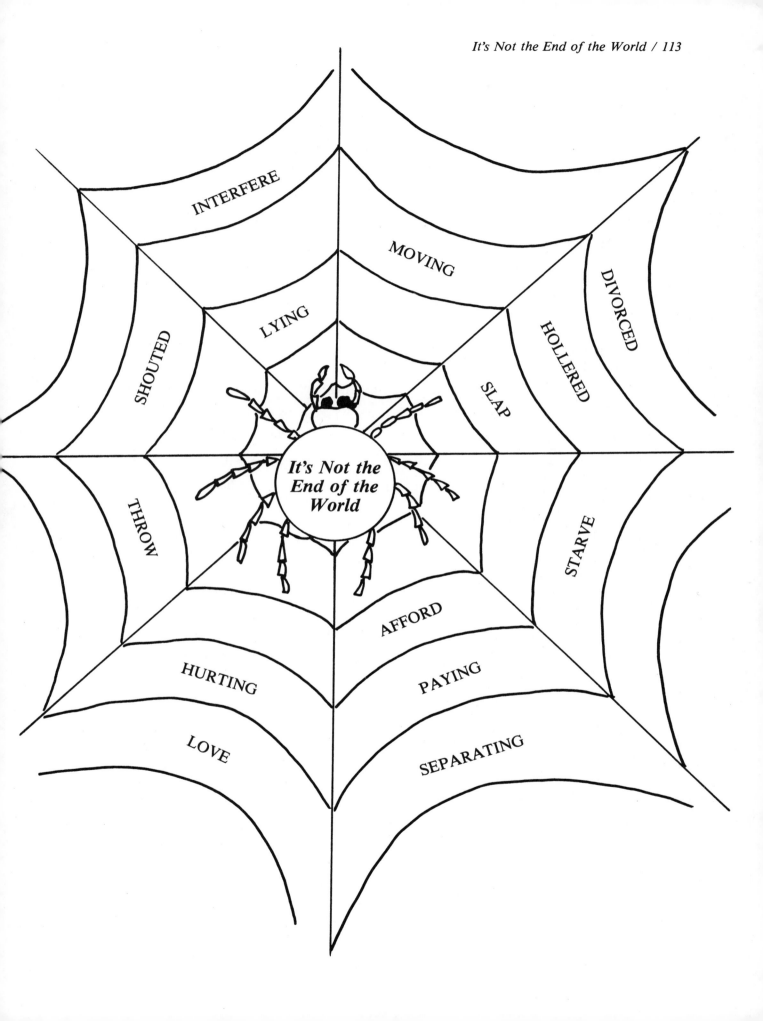

Chapters 1 through 7

Literal Thinking:

1. What does Jeff say that proves how worried he is about his parents?

2. What responsibility did Aunt Ruth remind Karen of?

3. Where will the children live?

4. How does Karen ensure she will know if someone reads her day book?

5. What did Karen think was the reason why her father was gone?

Interpretive Thinking:

1. Why does Karen keep making up reasons for her father not being at home?

2. What does her father mean by "I'm your father and I'll always love you. Divorce has nothing to do with that"?

3. What could a child who has gone through divorce learn from chapters 1 through 7?

4. Karen wanted to be alone to ponder when she pretended to be sick. Have you ever felt this way?

5. Why was the spilling of Amy's milk only a trigger for all the anger?

6. Is it correct that "the one who asks the most questions learns the most"? Why or why not?

7. Why do you think Karen wasn't at a point to be able to help her mother?

Creative Thinking:

1. Mime Karen, Jeff, and Amy. Show with facial expressions each one's reaction to the divorce.

2. Write about a time you felt happiness because someone else was making decisions for you. Share with a partner.

3. Keep a day report card for one week. Write reasons for each daily grade.

4. Have Karen write a letter to one of her parents expressing her feelings that she can't express face to face.

5. Role-play the scene where the father took the children out to dinner and talked with them about the divorce.

Critical Thinking:

1. Would it have been better if Karen's mother had talked with her about the separation before it occurred? Why?

2. In realistic fiction, the conversations of the characters seem real. Find examples of this in the story.

3. What is Karen's most positive personality trait?

4. Judge why the parents altered their usual Saturday night schedule. Predict what will happen.

5. The children were not told what was happening between their parents. Debate whether wondering and guessing is better than knowing.

6. Do you think most children would prefer to have verbal confrontations rather than a divorce in their family?

Chapters 8 through 15

Literal Thinking:

1. Give the name of the book Valerie read about in the *New York Times*.

2. Who is Karen worried her mother may want to marry?

3. Who is Karen's new friend? What do they have in common?

4. What happens to Karen's plan to get sick and get her parents together?

5. List the things that Karen is worried about concerning her parents.

Interpretive Thinking:

1. Is Aunt Ruth being helpful to Karen's mother?

2. Why did it make Karen feel so good to laugh?

3. Why is Jeff acting so angry toward his mother?

4. Have you ever felt angry but found it difficult to identify the real cause? Discuss.

5. Why do you think Amy was afraid that, if she went to sleep, everyone would be gone when she awakened?

6. Judge why children retelling something from one parent to another can create more of a misunderstanding.

Creative Thinking:

1. As Karen, write a letter to Dear Abby for advice on any aspect of the divorce that troubles you. Have a partner write Dear Abby's answer.

2. Tell the divorce from Karen's point of view by writing entries in her day book.

3. Illustrate an A+ day.

4. Create a house-warming invitation for the father's new apartment.

5. Draw a picture of Karen and Valerie in Valerie's room.

6. Design a newspaper advertisement for a college encouraging older women to return to school for a degree.

Critical Thinking:

1. What is the most positive step Karen's mother has taken for herself?

2. What do Karen's father and mother do in the story as good role models?

3. Was it a good idea for Karen to use the wedding napkins at dinner? Why or why not?

4. Do you think that Karen thinks too much about the divorce?

5. Why does Amy blame her mother for her father's leaving?

6. Judge why Grafa's solution might be an example of too little, too late?

7. Evaluate why Valerie might be the best person to help Karen deal with the situation. Cite a time when someone who has already been through something has helped you.

Chapters 16 through 23

Literal Thinking:

1. What were Uncle Dan and Aunt Ruth worried about concerning the children?

2. Which character disappears from the restaurant?

3. How did Karen's parents react to getting an anniversary card?

4. Where is Karen's father going to get the divorce? Why?

5. What did Karen's mother decide to call herself at work?

6. What did Debbie and Karen do to try to help Amy in case she got scared when she woke up?

Interpretive Thinking:

1. Why does Karen feel that her mother is selfish?

2. Do you think Valerie is really not interested in her father?

3. Why does talking out problems to a trusted friend usually help in a crisis?

4. Why did Karen finally react to the stress with hysteria?

5. Why did Karen feel lucky not to be anyone's favorite child?

6. Why do you think Karen's attitude toward solving her parents' divorce resembles a fairy tale?

7. How did Mrs. Singer show she understood some of Karen's concerns?

Creative Thinking:

1. Valerie is living alone. Write a paragraph as Valerie telling how you fantasize about a different home life.

2. Create impromptu speeches based on the positives of change. Examples of titles might be "Learning to Be More Independent Helped Me Grow" or "New Experiences and New Friends Changed My Life."

3. Have you ever wanted something so much that you ignored the negative aspects of your wish?

4. Write a letter to Karen suggesting what she might do to have a better adjustment.

5. Role-play the girls listening in on the extension to Jeff and Mary Louise Rumberger. Have two people offstage reciting the dialogue of Jeff and Mary Louise.

Critical Thinking:

1. Do grown-ups always know what they want to do?

2. Which view do you agree with concerning Karen's parents' anniversary, Karen's or Aunt Ruth's?

3. Does Karen know the difference between fantasy and reality? Give reasons for your opinion.

4. Do you think Valerie's book would always help a child? Cite reasons for your opinion.

5. Jeff is also having problems with the divorce. Why are they manifesting themselves in a different manner?

Chapters 24 through 31

Literal Thinking:

1. Why did Karen's father slap her?

2. What comforting thing does Grafa tell Karen about her dad?

3. What convinced Karen that getting her parents together was hopeless?

4. What concerns does Karen have about moving?

5. What was the family secret?

Interpretive Thinking:

1. Why does Karen now hate her Viking diorama? Why was destroying it an acceptance of reality?

2. Why was Debbie's gift very special to Karen?

3. Will the divorce book help an elderly person like Grafa better understand the divorce?

4. Why do you think that having the divorce book suddenly became so important to Karen after Jeff's disappearance?

5. How do you think Petey could be so certain Karen's brother wasn't dead?

Creative Thinking:

1. Draw a picture of Karen and her family in their new home in cartoon format. Each tells what they like about their new home life.

2. Which do you believe: "Absence makes the heart grow fonder" or "Out of sight, out of mind"? Why?

3. Design a missing persons bulletin for Jeff using the description given by his family.

4. Role-play the scene in which Jeff arrives back home.

Critical Thinking:

1. What one word would best describe Karen's feelings about the divorce in the last chapter?

2. Why would it be good for the family to move away from Aunt Ruth?

3. Analyze why Karen's mother's reaction to Jeff's return produced from Karen the statement "I always knew she loved him best." Do you agree?

4. Evaluate the signs that show that Karen's mother is beginning to take control of her own life.

Additional Activities

Visual Art:

1. Create illustrations for key scenes in the book. Make illustrations for a divorce manual.

2. Create a mosaic using words and pictures that deal with divorce.

3. As Karen, create a family shield. Include symbols that summarize each individual's personality.

4. Using pen and ink or colored markers, draw Jeff and his mother reunited.

Creative Writing:

1. Using Karen's concept of a day book, write down your feelings and what happens to you over one week. At the end of that time, reread it and evaluate if it helped you in any way.

2. Write an epilogue in which they do move to another area. Tell what changes occur over the next five years.

3. As Karen, write an article for teachers to read. Tell what a divorce is like and how teachers may help children.

4. Write a short manual for children who are either involved in a family divorce or have already gone through one.

5. Write a postcard to Karen from her dad explaining his actions.

Drama:

1. Role-play a conversation between Val and her mother.

2. As Karen dressed as a grandmother, tell about your parents' divorce and how you coped with it.

3. Learn what *resolve* and *climax* are in drama. Recreate the climax of the book by brainstorming new endings, then videotape them.

4. Have Amy perform a monologue about all the changes going on around her.

Music:

1. Create a rap song about either Karen and Debbie or Karen and Valerie.

2. Play music such as marches, lullabies, or rumbas. What section of the story does each remind you of?

3. Create a phone conversation between Karen and Valerie similar to the teenage conversation in *Bye, Bye, Birdie.*

Social Studies:

1. Research the Vikings and their origins, travels, customs, and so on. Make a diorama similar to the one Karen made for her class.

2. Nevada is the state known for its "quickie divorces." Research their laws and compare to the divorce laws of your own state.

3. Research Florida and its life-style. What would living there be like with all of its attractions, both natural and tourist? Prepare a mini-report for the class.

4. Have a professional speak to the class about the importance of communication.

5. Divide the class into cooperative teams to research causes and effects of divorce. Each team leader reports the findings of his/her group.

Science:

1. Investigate how feelings can affect your health and school performance.

2. Research how stress can be either positive or negative. What are some activities that reduce it? How could the stress of divorce be helped by exercise?

3. Val wanted to discover something important as a woman scientist. Read about discoveries and achievements of women in science-related fields. Share with your class.

4. Research hysteria. Discover what produces it and some possible ways to handle it.

Math:

1. Set up a budget for Karen's mother if she were to have a monthly income of $1,000. Keep in mind that you are to pay no more than one-third of your monthly income for housing.

Bulletin Board

It's Not the End of the World

Students write stories or about incidents in which they have thought it was the "end of the world" and how they coped with the situations.

Dear Mr. Henshaw

Beverly Cleary

Dear Mr. Henshaw

by

Beverly Cleary
William Morrow, 1983

Leigh Botts is required to write to an author for a school assignment in the sixth grade. He chose Boyd Henshaw. This correspondence turns into a disappointment for Leigh, because rather than answer the ten questions Leigh sends to the author, Mr. Henshaw sends ten questions for Leigh to answer.

Leigh gives a description of himself to Mr. Henshaw of being the "mediumest" in his class, that the kids like lunch better than they like him, and that his parents are divorced.

The custodian, Mr. Fridley, lets Leigh help raise the flag each morning and tries to suggest ways that Leigh can catch the thief that is stealing his lunch each day. He also suggests that Leigh develop a more positive attitude.

When Mr. Henshaw suggests that Leigh keep a diary, Leigh pretends he is still writing to Mr. Henshaw because he does not know how to keep a diary.

Leigh has not heard from his father, who is a truck driver and who has Leigh's dog, Bandit. In loneliness Leigh calls his father one evening while his mother is not at home. His father tells him that Bandit was lost in a snowstorm on his truck route. This is painful, but worse yet he hears a boy's voice in the background asking when they are going for pizza. Leigh is hurt and angry, and his feelings show in school. His mother tries to explain, but Leigh does not understand why his father left them.

When Mr. Fridley suggests that Leigh build a burglar alarm for his lunch box, a boy named Barry offers to help. This friendship is helpful to Leigh.

Leigh enters a creative writing contest and receives honorable mention. At a luncheon honoring the winners, Leigh gets compliments from the visiting guest author. Writing is a way Leigh can express his frustrations, loneliness, and lack of self-esteem.

After a visit from his father, Leigh accepts his father and the divorce.

This story of a boy going through a difficult time shows how expressing thoughts and feelings through journal writing is a healthy outlet.

DIVORCED

FICTITIOUS

SNITCH

BOTHERED

FOIL

LONGED

MISS

SUPPORT

CRIED

Dear Mr. Henshaw

SCOWLS

LETTERS

MOVED

FEELING

WRATH

NUISANCE

FORGETTING

Part 1

Literal Thinking:

1. Why is Leigh angry?

2. Why does Leigh not write to his father?

3. Why did Leigh's mother say he should answer the author's questions?

4. To whom did Leigh decide to address his diary?

5. List the writing tips Mr. Henshaw gave Leigh about becoming a writer.

Interpretive Thinking:

1. How do you feel writing to Mr. Henshaw was helping Leigh?

2. What leads you to think Leigh appreciates both sensitivity and humor?

3. Is Mr. Henshaw a substitute for Leigh's father? Discuss.

4. Why did Leigh want a letter in Mr. Henshaw's own handwriting rather than a printed one?

5. Why did Leigh sign his November 16th letter "Disgusted Reader"?

6. What greatest losses and changes are related to the divorce?

Creative Thinking:

1. Choose an author you enjoy and write him/her a letter. Compare responses with the rest of the class.

2. Using a map of California, mark each of the places Leigh has mentioned.

3. Most truckers sleep in the cabs of their trucks. These are small confined areas. Use graph paper to mark off a space, perhaps three feet by six feet, and create an environment for someone living on the road. How would you alter your design if the person was your age?

4. Start your own diary. Keep it for the amount of time your class spends on this book. How would you start each entry?

5. What is a manuscript? Invite a professional writer to your class to give pointers on how a manuscript is developed.

6. Create a saying like Leigh's "De liver de letter."

Critical Thinking:

1. Why do you think Leigh wants Mr. Henshaw for a pen pal?

2. Evaluate how Leigh signs his salutations in his letters to Mr. Henshaw. Do they give you information about Leigh's feelings?

3. Is it often easier to talk to an impartial person outside your family about a problem than to your family? Why?

4. Leigh had difficulty passing time before school in the morning. Share a creative way you could pass boring time; for example, while waiting for someone in a doctor's office. Share with the class.

Part 2

Literal Thinking:

1. What did Leigh's mother feel his father actually loved?

2. What was Leigh's mother's concern about marrying again?

3. How did Leigh's dad get his Christmas gift to him?

4. How was Bandit lost?

5. What makes Leigh feel that he is to blame for everything?

Interpretive Thinking:

1. What does the author do to arouse curiosity in this story?

2. Why was Leigh particularly sympathetic with the bear cubs in *Beggar Bears*?

3. Explain how Leigh's dad showed that he cared and thought about Leigh.

4. Relate a time when you could have "tripped over your lower lip."

5. How did one of Leigh's solutions to someone getting in his lunch bag nearly backfire on him?

6. Explain how the phrase "practice makes perfect" applies to Leigh's writing?

7. Why did Leigh put "Mr. Pretend Henshaw" in his December 22nd letter?

8. Why was Leigh angry about the note and money he received from his father?

Creative Thinking:

1. Write a story as the shoe left on the road: explain its life before, how it got there, and what it feels like to be out on the road.

2. Using famous people, such as Mikhail Gorbachev, Ronald Reagan, George Bush, George Washington, Madonna, Michael Jackson, Kirk Cameron, or Bill Cosby, create pen names for each. Select three additional choices your class would know. Write your creations on paper. Exchange with a friend to see how many they can identify.

3. Create a unique lunch container for Leigh and for yourself.

4. What do you bring to your mind that makes you know "that no matter how bad things seem, life will still go on?"

5. Leigh focused on the word *wrath* from his readings. Make a list of words from books you have read. Try to use one of the words each day in your vocabulary for a week. As a class, share reactions of people to your enriched vocabulary.

6. Organize a writing club in your class. Decide on the purpose of your club and the categories of writing to be accepted.

Critical Thinking:

1. Leigh's mother is excellent at analyzing a situation. What career would best showcase her talent?

2. In the initial stages of writing, which is more important, what you write or how you write?

3. Debate Leigh's handling of the theft of his lunch items. Do you agree or disagree? How would you have handled this situation?

4. Leigh said that he hated answers like "we'll see." Do you agree or disagree? Discuss with a partner.

5. Leigh's mother talked about how both parents changed and their marriage didn't survive. Cite ways in which your interests and outlooks have altered during your life. Discuss as a class how this would magnify as an adult.

6. What was Leigh's feeling when he heard the boy's voice in the background as he was talking to his father on the phone?

Part 3

Literal Thinking:

1. Describe what is worrying Leigh about the boy who wanted pizza.

2. What does Mrs. Badger think is an attribute of a good writer?

3. What is Leigh's mother studying in school?

4. What award did Leigh receive for his story?

5. Why was the winning poem disqualified?

6. How did Leigh manage to get everyone's attention at lunch?

7. How did the children know Mrs. Badger had actually read their stories?

Interpretive Thinking:

1. Leigh complained that others did not like him. How do you think his actions affected their feelings toward him?

2. Why, once the problem was corrected, did Leigh begin to think of reasons for their behavior and be more understanding?

3. In Mrs. Badger's opinion, what made Leigh's story good?

4. How did Mrs. Badger reconfirm Leigh's attitude toward Mr. Henshaw?

5. Why is Leigh happy he did not catch the lunch box thief?

6. Has having a friend helped Leigh adjust to the divorce?

Creative Thinking:

1. Design a warning for the lunch storage area telling thieves to beware, similar to those in stores to warn shoplifters.

2. Write a humorous Western adventure story about Black Bart and his gang. Include Leigh as the sheriff, Bandit as his partner, and Mr. Fridley as the thief.

3. Do you think Beverly Cleary is extremely perceptive in her understanding of children? Read books to support your views. Write a letter to Beverly Cleary telling her of your class's opinion.

4. Write a final letter to Mr. Henshaw from Leigh.

5. Create a sign for your room to keep others out.

Critical Thinking:

1. What one gesture by Leigh's mother most reflected her acceptance of Leigh's father?

2. What parts of the story show that almost nothing in life is either black or white but shades of gray?

3. Leigh's alarm did not catch the thief, but it ended the problem. Can you think of an instance in which something didn't turn out as you had planned but it still worked? Have a class discussion.

4. Judge why disappointment over something might make one not even want to try again. Brainstorm more positive alternatives to cope with disappointment.

5. Why did Leigh give Bandit to his father?

6. Explain why Leigh felt "sad and a whole lot better at the same time" after his father ended his visit.

Additional Activities

Visual Art:

1. Have students create pictures of what they think Mr. Henshaw looks like.

2. Create a class poster on "Tips for Writers."

3. Students create two portraits. One depicts what Leigh thought his dad looked like while he was writing to Mr. Henshaw, and the other what his dad actually turned out to look like.

4. Study various illustrators' styles, such as Arnold Lobell's. Choose a favorite style. Incorporate parts of it into illustrations for your own publication.

5. Illustrators must submit portfolios of their illustrations to editors. Create a portfolio of three illustrations you have drawn for *Dear Mr. Henshaw*.

6. Draw an illustration for a future book jacket of a famous author at home. The author is Leigh telling how he was inspired by Mr. Henshaw.

Creative Writing:

1. Have each student answer the questions that Mr. Henshaw asked Leigh.

2. Have students write an epilogue to the book.

3. Mr. Henshaw was a mentor to Leigh. Design a thank-you card for your mentor who has encouraged your talents and skills.

4. Invite writers of various types to your class. For example, hear from script, newspaper, and novel writers. Prepare interview questions to ask about (1) how to get started, (2) the process of publication for each, and (3) addresses of publishers for children's writing.

5. Write a letter as a pen pal to Leigh Botts. Include aspects of his personality that are similar to yours.

Drama:

1. Improvise a discussion between various class members about items being stolen from their lunches. Think of solutions. Be humorous.

2. Practice ad-libbing. Improvise lines based on the humorous scene of the lunch box alarm. Add a character from another book to the scene.

3. Create a C.B. conversation between Leigh and his father on Highway 80 in the snow.

4. Have students give performances of their winning creative writing stories using the readers' theatre format.

Music:

1. Truck drivers listen to music while on the road. If possible, call a trucking line or get a trucker interview. Find out about the preferences of truckers. Possible questions might be about a favorite song, or if the trucker prefers certain music at certain times.

2. Write an original song about your choice of shoes. This song could be about famous shoes, clown shoes, sneakers, boots, or others. Combine the lyrics with a well-known melody to teach to your class.

3. Listen to a country-western song. Note how the lyrics tell a story. Using a country-western melody, write lyrics to tell the story of Bandit's adventure.

4. Survey your class to determine what music is the most popular.

5. Observe butterflies. Play any music and discover how their movements tend to fit the rhythm.

Social Studies:

1. Interview a truck driver. Discover how this occupation affects family life.

2. How are beets refined in a sugar refinery? Write to a refinery to learn more about the process.

3. Find out the symbolism of the bear on the California flag. What does the design on your state flag signify?

4. Research the economic base of the central valley of California. Investigate its farming, livestock, and business, and why trucking is so important.

5. On a map of California, mark the principal agricultural areas and their crops. Include livestock and oil areas.

Science:

1. Create a week of exotic meals Leigh might find in his lunch box.

2. Research hawks and peregrine falcons: their life patterns, hunting, nesting, special abilities, and so on. Include the effect society is having on birds of prey.

3. Truckers use C.B. radios to communicate with each other. Create a system to communicate with someone in another room.

4. Research monarch butterflies and their migrating patterns. Discover what times of year you would find them in the setting of *Dear Mr. Henshaw*.

5. Compare the differences between making sugar from sugar cane versus sugar beets.

6. How important are pets to people who live alone? What is research telling us about the importance of touch in our lives?

Math:

1. Calculate the mileage of a truck driver from Los Angeles to San Francisco. Determine the cost. Assume that gasoline is $1.00 per gallon and the driver gets 15 miles per gallon.

2. How does a union in a factory help determine the employees' salaries? Create a math problem based on extra pay for extra work as opposed to wages at the beet factory.

Bulletin Board

Dear Mr. Henshaw

Create a large butterfly tree. Each student creates a butterfly. A simple butterfly shape can be cut from an 8½-by-11-inch piece of paper by folding the paper in half and cutting half of the butterfly. Place a special message or thought that the butterfly could carry to people faraway.

DeDe Takes Charge!

Johanna Hurwitz

DeDe Takes Charge!

by

Johanna Hurwitz
William Morrow, 1984

There are inevitable changes in DeDe's life because of her parents' divorce. The events in her life are divided between B.D. (before divorce) and A.D. (after divorce). Because of additional responsibilities and jobs both parents now have less time for her. Visits to her father are infrequent and arranged. DeDe's mother is preoccupied with the social as well as the economic changes of the divorce. The only constants in the child's life seem to be Aldo, a friend, and her dog, Cookie.

DeDe decides that she, a creative and persistent person, can think of ways to improve life for herself and her mother. Many of her ideas produce comic results, such as the Vegetable Club and the matchmaking with Mr. Evans. However, with resourcefulness, DeDe's ideas have a surprisingly positive effect upon many negative situations. A poignant, humorous account of the trials and adjustments of divorce.

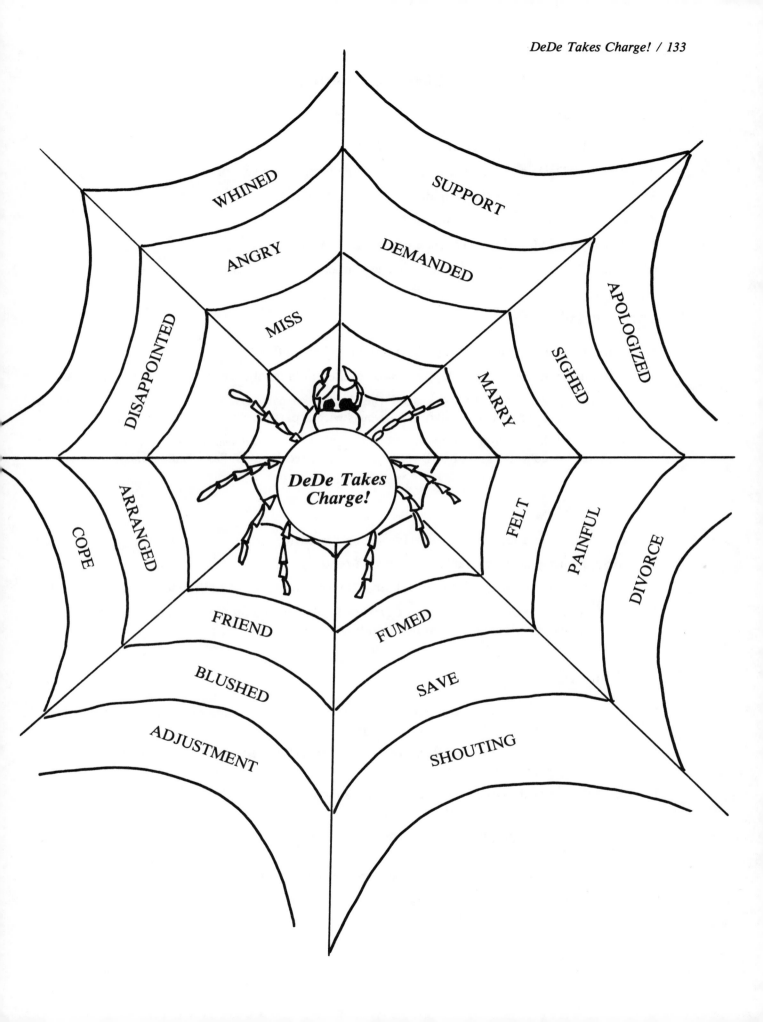

Chapters 1 through 4

Literal Thinking:

1. What does A.D. and B.D. mean to DeDe?

2. Why was DeDe embarrassed when Aldo came home from school with her?

3. What did her mother think made the noise in the attic?

4. What really caused the commotion?

5. Explain why Mrs. Rawson's work hours changed frequently.

6. When did DeDe spend weekends with her father?

Interpretive Thinking:

1. In what sense was DeDe acting like a parent to her mother?

2. Relate an experience in which your plans resulted in laughable confusion despite organization.

3. Mrs. Rawson returned to work after the divorce to earn extra money. Why is this such a common occurrence after a divorce? Discuss with a partner.

4. Because her sleep had been interrupted, the next day at school seemed endless. When was your ability to concentrate and absorb information affected by a similar circumstance?

Creative Thinking:

1. As DeDe, write a letter to a counselor asking for advice.

2. Create papier-mâché vegetables and make a centerpiece.

3. Illustrate an A.D. and B.D. family album. Draw candid views of both times in the family's life.

4. Draw caricatures of each member of DeDe's family, including Cookie. For example, DeDe's mother could be shown engulfed in vegetables.

Critical Thinking:

1. DeDe's father appeared to be a perfectionist. Research the meaning of the word and the effect this would have on family life and marriage.

2. Judge why DeDe's father's rejection of her mother has made DeDe uncertain of her continued acceptance by her father.

3. Do you agree or disagree that a person can be missed even though the person is still near you? Discuss this feeling with a partner.

4. Write a brief paragraph discussing your attitude toward DeDe's father. Do you find him a realistic character? Explain.

5. How can divorce sometimes encourage resourcefulness and creativity?

6. Was DeDe beginning to see her parents as individual people? Find sentences in the story to support your view.

Chapters 5 through 8

Literal Thinking:

1. What did Mrs. Rawson help DeDe create for her social studies class?

2. Where did DeDe and her mother eat Thanksgiving lunch?

3. Why couldn't DeDe smile at her father when she saw him in the cafetorium?

4. Why did everyone laugh when Robespierre walked the headless Marie Antoinette offstage?

Interpretive Thinking:

1. Do you agree with DeDe that the party fiasco was her fault? Why or why not?

2. Should DeDe's mother stay at home if her father attends the play? Explain.

3. Have you ever planned an event but the alternate plan turned out to be surprisingly better? Share your experiences with the class.

4. Demonstrate what you would have done had your guests disappointed you as Mrs. Rawson's did.

5. What leads you to think DeDe is a resourceful person?

Creative Thinking:

1. Draw your concept of a unique birdhouse DeDe might make.

2. Create a papier-mâché or clay head of a famous person. Display it in your classroom.

3. Brainstorm ideas for gifts that are original yet inexpensive to make. Some examples are to make pomanders, by sticking cloves in oranges and attaching a ribbon; or to make certificates for cleaning the house, calling a truce with a sibling, and so on.

4. Write a description and demonstrate a skill that a member of your family has taught you, such as weaving or carving.

5. DeDe was frustrated with the cold responses of her father's answering machine. Create a conversation between DeDe and her father about the school play that would have been more satisfying.

Critical Thinking:

1. Friends sometimes change after a divorce. Discuss why the party turned out as it did.

2. Explain why children often wish their divorced parents might reconcile. Discuss.

3. Explain how the family in the restaurant showed DeDe that appearances can be deceiving. Why did this make DeDe reevaluate how she was acting toward her mother?

4. Why is it important to have alternative plans in any situation?

5. If you were a reporter, which character would you choose to interview? Why?

Chapters 9 through 11

Literal Thinking:

1. Who does DeDe want her mother to meet?

2. Instead of going out to dinner, what does DeDe want to do with the extra money?

3. What had Mrs. Rawson done to use the vegetables in a creative way?

4. What performance did DeDe and her mother see?

Interpretive Thinking:

1. Some of DeDe's reactions are becoming more mature. Find examples in the story and discuss.

2. Why didn't DeDe's mother bring up the subject of Mr. Evans and the birdhouse?

3. Why had DeDe always known how well her father did at his job yet never realized her mother's talents until someone else recognized them?

4. Why did DeDe feel it was her responsibility to find a companion for her mother?

5. Did Mr. Evans suspect that DeDe had an ulterior motive in introducing him to her mother? Discuss.

Creative Thinking:

1. As DeDe, write a note to each parent, telling each the unique qualities you appreciate in them.

2. Write about a special time you have had alone with a parent.

3. Recreate in color the scene in which Mr. Evans met Mrs. Rawson. Accentuate Mrs. Rawson's green face, DeDe's embarrassment, and Mr. Evans's astonishment.

4. Role-play a conversation between Mr. Evans and one of his teacher friends. Describe the strange meeting with Mrs. Rawson.

5. Role-play a conversation between DeDe and her mother about the positive aspects of the divorce.

Critical Thinking:

1. If DeDe and her mother had lived on a farm, how would their reactions to the divorce have been different? Discuss.

2. Was it right for DeDe to delude Mr. Evans in order to introduce him to her mother?

3. Why is a candid look at a new acquaintance sometimes better for the friendship than a planned meeting? Discuss.

4. Why do first impressions of people need to be evaluated?

5. DeDe helped her mother but not in the way she had intended. Relate a situation in which trying to force or lead something to happen produced a less desirable result than allowing it to happen.

6. The selling of the planters will benefit Mrs. Rawson economically, but a deeper result may follow. Discuss why the psychological effect of success may help Mrs. Rawson more than the added income.

Additional Activities

Visual Art:

1. Using ice-cream sticks, create your own bird cage.

2. Braces are something many teenagers wear. Create some unique braces.

3. Locate famous still lifes of fruits and vegetables. Draw facsimiles to display in your classroom.

4. Using vegetables such as potatoes, cut designs. Dip the vegetables in tempera and press them on paper for unique designs.

Creative Writing:

1. What if the noise in the attic had been a goose? How would the story have been changed? Write a madcap adventure.

2. Write a letter to Johanna Hurwitz. Express your opinion about the book and the new things you learned about divorce.

3. Write a diamante poem about the contrast of relationships. Write about the differences between those that are arranged and those that grow naturally.

4. Create a "care line." Place a box in a familiar location in the classroom. Students can write their concerns and needs for advice on slips of paper that they put in the box. Create a small radio show to discuss the issues.

5. As DeDe's parents, design a card to your daughter expressing your care and concern for her future.

Drama:

1. DeDe said that the family in the restaurant looked as though they could do a TV commercial for soap or tomato sauce. Role-play the family doing such a commercial. Emphasize comic side-effects because grandmother or the children won't cooperate.

2. Create a monologue of DeDe talking to Cookie about the events in her life at the time of her greatest confusion.

Music:

1. Create a humorous jingle designed to encourage children to eat their vegetables. Adapt it to a familiar tune.

Social Studies:

1. Learn more about Marie Antoinette and the French Revolution. Report to your class.

2. What are some of the difficulties and joys of being a single parent? Chart your ideas from examples in the book.

3. Who was Robespierre? What part did he play in the court of Louis XVI of France? Research to find out.

4. Vegetarians are people who restrict meat from their diets. Research some of the reasons they select this eating pattern. Interview a vegetarian or go to a health food store to find more information.

Science:

1. Grow vegetables from seeds in your classroom. Learn about the best light, watering, and fertilizing for the plants.

2. Look in the *Guinness Book of World Records*. What and when were the largest vegetables ever grown? Share the information with your class.

3. Become chefs! Find simple vegetable recipes. As groups, prepare recipes for a tasting party.

4. Research the particular food value and vitamins found in various vegetables. How do each of the primary vitamins help the body?

5. Throughout history, the extracts of various plants have been used to control certain medical ailments. For example, aloe juice is known to help burns. Research medicinal properties of other plants. Share the information with your class.

6. Research some unusual fruits and vegetables. Examples are ugli fruit, bean curd, coconut milk, mangoes, kiwifruit, and spaghetti squash.

Bulletin Board

DeDe Takes Charge!

Cut large letters spelling *serendipity* backed by a banner. Discuss the meaning of serendipity. Each child writes a story and illustrates a picture about a time when alternative plans were better than the original and an interesting discovery was made. The stories are based on experiences with friends and families in various situations.

Crossword

DeDe Takes Charge!

Across

3. Type of book Mr. Rawson was given as a gift.

5. Man DeDe wants her mother to meet.

7. A difficult day for DeDe.

9. The Vegetable Club was considered a food _____.

10. Type of store where Mrs. Rawson worked.

11. Time DeDe spent with her father.

12. The only kind of woman for Mr. Rawson.

Down

1. Something between people that can't be arranged.

2. Unique color of Mrs. Rawson's face.

3. Vegetable that could be found at co-op.

4. A kind of cake made out of a vegetable.

6. Dissolution of a marriage.

8. Classes Mr. Evans taught.

Words: DeDe Takes Charge!

ADDRESS	DIVORCE	RELATIONSHIPS
OKRA	EVANS	SHOP
CARROT	GREEN	THANKSGIVING
CO-OP	PERFECT	WEEKENDS
DEPARTMENT		

Puzzle Answers: DeDe Takes Charge!

ADDITIONAL BOOKS ON DIVORCE

1. *The Boys and Girls Book about Divorce.* Richard Gardner. Jason Aronson, 1970.

   Dr. Gardner, a child psychiatrist, discusses the problems of divorce, including such topics as blame, anger, and fear of being alone. The book can be read independently by an average reader or by an adult to a child.

2. *Bring to Boil and Separate.* Hadley Irwin. Atheneum, 1980.

   Fearful of her parents' divorce, Katie Warner dreads her friend's month-long absence. The friend returns, and Katie accepts the divorce after having experienced many emotional upheavals.

3. *Davey Come Home.* Margaret Teible. Harper & Row, 1979.

   Davey lives with his father after his parents divorce. His teenaged baby-sitter never makes him come home for dinner. Mealtime is the essence of love for Davey. When the baby-sitter is replaced with responsible Mrs. Summers, Davey thrives in his new circumstances.

4. *Don't Make Me Smile.* Barbara Park. Knopf, 1981.

   A troubled boy, emotionally upset by his parents' divorce, is helped by an empathetic psychologist. He learns to adjust through honest communication.

5. *The Great Male Conspiracy.* Betty Bates. Holiday House, 1986.

   Maggie's sister's husband abandons her. Maggie becomes disillusioned and thinks all men are worthless. She finds stereotyping is useless as no group can be judged by the actions of an individual.

6. *Just Like Sisters.* LouAnn Bigge Gaeddert. E. P. Dutton, 1983.

   The unpredictable behavior of a child of recently divorced parents is candidly explored. The transition reflects on the cousins that were much like sisters.

7. *Out of Love.* Hilma Wolitzer. Farrar, Straus and Giroux, 1976.

   This is a first-person narrative of a child trying to understand the underlying reason for her parents' divorce. Wit and humor bring the problems into perspective.

8. *A Room Made of Windows.* Elenor Cameron. Little, Brown, 1971.

   Julia Redfern's emerging understanding of life's problems and her ultimate acceptance of her mother's remarriage are recounted. This is a realistic search for maturity.

9. *The Silver Coach.* Carol Schwerdtfeger. Adler, Coward, Cann and Geoghegan, 1979.

   Chris sees her parents' divorce in a new way as she learns to look realistically at her father's participation in the separation.

10. *Will Dad Ever Move Back Home?* Paula Hogan. Raintree, 1980.

    Laura runs away from her divorced parents. The crisis is resolved with both parents committed to giving more understanding to a child desperately needing to communicate.

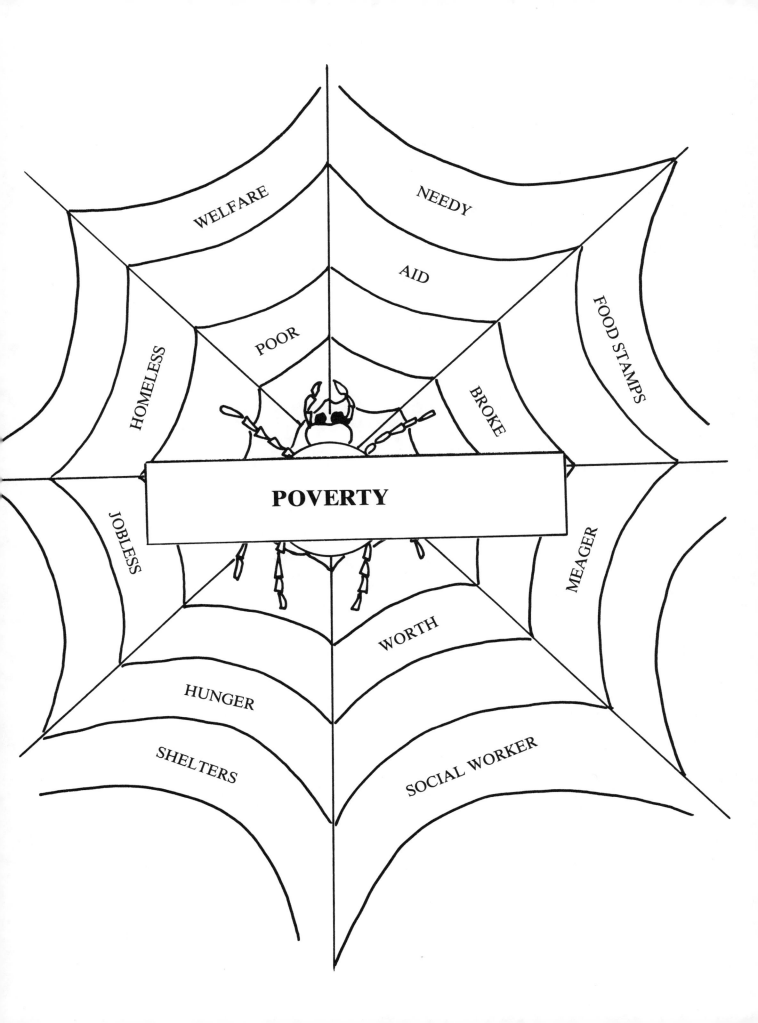

Sounder

William H. Armstrong

Sounder

by

William H. Armstrong
Cornerstone Books, 1969

Sounder is the poignant story of a coon dog's loyalty to his master.

His master is an extremely poor sharecropper with a growing family. Driven by poverty, he steals food from the local store. He is subsequently arrested by the sheriff. Later, he is sent to work gangs in several locations. Sounder tries to save his master from his fate, with disastrous results to the dog.

Disfigured, Sounder finally rejoins the family. He seems to have almost lost his voice but accompanies the boy in finding his master.

The fateful day arrives when the master comes home. He, too, has been disfigured in a work-gang accident. Sounder regains his voice to bark in joy to be reunited with his master.

As the story progresses, the master finally dies. Sounder's partner is gone. He feels such grief that he loses his spirit to live.

A picture of poverty, degradation, and hopelessness is clearly drawn in this book. Finally, however, the resilience of the human spirit triumphs.

TRASH

HERITAGE

LOYALTY

PATCHES

ADDLED

COLD

CABIN

TANNERY

FAITHFUL

PALLET

JAIL

Sounder

MONGREL

SHARECROPPERS

FAMISHED

POULTICE

MUSH

DEFIANT

CLOTHESLINE

FRIEND

MIMICKED

HARDSHIPS

SCRAPS

Chapters 1 and 2

Literal Thinking:

1. Why didn't the boy continue going to school?

2. What had inspired the boy to want to read?

3. Why was Sounder well named?

4. Why does the presence of wind make animals uneasy?

5. Why hadn't Sounder warned them of the approach of the men?

Interpretive Thinking:

1. Why do you think the mother's singing kept the boy from being lonely?

2. What is the approximate age of the narrator? Give reasons for your opinion.

3. What is the meaning of "night loneliness"?

4. Do you think the father was a thief?

Creative Thinking:

1. Research the type of dog commonly called a "coon" dog. Learn about its particular talents, its uses, and the areas in which it is most commonly found. Report to the class.

2. Using the title "Speck on the Horizon," write a letter or simple poem about the feelings of the children as they watch the speck slowly enlarging.

3. Design a poster that the sheriff, to catch the thief, would have nailed on a tree. List information and a suspect's picture on the poster.

4. Read *Where the Red Fern Grows* by Wilson Rawls. Create a conversation between Old Dan and Sounder about their adventurous hunts.

5. You are the boy in *Sounder*. Make a telephone call to your attorney about the arrest of your father. A partner replies as the attorney.

Critical Thinking:

1. Interview the sheriff and deputies. What was the real reason they shot Sounder?

2. What was the greatest lesson the boy learned about law enforcement in chapters 1 and 2?

3. What character traits did the boy admire the most in his mother and father?

4. Was the sheriff treating the family fairly? Discuss.

5. Evaluate why having a good coon dog would be so important to a family in this situation.

6. Evaluate why the boy followed the example of his father in lighting the lantern. Was this acceptance of fate? Discuss.

7. Why was fixing food for Sounder as usual important to the boy?

Chapters 3 and 4

Literal Thinking:

1. What did the boy wish his mother could get for Christmas from the big houses?

2. Who does the boy's father say will bring messages to the family?

3. What did the boy's mother take back to the store?

4. Where does the boy hope Sounder has gone?

5. Why didn't the boy's mother take the cake to the jail?

6. Explain the mother's view of using oak leaves as a healing agent.

Interpretive Thinking:

1. Have you ever had to go to a strange new place to fulfill a responsibility? Share your experiences.

2. What did the boy learn by observing his mother returning the food?

3. Why did the boy feel he had let his mother down and "grieved" his father?

4. In what ways did the mother show she was a loving person?

5. Why would the boy not allow himself to cry? Did this have anything to do with his new role in the family?

6. Why did the mother act casually when with the children but differently when alone?

Creative Thinking:

1. Create a gold medal for the boy. Celebrate his courage, persistence, and self-control.

2. What could the boy have done to earn money for the family? Brainstorm answers.

3. You are the boy's father. Tell of your feelings about the meeting with your son in the jail.

4. The boy felt he could learn to read if he had a book. Create a very simple picture I Can Read book for him.

5. The boy had no concept of what sea foam might be. Brainstorm ways you could recreate sea foam to show him. For example, root beer could be poured into a container, or liquid detergent beaten. Share the most realistic results.

Critical Thinking:

1. Who was the bravest character in chapters 3 and 4?

2. Could the boy's mother have been a teacher? Find examples in the story to prove your point.

3. Judge what the boy's reaction would have been to his father's arrest had the boy been a teenager.

4. Evaluate why the boy sensed his mother wasn't satisfied with her trip to town.

5. Why were most of the mother's stories from the Bible?

6. Judge the action that indicated the mother felt her husband had been guilty.

7. Why did the boy's mother want him to act "perkish" and not grieve his father?

Chapters 5 and 6

Literal Thinking:

1. What sentence did the boy's father receive for stealing the ham?

2. Why did the jailer destroy the cake?

3. List the possible choices of where the boy's father might serve his sentence.

4. How did the family find out what happened at the father's trial?

5. What wonderful things did the boy find during the search for his father?

6. How long had Sounder been away from home?

Interpretive Thinking:

1. What leads you to think that the boy is sensitive to feelings?

2. Have you ever desperately wanted to learn a skill as the boy did? What action did you take?

3. Why did loneliness put its stamp on everything in the cabin?

4. Why did the boy use stories from the Bible to convince his mother to allow him to go find his father?

5. Why did the father tell the boy to not come to the jail?

6. Why did the boy decide to not tell his mother about the jailer and the cake?

7. How could the boy sense his mother was becoming more upset and depressed about the situation?

8. What makes you think Sounder was never far from his mind?

Creative Thinking:

1. Make an acrostic poem about Sounder and his special qualities.

2. Write and perform a scene in which the younger children talk among themselves about the crisis in the family.

3. Find a newspaper story and create a new story from it as the boy did.

4. As the boy, write a letter to your father describing Sounder's return.

5. Practice storytelling. As the boy's mother, tell him a fairy tale or fable that would teach a lesson.

Critical Thinking:

1. Which character have you liked or disliked the most in the book? Give reasons for your answer.

2. If the father returns, will his and the boy's relationship have changed?

3. Analyze why the boy's mother wasn't more active in getting help for her husband.

4. Walking home, the boy went over the day's events. Do you have a certain time to review what has happened in a given day? Share and compare answers with a partner.

5. Analyze why one's actual age would mean very little in this situation. Evaluate why his reaction was that "he had lived a long, long time."

Chapters 7 and 8

Literal Thinking:

1. After the guard hurt him, how did the boy know his father was not in the crew?

2. How was the boy's father injured?

3. Describe the boy's father when he returned home.

4. When did Sounder finally demonstrate he had a full voice?

5. What does the boy's mother think dog days means?

6. Why did Sounder die?

Interpretive Thinking:

1. How did the incident with the guard show how brave the boy could be?

2. Why was the boy glad his father was not in that particular gang?

3. Why did the boy's mother allow him to go to the teacher's home?

4. Compare Sounder's condition to that of the boy's father.

5. What was the ultimate proof of Sounder's love for his master?

6. What leads you to think that the teacher was very concerned about the boy's education?

Creative Thinking:

1. Tell of an experience you have had that relates to the song the mother sings, "Ain't nobody gonna walk it for you. You gotta walk it by yourself."

2. Draw an illustration of the schoolhouse in charcoal or colored markers.

3. Draw your impression of the scarecrow that the boy imagined.

4. Create a bookmark for the boy that would encourage him to read.

5. What is *serendipity*? Write a paragraph telling how this word applies to the boy in *Sounder*.

Critical Thinking:

1. Do you think this book deserved the Newbery Award? Why or why not?

2. Debate the sentence his father received given the severity of the crime. Do you feel it was fair? Why or why not?

3. Evaluate why his particular book set him apart from the other children. How could it aid him in forming new relationships?

4. The teacher helped the young boy by being interested, caring, and attentive. Cite a time in your life when someone did the same for you. Share with a partner.

5. Is cowardice the mother of cruelty? Discuss.

6. How did the boy feel about himself after talking to the teacher?

7. Why was it healthier for the boy to fantasize about the guard instead of taking action?

Additional Activities

Visual Art:

1. Draw three buildings — a shack, a jail, and a school. Under each write a sentence summarizing its significance in *Sounder*.

2. Create a new cover for the boy's treasured book.

3. Make a scroll of every person's rights.

4. Create a headstone for Sounder from clay or papier-mâché.

5. Using a burlap background, cut designs from scrap fabric for favorite scenes from *Sounder*.

Creative Writing:

1. Brainstorm ways to find a missing person. You are a famous sleuth and find the boy's father. Write a report to your supervisor describing your methods.

2. How was the boy a model for his brothers and sisters? Write a thank-you note from one of his brothers to him.

3. Research the Uncle Remus stories by Joel Chandler Harris. Create a new adventure of Brer Rabbit based on an aspect of this story.

4. Write an eulogy the young boy might give for his father, and for Sounder.

5. Write a letter nominating Sounder as the Most Memorable Pet.

6. Write a short epilogue focusing on the education of the boy.

Drama:

1. Prepare a speech by the boy on civil rights.

2. Recreate the scene in which the boy gives his father the cake. Remember his actions and feelings while walking through town until he leaves the jail.

3. As the boy, now a grandfather, tell your grandchildren about your childhood and your wonderful dog Sounder.

4. As the boy's mother read excerpts from your journal about turning points in the beginning, middle, and end of the story.

5. As the boy, now a teacher, counsel a student who wants to read but is having difficulty and thinks learning to read is boring. How would your childhood experiences concerning reading aid you in counseling?

Music:

1. Investigate gospel singing of Afro-Americans in the nineteenth century. Discover how their faith helped them survive.

2. Change the lyrics of a gospel song to depict a cause you feel strongly about.

3. Find music for various moods—nostalgic, sad, happy, mysterious. Play the recordings and find appropriate sections in the book that also reflect these moods.

4. Create your own song about life on a plantation from the viewpoint of an Afro-American.

5. Listen to music from *Song of the South* by Disney. Learn favorite songs as a class.

Social Studies:

1. It is said that throughout history the greatest resources are children's minds. Is this statement true? Discuss.

2. Interview teachers in your school. Find out why they encourage reading, what books they recommend, and their personal favorite stories.

3. Research the history of coon dogs, the areas in which they were used, and how they were taught to hunt.

4. Evaluate poverty today compared to the nineteenth century. Compare and contrast conditions.

Science:

1. Research mistletoe and bittersweet, including the origins of both. Draw an example, marking the stamen, pistil, stem, bloom, and leaves.

2. Herbs have been used throughout history for healing. Research various healing herbs, including oak leaves.

3. Does nutrition affect mental ability? Is poverty perpetuated, to some extent, by the lack of balanced diets? Research to see if there is a connection.

4. Sounder learned to compensate for his lost senses. How do people compensate for a weakened or lost sense? Research to see if the blind have a heightened sense of touch or hearing.

5. Find out the typical crop grown by the sharecroppers.

6. Research the Dog Star, including its location and some of the superstitions associated with it throughout history.

Math:

1. The value of walnuts is mentioned in the story. How many pounds would it take to earn 90¢, $2.70, $9.60? If you had 25 pounds, how much money would you earn? 100 pounds?

Bulletin Board

Sounder

The boy in *Sounder* learned much from the well-known truths of his book. Locate famous truths such as "You can't judge a book by its cover." Write a fable about the truth and restate the truth at the bottom of the fable.

No Promises in the Wind

Irene Hunt

No Promises in the Wind

by

Irene Hunt
Follett, 1970

The story takes place during the depression years in Chicago. Josh, following a confrontation with his mother, decides to leave home and make his own way in the world. His younger brother Joey and his friend Howie accompany him.

Howie is killed while attempting to board a freight train. The boys manage to save his most prized possession, a banjo, and carry it with them on their journey.

This story tells of the brothers' hardships and the people they encounter until they are finally reunited with their parents.

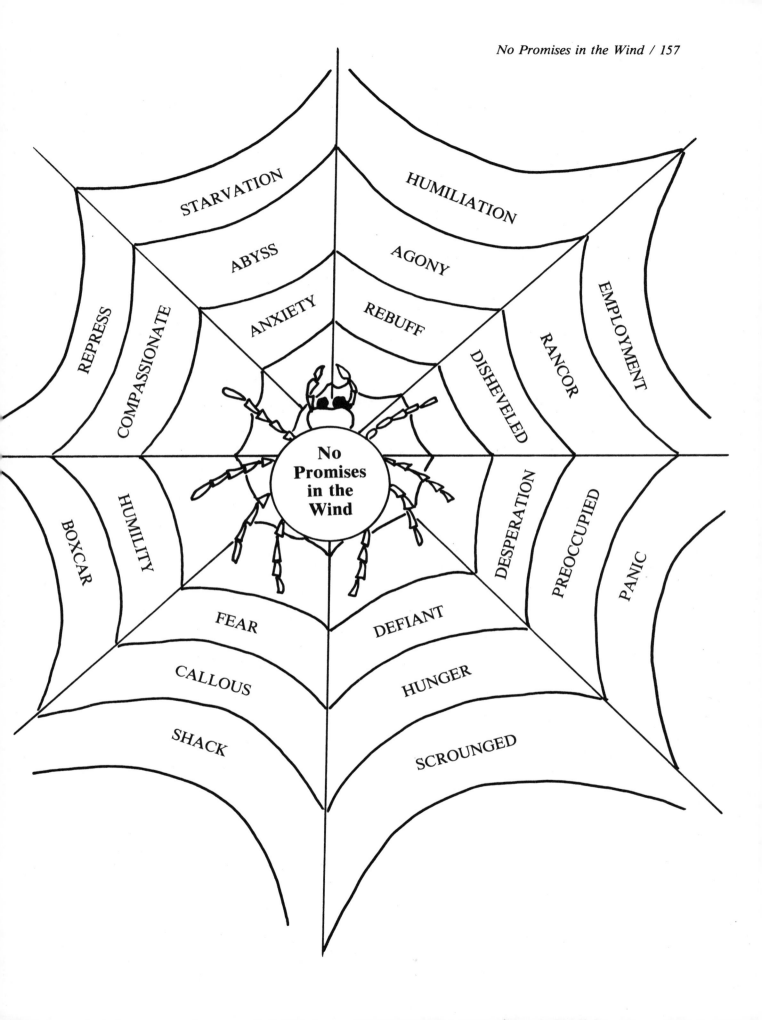

Chapters 1 through 3

Literal Thinking:

1. What nationality was Josh?

2. What was the balm to Josh's soul?

3. Why did Kitty have such a special place in her father's heart?

4. What were the railroad detectives called?

5. Why were jobs so scarce in Chicago in 1932?

6. How did Howie die?

7. Who attacked Joey and Josh while they were in the woods?

Interpretive Thinking:

1. Music can be a great healer. What sentence in the story relates this?

2. How do people's personalities change when their basic needs are not met?

3. How did the desire for freedom and self-worth enter into Josh's decision to leave home?

4. Why do you think Josh felt the way he did about Joey? Do you think he was justified?

5. Why did Josh's mother have the worst time of any of the family members?

6. Why, when the decision to leave was such a serious matter, did both of the boys also feel optimistic and excited?

7. Why was riding the rails so popular?

8. What characteristics of Howie tell you that he was warm and caring?

Creative Thinking:

1. Create a conversation between a railroad bull and his supervisor. What would each say about the boys being on the train?

2. Role-play the confrontation between Josh and his mother.

3. Recreate the scene between the three boys while Joey tried to go with them. Keep in mind the relationships among all three, and the techniques they might use to influence each other.

4. Role-play a scene between the boys and the hobo, with the latter telling them about the pitfalls of riding the rails.

5. Draw a scene from this time depicting the feeling and attitude of the people, such as a hobo in a shantytown.

6. Using dark and somber colors, draw a picture of the city during the depression.

7. Interview Josh, Joey, their father and mother, and the hobo. What do they have to say about events thus far?

Critical Thinking:

1. Josh felt school had become his refuge. Have you sometimes needed or had such a place? Where was it located? Discuss with a partner.

2. Evaluate why Josh's mother always made special allowances for his father. Do you agree or disagree with her?

3. Evaluate why Howie might not have been sympathetic to Josh's problems. Do your own problems influence your evaluation of others? Discuss as a class.

4. Was Josh's mother right to encourage Josh to leave? Why?

5. Was Josh's decision to leave home wise? Debate.

6. After Howie's death, why didn't the boys go home? Should they have?

7. Should Josh and Joey have been punished for stealing the rooster? Discuss.

8. Why was Joey most vulnerable to an attack by the gang of boys?

Chapters 4 through 6

Literal Thinking:

1. Where did Josh look for food, something he never thought he could bring himself to do?

2. What humiliation was hardest for Josh to bear?

3. What was always the boys' most pressing problem?

4. What was the most wonderful thing the old lady let them have?

5. What were the rules for staying anywhere?

6. Where did Lonnie suggest that the boys work?

7. Why did the clown prefer to be called Bongo?

8. Why was the Christmas Eve celebration at Emily's not a happy one for Josh?

Interpretive Thinking:

1. Why couldn't Josh allow himself to feel anything toward his father?

2. Why does Lonnie feel empathy toward Josh's father?

3. How did Lonnie give Josh some of his self-respect back?

4. How did Josh show he still had not forgiven his parents?

5. Why did people find it hard to turn Joey away from their doors when he was begging?

6. Why does Josh want to pay Lonnie back for the food and the ride?

7. Why did Josh write Lon Bromer in his wallet identification rather than Stefan Grondowski?

8. Visually, why was the carnival a magical place to boys with Josh and Joey's background?

9. How did Emily's reactions after the fire show that she was a survivor? Was Florida?

Creative Thinking:

1. Write a letter from Josh to his parents. Include what you think he would have written given his attitude. Rewrite the letter with what you believe he really would have liked to tell them.

2. Describe a time when you were alone and felt isolated from those around you. Write or verbally share your experience.

3. Using pastel chalk, draw a mural of the carnival and its varied scenes.

4. Invite a clown makeup artist to your class. Learn how to apply the makeup. Understand the importance of individuality in clown makeup.

5. Have students choose characters from the circus. Develop the mannerisms and a background for your character. Introduce yourself to the boys and include how you joined the circus.

6. Mime the way in which Josh was to play the piano.

7. Draw a Christmas tree for the circus. Decorate it with items designed to represent everyone important to the boys. Exchange and show how many items others can connect to the correct person.

Critical Thinking:

1. Evaluate the wisdom and compassion of the old lady, her respect for the boys and concern for the parents. What would you have done in a similar situation? Discuss with the class.

2. What does Lonnie mean by "But you somehow got the idea that men have no right to make mistakes? That's just a privilege of kids?" Is he right?

3. Do you think that Josh is carrying his anger for his father too long?

4. Analyze why the boys might be helping Lonnie as much or more than he has them. Choose a point from the story to support your opinion. From your life or something you have heard about, cite another example in which helping others really helped the giver the most. Share with the class.

5. The boys felt strange when they first joined the circus, as they felt they were the only ones not knowing what to do. Relate a time when you were in a new situation and felt at a real loss. Compare with a partner. Were your basic concerns and feelings alike?

6. Analyze why Josh's stubbornness gave him heartache more than anyone else. Evaluate a time when the phrase "You're your own worst enemy" could have been true of you.

7. What word would describe Pete Harris?

8. Which character of the carnival did you find the most fascinating?

9. Predict what will happen to Josh and Joey after the fire.

Chapters 7 through 9

Literal Thinking:

1. Why did Pete Harris say that he could not employ the boys for six months?

2. Who visited and cared for Josh the most during his convalescence?

3. Josh started out being Joey's protector. Cite examples in which this is no longer true.

4. How had Josh been reduced to the "lowest common denominator"?

5. Even though Josh is warm and comfortable at Lonnie's, it is meaningless and he is still miserable. Why?

6. What was the children's army?

Interpretive Thinking:

1. List ten verbs that describe the depression.

2. What is the difference between dominating and convincing people?

3. Why would a shoe salesman swindle two homeless boys out of their money?

4. What role did humor play in dealing with the shoe salesman's dishonesty?

5. What was comforting about President Roosevelt's inaugural speech?

6. Why do you think the sheriff agreed with the store owner?

7. Why didn't Josh feel he deserved breakfast?

8. How had Josh's life changed so that it revolved around Joey?

Creative Thinking:

1. Have one of the boys write a letter to someone special from the circus. Include the reasons he feels that the person has been special for him.

2. Analyze why the boys felt poor people would be more likely to share. Defend your position.

3. Role-play the scene between Josh and Joey in which the latter has had enough of his brother's behavior.

4. Why do you suppose President Roosevelt brought renewed hope to so many? Compare that to the feeling people have today with a change of leadership. Interview a grandparent or someone who remembers Roosevelt coming into office.

5. Create a news broadcast about a missing boy. Include aspects of Joey's personality that might help someone recognize him.

6. Draw two pictures depicting Josh's concepts of life with and without Lonnie. In the first, use bright colors to reflect the joy of the reunion with Lonnie. In the second illustration, use dark colors, reflecting the blackness of living alone without Lonnie.

7. Plan a welcome-home party for Joey from Josh and Janey. Create invitations, decorations, and a banner. Role-play the party, and videotape it.

8. Imagine what would have happened had Lonnie not found Joey. Draw an illustration of your idea.

9. Do you feel better when you are able to laugh at something unfortunate that happens to you?

Critical Thinking:

1. Should Josh have confronted the shoe salesman verbally or physically? Brainstorm more creative ways for Josh to have recovered his money.

2. Does Josh really have things more valuable than money in his life? Read the story *The Midas Touch*. How could this story have helped Josh appreciate what he had? Discuss.

3. What was the most important thing Josh learned from Joey's running away?

4. Why does Josh have such difficulty expressing his feelings to Joey?

5. Evaluate the mental and emotional growth of both Josh and Joey since they started their trek. Debate which has shown the most growth. Were there indications of this before they left? Cite examples.

Chapters 10 and 11

Literal Thinking:

1. What in Joey's actions showed that he had forgiven his brother?

2. Tell why Josh questioned Mrs. Arthur's story about the clothes?

3. Why had Joey not called Lonnie?

4. What would be Josh's proudest moment?

5. When was Josh employed playing the piano?

6. Who wrote a letter encouraging Josh to go home?

Interpretive Thinking:

1. How has Josh's attitude toward his father changed?

2. What kind of piano music would Mrs. Arthur probably prefer?

3. What word would describe Josh's feelings about Mr. Ericson's publicity?

4. How did Janey show she really cared for the two boys?

5. Project what you feel will happen to the relationship between Josh and Janey; the boys and Lonnie; Josh and Emily.

6. Contrast the train ride when Josh, Joey, and Howie started out and the train trip home.

7. Is Lonnie an understanding person? Explain.

Creative Thinking:

1. As Josh, write a message to Janey that will fully convince her of your return.

2. If you were Josh's parents, what changes would you hope had occurred in your son's attitude?

3. Write a letter from the boys to their parents telling of their return. Try to clear up some of the misunderstandings in order to make their initial meeting easier for them all.

4. Create a limerick about "The two boys from the Windy City." Keep in mind that a limerick consists of five chiefly anapestic lines (one anapest or foot being *short, short, long*). The first two lines and the last one must rhyme, each consist of three feet. The second and third lines must rhyme, and each consist of two feet. Before you begin, read some examples of limericks.

5. Create a placard or poster with the slogan "As right as Roosevelt."

6. What suggestions do you have that might help Josh and his father improve their relationship?

7. Imagine you are Josh. Write a thank-you letter to Lonnie.

Critical Thinking:

1. Why does imaginative improvisation usually indicate talent in a musician?

2. Was Mr. Ericson mainly interested in promoting Josh's talent or in a personal business venture? Explain your opinion.

3. What was the feeling Josh expressed to Emily when he said she need not wear earrings?

4. Do you agree with Josh that you should not blame your father for weaknesses, but rather work on self-discipline and understanding?

5. Why does Emily urge Josh and Joey to go home?

6. Do you agree with Mr. Ericson's putting the page with "Our Wild Boy" inside the menus? Explain your attitude and if there was another way that could have been used to handle the situation.

7. Analyze the fatalism Janey showed toward relationships. Why would those times promote such attitudes? Discuss with a partner.

8. Judge the changes Josh has undergone. Compare a statement from the last few pages regarding his feeling about someone to a statement about the same person from earlier in the book. Evaluate the difference in attitude. In your own life can you think of an example in which reevaluating something caused you to see it from a different perspective?

Additional Activities

Visual Art:

1. Create a newspaper front page signaling the 1929 stock market crash. Research information of that date and use associative information, such as weather for that area.

2. The cartoon strip "Little Orphan Annie" was very popular during this time, possibly because it dealt with conditions people could relate to. Research its style and uniqueness. Using those characters and visuals, create a cartoon depicting a particular situation from the story.

3. Create a visual display of the depression, using newspaper articles, pictures, and journals.

4. Create a bulletin board about the homeless in the United States today. Brainstorm solutions for the problem.

Creative Writing:

1. Write a brief essay of what the title *No Promises in the Wind* means.

2. Read a biography of Franklin D. Roosevelt. Write an essay on his coming into office during the depression era.

3. Write a short article for the newspaper urging runaways to return home or at least to seek help.

4. Write what you think about the symbolism of the banjo. Why did it become so important to the boys and what did it signify to them about life and Howie?

5. Bring a photograph of early childhood. Each child in the class writes a story about what is happening in the picture, emphasizing positive family memories.

6. Investigate writers during the depression. What great literary works were written during that period?

Drama:

1. Interview senior citizens about the years of the depression. Retell the stories for your class.

2. Create a dialogue between Josh and Lonnie ten years after the boys return home.

3. During the time of this book's setting, entertainment was very limited because of lack of money. The mayor of New York City even took to reading each Sunday's newspaper to children, as most of the families could not afford to buy a newspaper but might have access to a radio. Look over the newspaper for two or three weeks. Save the cartoons you feel might best fit this situation. You might use a comic book or anthology. Keep in mind you will have to completely set up each frame verbally for your listeners. Perform a radio show. Give yourself a name, show title, and theme music.

4. Have students present campaign speeches by Hoover and Roosevelt.

Music:

1. Jazz had been popular in certain areas and with certain groups long before this time. During these years its popularity and base of followers broadened. Research and listen to some of the classical jazz, such as that from New Orleans, and follow the life of Louis Armstrong.

2. Investigate the banjo. Have a guest performance.

3. Think of songs that were comforting and meaningful to you as a young child. Teach one of these songs to your class and tell why it was meaningful.

4. Learn the Polish song on the last page. Sing it together as a class.

5. Lullabies are often sung to children and the memories bring comfort even as adults. Listen to a recording of Brahms's "Lullaby" as you read excerpts of Josh's memories of his father.

Social Studies:

1. Different times and conditions have produced other hardships. Research the Dust Bowl and its impact on people.

2. Shantytowns and squatter cities illegally cropped up during the depression. Research, compare, and contrast those conditions to the situation with the homeless in this country today.

3. Research the causes of the Great Depression. What measures did President Roosevelt take to aid jobless people?

4. Collect famous sayings of presidents similar to President Roosevelt's "The only thing we have to fear is fear itself."

5. Have a debate on how the depression could have been prevented.

Science:

1. What does science say about the correlation between mental attitude and physical health? Explain.

2. Evaluate the quality of medical care at the time Joey was ill. How has medical treatment changed?

3. There are some very distinct differences between midgets and dwarfs. Research the causes of each condition and the medical discoveries that aid in the treatment of these conditions. Billy

Barty is a famous actor who has this irregularity. He does a lot of volunteer work and has made great strides in informing the public. Research some of his interviews and share with the class.

4. Inverse air pressure creates suction when one train passes another. This proved to be dangerous because it caused the death of Howie. Research this and present a short scientific explanation to the class. Explain how a similar effect and problem can be encountered in an airplane at high altitudes.

5. Investigate what discoveries and inventions in science were made during the depression.

Math:

1. Lack of money was a major problem during the depression. Learn how compound interest works. Create math problems with paper money to demonstrate.

2. The boys were able to buy a lot of food for less than one dollar. Prices were much lower in the 1930s. Research and compare the cost of common grocery items then and now. Compute the percentage increases and chart them on a graph.

3. The author discusses the age differences between Josh, Emily, and Peter. Translate the given information into their actual ages.

4. Create a graph showing the following between 1929 and 1933: (1) the stock market, (2) unemployment, and (3) public service agencies.

Bulletin Board

No Promises in the Wind

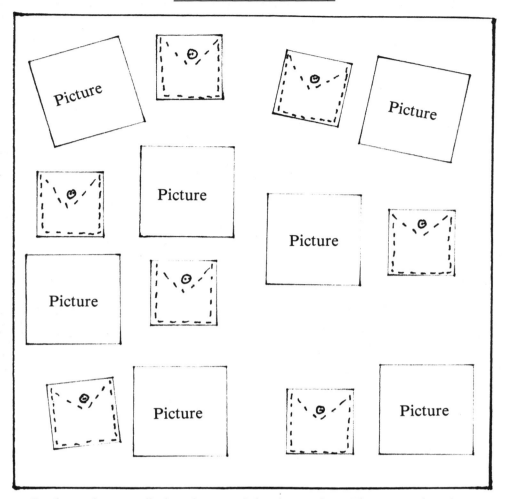

Students draw or find a picture of the depression. These are placed on the board. Students do research on the dynamics of the depression that relate to the pictures. Reports are displayed in the pockets after the oral presentations. Pockets can be real ones cut from old shirts or jeans, or pockets made by students from construction paper.

The Noonday Friends

Mary Stolz

The Noonday Friends

by

Mary Stolz
Harper & Row, 1965

The Noonday Friends is a story about two young girls who live in a Hispanic neighborhood. Franny, the main character, lives with her parents and two brothers. Her father is an artist who has trouble keeping a job because of his dream of being a great artist. The family has difficulty meeting their basic needs because of illness and the father's dreaming. Franny's older brother is frustrated with the lack of money and makes wisecracks about their situation. Marshall, Franny's younger brother, is a joy to her. She teaches him while playing "school" and has high hopes for his future.

Franny is embarrassed to be on the free lunch program at school. She is frustrated that she does not have pretty clothes to wear as some of the children, especially a girl named Lila. Franny's best friend is Simone. The two girls have a common bond—helping their own families with the day-to-day living of the poor. Because of a silly misunderstanding, the friends do not communicate their true feelings. Both girls suffer from loneliness, but are unwilling to give up their pride for a reconciliation.

A bit of luck and fate help the father achieve his dream and the family is once again on the road to success.

This is a touching, realistic book that shows the importance of communication with family and friends.

GLOOMY

SCARED

AWFUL

MOODY

CROWDED

FREE

The Noonday Friends

POVERTY

THIN

NARROW

SHARP–FEATURED

LONELY

Chapters 1 through 3

Literal Thinking:

1. Why was Franny afraid of the sirens of ambulances?

2. Tell why Mr. Davis continually lost his job.

3. Why could Franny not see her friends after school?

4. How did Lila react when Simone beat her at hopscotch?

5. In what part of New York City did the Davis family live?

6. Why did Franny want to return the free lunch pass to the teacher saying she didn't need it?

7. What was Mr. Davis's latest job?

Interpretive Thinking:

1. What is worrying Franny and Jim about Marshall's saying people always have birthday parties?

2. What does it mean that Mr. Davis has dreams that are reasonable and impossible at once?

3. What leads you to think the Davis parents are very concerned about their children?

4. Have you ever sketched or daydreamed when you were bored? Share your experience with a friend.

5. Given Franny's information about Simone, from what country do you think her family originated?

6. Why do you think Marshall was so much closer to Franny than anyone else in the family?

7. Do you feel that the name the family gave their cat was an interesting choice given their economic conditions? Discuss.

Creative Thinking:

1. Design a lunch box for Franny.

2. Compose a short, silly poem similar to the ones Franny and Marshall enjoyed.

3. Draw a picture of Franny looking out the window at the rain. Under the picture, write what Franny is thinking.

4. Create a collage from magazine pictures showing the various emotions Franny felt in chapters 1 through 3.

5. Design an original front cover for *The Noonday Friends*.

Critical Thinking:

1. You are a job counselor with Mr. Davis. Suggest jobs that would incorporate his artistic talents.

2. Which character in this story seems to have the most potential to learn from mistakes? Explain your choice.

3. Speculate why the ambulance might have come for Mr. Davis.

4. Franny was upset that she couldn't go to her friends' homes after school. Compare this to a time when you were not allowed to do something with a friend. Remember your feelings and disappointment. Share with a partner.

5. Is Mr. Davis a reliable character? Discuss.

Chapters 4 through 6

Literal Thinking:

1. Why did Marshall throw a tantrum about getting a picture book at the store?

2. Explain why Marshall had fallen into an ambush.

3. What caused Mr. Davis to abandon his job and revert to being a father?

4. Mrs. Mundy and Marshall both got pains, but from different things. What gave them to each?

5. Why did Franny believe everyone so carefully listened to Mrs. Davis?

6. What was a minor blessing of poverty according to Mr. Davis?

Interpretive Thinking:

1. Do you feel Mr. Davis is an intelligent man? Find a portion of the story to prove your point.

2. What does Simone mean by "New York has a cold heart"?

3. Why does Franny feel insecure in her friendship with Simone?

4. What do you know about Franny's and Simone's families by reading the story? List the main characteristics of each.

5. Pretend to interview Franny and Simone to find the things they like and dislike about each other.

6. Why do people lose their educational goals? Discuss.

Creative Thinking:

1. Write a job-wanted ad for a newspaper for Mr. Davis and Francisco, telling what abilities they have.

2. Mrs. Davis had dreams of becoming an astronomer but didn't take action to become one. What career do you dream of? What course of action will you pursue to obtain your career? Write a plan of action.

3. Think of how Franny's life could have been different had she had a way to earn money.

4. Design a cereal box with a special surprise inside.

5. Duplicate your impression of Mr. Davis's drawing of Mr. Horney.

6. Using all the grocery items Marshall loved, cut out wrappers and advertisements to make a collage. An alternative would be to create overlapping drawings of all of the items.

7. Draw Pipi with his pushcart. Emphasize his grand moustache.

Critical Thinking:

1. What was the best part of living in a large family like Simone's? The worst?

2. Which character emphasizes most clearly the need for an education? Discuss.

3. How would you have reacted had you been Peter's mother in the grocery store? Evaluate how your impression of such an incident has changed since you were four years old.

4. Why was Marshall upset with Franny's idea of being a mermaid? Why did his opinion differ with her second choice?

5. Receiving an answer of "just because" can be very frustrating. Evaluate why, to Marshall and Franny, it was a reasonable explanation.

6. Do you think Mr. Davis's explanation of why foreigners have more difficulty getting a job is correct?

Chapters 7 through 10

Literal Thinking:

1. What scheme had the boys devised to get money?

2. Explain Mr. Davis's idea about how to pay for the shoes.

3. Why did Mr. Davis choose the color he did for Mr. Horney's face in the portrait?

4. Why had Franny and Simone quarreled?

5. Why was Mr. Horney pleased that Francisco spoke Spanish?

6. Why did Mr. Davis's triumph of helping Francisco turn dim and hollow when he returned to his home?

Interpretive Thinking:

1. How did the change in name for the Horney canvas reflect a change in Mr. Davis's attitude toward Mr. Horney?

2. How did Lila try to undermine Franny's and Simone's friendship?

3. How did Marshall's announcement about someone getting a job make the family lose sight of what a nice thing Mr. Davis had done for two other people?

4. Was Franny crying only about Simone?

5. Why is *promise* a meaningless word to Mrs. Davis?

6. Analyze the statement "Having a lot to live for is a better guarantee of long life than promises can be."

7. Have you ever experienced a misunderstanding when you were the generous one who tried to first apologize? Discuss.

8. Why did Mr. Davis suddenly have the confidence to recommend Francisco for his job?

Creative Thinking:

1. Role-play a quiet conversation between Mr. and Mrs. Davis concerning his job losses. Role-play another conversation with Francisco telling his family about finding a job. Contrast the styles of the two conversations.

2. Green was a reflective color to the artist. Create a color wheel and write a short analysis of how each color makes you feel. Survey your class to assess their opinions.

3. Have a cooking class. Create the s'mores that Jim made. They are a combination of graham crackers, chocolate chips, and marshmallows. Heat in a regular oven or microwave. Each student, using simple ingredients at home, can create new variations. Bring examples to the class.

4. As Mr. Horney, try the "sandwich" form of criticism to help Mr. Davis learn to keep a job. First congratulate him on his talent, then tell him how he can improve. Finally, again, tell him how talented he is.

5. Franny states that "silence can be so lonely." Give examples of your experiences when silence was lonely.

6. Create a "souvenir" of one of the following: Mr. Davis's time at the shoe store; Franny and Simone's friendship; or the Davis family, themselves.

Critical Thinking:

1. Evaluate if more communication between Mr. and Mrs. Davis would have made a difference in Mr. Davis's ability to keep a job.

2. Was Mrs. Davis's reply to Franny's question about death comforting? Why or why not?

3. Are flattery and rewards more productive than negative criticism? Discuss.

4. Evaluate why Jim couldn't even look at his father after talking about him to the stranger. In your journal, write about a situation in which you reacted in a way that you later regretted.

5. Mr. Davis had difficulty holding a job. Did his irresponsibility extend to his family? Validate your opinion by citing examples from the book.

6. Mr. Davis was fired because he was honest about his opinion concerning the woman's shoes. In sales, where does professional ethics enter in? Extend this to ethics in government. Debate.

7. Analyze how you handle an argument. Do you discuss it, get angry, or simply leave the situation? What do you particularly dislike about the responses of others? In a group discussion, develop a response that would be most comfortable but still solve problems effectively.

8. Is it true that when negative experiences happen to people, the people tend to pull together? Discuss.

Chapters 11 through 14

Literal Thinking:

1. What was Jim's most peculiar birthday present for Marshall?

2. How did Marshall show that he was indeed a very unusual boy?

3. Why would Franny have some extra time to be with Lila and Simone?

4. Why was Franny excited about carrying her lunch to school?

Interpretive Thinking:

1. Have you ever had an unusual birthday party? Explain.

2. Have you ever been grateful for what you have after comparison? Share with a partner.

3. Why was Franny's father's gesture so important to her?

4. How did the green color add interest to Mr. Horney that he didn't already have?

5. Why, after a period of time, does it not matter who started an argument?

6. How was the entire family showing the stress of Mr. Davis's not having a job again?

7. How did Mr. Davis show that he was too honest to take credit for something that he felt he did not deserve?

Creative Thinking:

1. Write a letter from Franny to Simone attempting to clear up the misunderstanding. As Simone, reply to Franny.

2. Decorate a birthday banner for Marshall. Each child in the class signs it with well wishes.

3. Write an additional chapter telling what happened between the friends and with Mr. Davis's painting career.

4. Design for a friend a unique birthday present that does not require much money.

Additional Activities

Visual Art:

1. Look carefully at advertising symbols for American businesses such as the *M* for McDonald's. What would you do to add to or improve the symbols? Draw pictures of your ideas.

2. With a partner, draw each other's portraits. Make a portrait gallery for your classroom.

3. Look at works by modern artists such as Picasso. Learn how color influenced the periods he painted. Create a portrait in the Picasso style.

4. Design a poster advertising an art show by Mr. Davis.

5. Create a scrapbook of things you like and dream of.

Creative Writing:

1. Create a mobile about yourself. Include symbols of your family, interests, school, hobbies, and hopes for the future.

2. Choose the name of someone in your class and compile a scrapbook for the person. Get information and pictures from parents, former teachers, and others. Include humorous anecdotes, likes and dislikes, favorite songs and singing groups, and so on.

3. Write a list of wise sayings and philosophies from *The Noonday Friends*. Create questions about them for classmates to answer.

4. Gifts are best when they are what the recipient wants, not what the giver wants him/her to have. Make a gift list for special people. Think of very individual gifts for them.

5. Write a story of how life would have been different for the Davis family had they lived in a small town or on a farm.

6. Write an epilogue to this story.

Drama:

1. Role-play each of the characters in the story by pantomiming their outstanding characteristics. The class guesses which character is presented.

2. Write a short speech by Jim telling of his feelings about his role in the family.

3. Suppose Simone and Lila had been unfriendly with Franny at the end of the book. Role-play Franny's creative reaction.

4. Read *The Bears' House* by Marilyn Sachs. Role-play a conversation between Franny and Fran Ellen's teachers after visiting their homes and learning of their students' difficult home lives.

5. Create a television interview program. Interview famous artists, such as Picasso, O'Keeffe, and Monet. Ask questions, such as what are their main contributions to the world of art.

Music:

1. Give Franny a taste of different kinds of world music. Play recordings of different types of ethnic music. Decide on your favorite.

2. Franny and Simone both wanted beauty in their lives. Find songs that celebrate beauty and sing them as a class.

3. Mr. Davis says the American Indian was mistreated. What stories did American Indians tell in their songs? Locate Indian songs to teach to your class.

4. Research and collect songs about New York City. Listen to them as a class and discuss the collective picture they give of the city.

Social Studies:

1. Devise a system that schools can use so that free lunches are not so obvious.

2. Learn more about the subject of illegal aliens in the United States. Brainstorm ways to solve the problem.

3. Learn about Greenwich Village in New York City. Write to the chamber of commerce for information.

4. Simone's parents were not originally from the United States. Most of our relatives were also from other countries. Research the migration coming through Ellis Island in the early 1900s. Interview a member of your family who remembers the arrivals, or research information on your nationality (German, Irish, Dutch, etc.). Report to the class.

5. Research bartering and how it has been used historically. Money is a medium of exchange today but bartering is common in many parts of the world.

Science:

1. The girls discuss chinchilla in the story. Research chinchillas, minks, and sables. Include facts about their natural habitat, varieties, and availability of pelts, as well as a unique characteristic of each.

2. Mrs. Davis was interested in astronomy. Ask an astronomer to visit your class. Make a list of questions to ask.

3. Concentrate on the location of the planets in the universe. Arrange students in relationship to the location of the planets. Assume the characteristic of your planet with facial expression and movement.

4. Devise a creative verbal game to learn the names of the planets. Teach it to your class.

5. Develop a week's menu of very inexpensive, nutritious meals.

Math:

1. Find statistics that show the percentages of various cultures living in a large metropolitan area.

2. Discover the highest price ever paid for a painting. Report to your class.

Bulletin Board

The Noonday Friends

Draw a large book, an apple, and a ruler for the center of the bulletin board. Each child interviews another classmate to find why he/she thinks education is important. The interviewer draws a picture of the classmate at the top of the interview. Interviews and pictures may be backed by small paper sacks.

ADDITIONAL BOOKS
ON POVERTY

1. *Andrew Carnegie.* Clara Ingram Judson. Follett, 1965.

   This is the biography of a boy born in desperate poverty. He pulled himself out of his surroundings and ultimately built a fortune which he donated to humanity and world peace.

2. *Blue Willow.* Doris Gates. Viking Press, 1940.

   This classic focuses on a migrant girl who dreams of permanence and an education.

3. *The Boxcar Children.* Gertrude Chandler Warner. Scott Foresman, 1960.

   Having nowhere else to go, four children, two boys and two girls, decide to set up housekeeping in a boxcar.

4. *The Complete Grimm's Fairy Tales.* Jacob and Wilhelm Grimm. Pantheon, 1974.

   Many of these well-known fairy tales deal with aspects of poverty and the goals and schemes to rise above it.

5. *Gooseberries to Oranges.* Beverly Brodsky. Lothrop, 1982.

   Eight-year-old Fanny leaves her cholera-infested Russian village to join her father in America. In spite of her father's promise of a golden land, she finds poverty and suffering. She doesn't feel America is home until she discovers that the taste of an orange will replace her familiar taste of Russian gooseberries.

6. *Hi, Mrs. Mallory!* Ianthe Thomas. Harper & Row, 1979.

   This story tells of a special friendship between a black child and an impoverished, older white woman. Mrs. Mallory teaches Li'l Bits tricks to learning the alphabet as well as telling her wonderful stories. Li'l Bits, in turn, makes out her checks and gets wood for her.

7. *Poverty in America.* Milton Meltzer. William Morrow, 1986.

   This is a survey of the history of the poor in the United States. Meltzer sums up a disturbing current problem.

8. *Stories from the Blue Room.* Emily Crofford. Carolrhoda, 1982.

   Meg tells stories of Arkansas during the depression. Accompanying photographs vividly portray the life of the people and countryside.

9. *Under the Haystack.* P. A. Engebrecht. Nelson, 1973.

   Thirteen-year-old Sandy discovers that her mother and stepfather have left and tries to keep her two sisters from realizing that they have been abandoned.

10. *Where the Lilies Bloom.* Vera and Bill Cleaver. Lippincott, 1969.

   An Appalachian girl, the eldest of an orphaned family, has pride in the face of abject poverty and interfering neighbors.

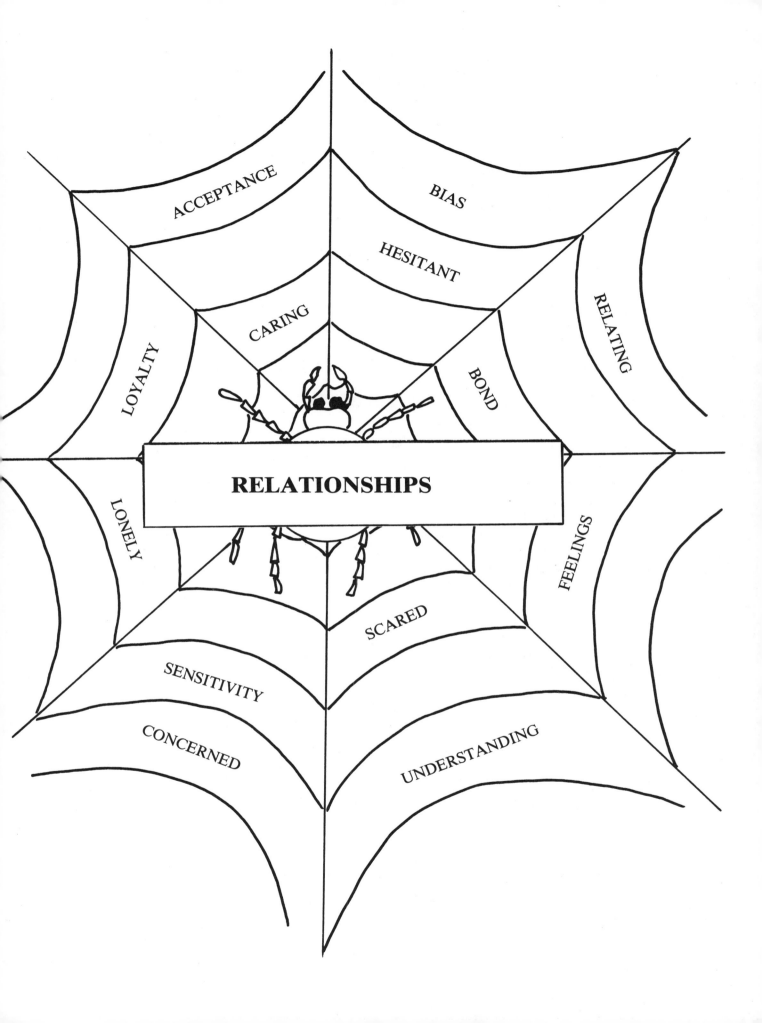

Between Friends

Sheila Garrigue

Between Friends

by

Sheila Garrigue
Bradbury, 1978

Jill Harvey has moved to Massachusetts from California. Here, at first, she has trouble meeting friends.

After a while, Jill meets DeDe Atkins, a girl with Down's syndrome. A real friendship develops between the two girls, but a problem arises with Jill's peers. They do not accept anyone who is different, especially someone who has a handicap.

Jill's friendship is severely tested when she is invited to DeDe's Christmas party at DeDe's school. Her own fears, coupled with the rejection of her peers, torture her. After discussing her problem with her parents, Jill makes the decision to attend DeDe's party.

Soon after the party, DeDe becomes very ill. Her mother decides they must move to a better climate in Arizona. Jill misses that person who has taught her much about fear, prejudice, love, and friendship.

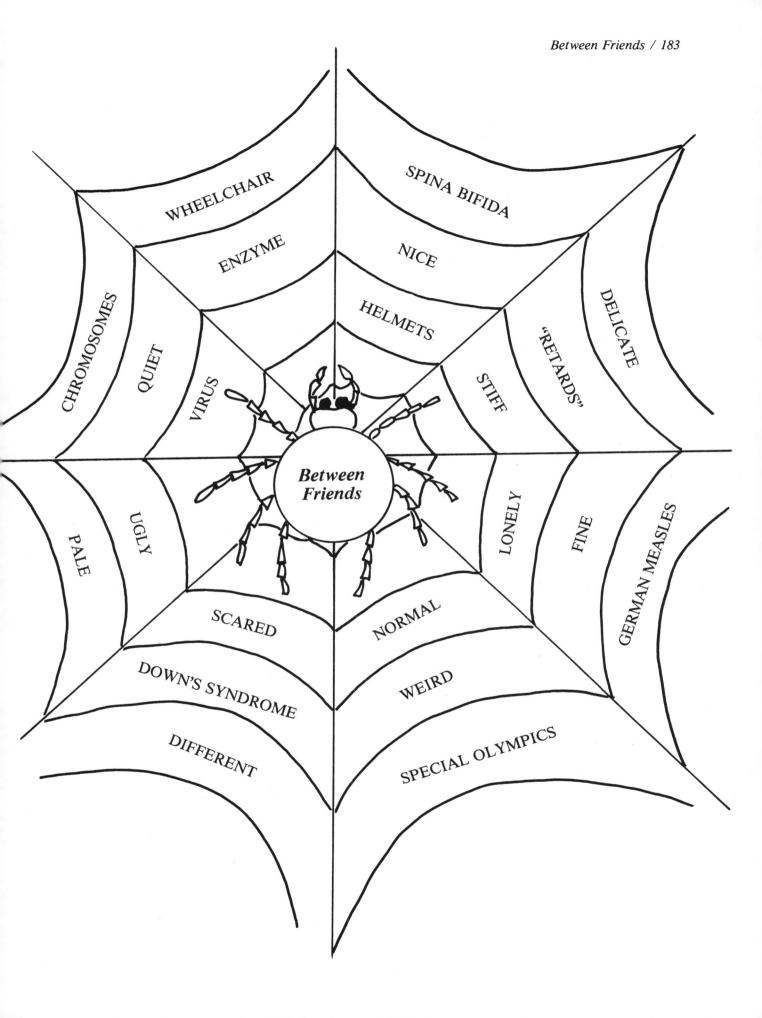

WHEELCHAIR
SPINA BIFIDA
ENZYME
NICE
CHROMOSOMES
HELMETS
DELICATE
QUIET
"RETARDS"
VIRUS
STIFF

Between Friends

UGLY
LONELY
FINE
PALE
GERMAN MEASLES
SCARED
NORMAL
DOWN'S SYNDROME
WEIRD
DIFFERENT
SPECIAL OLYMPICS

Chapters 1 through 4

Literal Thinking:

1. Where did Jill live previously and where does she live now?

2. Why had Jill and her family moved from San Diego?

3. Which character died unexpectedly?

4. Where did Jill first meet DeDe?

5. How did Jill define the term *retards*?

6. Who was the person who knew all the information about the block?

Interpretive Thinking:

1. What was really bothering Jill's mother after Jill had returned the ball to the girl?

2. Do you think DeDe knows the boys are making fun of her?

3. Why was this period in Jill's family life difficult?

4. Recall a move to a new town, school, or community. Describe your feelings and how you made new friends.

5. Explain what the term *family circle* signifies to you.

Creative Thinking:

1. Mrs. Lacey and Jill could just sit together and without feeling the need to talk still feel comfortable. Do you have a person you are that comfortable with? Discuss with a friend.

2. Create a cartoon illustrating the phrase "Low man on the totem pole."

3. Are there unspoken rules concerning friendships with retarded children that you feel need to be changed? Make a new list of rules that would promote friendship.

4. Perhaps this story reminds you of someone from whom you feel alienated or different. Brainstorm ways you can learn more about each other to become friends.

5. What is friendship? Each student draws around his/her hand. Above each finger, write an attribute of friendship. On a large piece of paper, join every two hands to symbolize friendship.

6. Describe an experience that was sad and frightening to you, similar to Jill's finding Mrs. Lacey deceased.

Critical Thinking:

1. What do you think the title *Between Friends* means?

2. Judge why people can feel so uncomfortable around mentally or physically handicapped people? Discuss class opinions.

3. Analyze which parent seemed to be most concerned with Jill's adjustment after Mrs. Lacey's death. Compare this to a traumatic incident you have had in which someone helped you through it.

4. Why do you think Sheila Garrigue wrote this book? Bring a list of reasons to a class discussion.

Chapters 5 through 8

Literal Thinking:

1. For what special event is DeDe training?

2. What things does Jill like about DeDe?

3. Describe Jill's friend, Marla.

4. What did Jill start doing with DeDe every day?

5. Why was Jill's mother unhappy with her after the Karen McCluskey incident?

6. How did Jill's father handle any question he did not want to answer?

Interpretive Thinking:

1. Why do you think Jill's and DeDe's getting along seemed to be so important to Mrs. Adkins?

2. How would you feel if you led Marla's life? Share your opinions with a partner.

3. Regarding Susan, what shows that Jill is adjusting to her new life?

4. Has a fearful experience in your past ever colored a meeting with someone new in a negative way until you learned more about him/her? Share your views in a journal entry.

5. How does Jill show that she is an independent thinker concerning DeDe? Share your views with a partner.

6. Why was it so important to DeDe to go to the party?

7. After Jill's mother tells her family about being frightened of DeDe, because she is pregnant, does she feel relieved?

Creative Thinking:

1. Create a paper balloon bouquet and notes written by your classmates to Jill. Congratulate her on her birthday and her thoughtfulness in accepting DeDe.

2. Prepare a session with a partner in which you answer a question with a question.

3. Create a small fashion show with either drawings or models showing the clothing trends in the 1960s, the 1970s, and the future.

4. Role-play the scene between DeDe and Jill playing in the leaves.

5. How does your Saturday schedule differ from Marla's, or is it the same? Prepare a schedule for your Saturdays for one month.

Critical Thinking:

1. Discuss Jill's actions regarding not wanting to go with DeDe to Charlie's when she and Karen were going to have ice cream at Charlie's.

2. Predict what you believe will happen with the three girls and their friendship.

3. Judge the similarities between Jill's mother and her friends regarding DeDe. Discuss possible reasons for their attitudes.

4. What makes this story realistic fiction as opposed to fantasy? List the components of both types of writing. Do you prefer one over the other? Why?

5. Do you think Jill's example of accepting DeDe will encourage her friends to do the same? Why or why not?

6. Tell the story of *The Ugly Duckling* by Hans Christian Andersen. Ask each classmate to write a paragraph about how the story relates to *Between Friends*.

Chapters 9 through 13

Literal Thinking:

1. What weight did Jill feel concerning DeDe's love?

2. What exciting secret did Marla tell Jill?

3. How did the baby send Jill a message?

4. List some of the forms of retardation and their causes.

5. What made Jill feel better about going to DeDe's school party?

Interpretive Thinking:

1. Think about a time you felt uncertain about a friendship with a person most people viewed as different. Could your relationship be called a "magic meeting"? Discuss.

2. How do you think the author felt about retardation and schools that educate handicapped children? Discuss.

3. What does it mean that Mrs. Adkins was smiling, but not in her eyes?

4. Why do you think DeDe was freer in expressing her emotions than the other girls?

5. How did the act of Jill telling Marla she wasn't going alter the way Marla was presenting the picture of her big dancing debut?

6. Why do you believe Jill changed her mind about going to Boston? Discuss.

Creative Thinking:

1. Draw a poster advertising the *Nutcracker* ballet as Marla would have designed it.

2. Construct a paper banner for DeDe's and her classmates' party. Write words of congratulations and encouragement for the children in DeDe's school.

3. How else could Marla have reacted to Jill's apology? Practice ad-lib by interpreting Marla's reaction humorously, sympathetically, and sadly.

4. List the little things that give you pleasure.

Critical Thinking:

1. Some of the hesitancy toward DeDe was the fear of the unknown or being different. Cite an example from your life in which not knowing made you hesitant to try something different.

2. How would you have responded had DeDe asked you to attend her Christmas party? Discuss as a class.

3. Why is it so difficult for Jill to accept DeDe's love?

4. Was the Christmas party a success? Why or why not?

Chapters 14 through 17

Literal Thinking:

1. Why did DeDe move to Arizona?

2. What was DeDe doing secretly?

3. What was on the windows of DeDe's school? What had Jill expected?

4. Explain some of the ways the school helps students to learn to deal with life.

5. What was DeDe's special area in the Olympics?

Interpretive Thinking:

1. Why did Marla react as she did about Jill's Christmas card?

2. Offer two reasons why DeDe may be more successful with relationships in Arizona.

3. In the beginning, Jill did not want to be near DeDe. Why does she now feel empty inside at DeDe's leaving?

4. How did going to DeDe's school alter Jill's opinion?

5. How did the helpers assist in the training of the children at DeDe's school both emotionally and physically?

Creative Thinking:

1. Create a flyer for an open house at the Pearson School.

2. As if to use 911, create an emergency phone call to get help for Jill's mother or for DeDe.

3. In realistic fiction, the actions seem real. How could the story have changed if DeDe had not had pneumonia or if Marla had not danced in the *Nutcracker*? Write new endings to show the changes in the plot.

4. What careers will DeDe and Marla pursue? Videotape each of the girls as adults at their college reunion.

5. Think of one of your friends. What qualities does your friend have that makes him/her special?

Critical Thinking:

1. Would you like to be a volunteer helper in a school like DeDe's? Why or why not?

2. Do you think Jill is "between friends" again?

3. What was the most important lesson Jill learned from DeDe? Survey classmates' opinions and chart the results.

4. Actions speak louder than words. Compare Marla's and DeDe's personalities by listing actions of both girls in chapters 14 through 17. What did their actions say about their concept of friendship?

5. Analyze what this book said about the needs and desires of the mentally handicapped.

6. Evaluate how Jill felt she could help her dad with his first visit to Pearson School. Compare that to a time when you, having already had a particular experience, were able to help someone else with the same situation.

7. Everyone has strengths. Marla felt hers was being a ballerina; DeDe's was being a friend. Write a short story about your strength and have either a friend or family member write another about your strength, then compare the two versions. Were they the same? Did you learn something new about yourself?

Additional Activities

Visual Art:

1. Draw a three-panel illustration for the beginning, middle, and end of the book. Summarize the story in cartoon format with only Barney and Squeak speaking.

2. Create an original oversized book cover for *Between Friends* for your media center.

3. Create a cartoon depicting Marla as a dancer.

4. Create a "missing-you" card for DeDe to receive when she gets to her grandmother's in Arizona.

Creative Writing:

1. As Jill, write a story about the person you admire most and why.

2. Write a letter to the national headquarters of the Special Olympics requesting information. Share it as a class.

3. Write a short essay on the characteristics of a good friend.

4. What were the saddest and most exciting times DeDe experienced during the story? Write about your own saddest or most exciting experiences with friends.

Drama:

1. Write a review of a play you have produced based on *Between Friends*. Answer the following questions:

   - Did the actors speak loudly enough?

   - Did the actors stay in character?

   - Did the script clearly follow the story?

   - What was an outstanding feature of the play? Describe it.

2. For the production of a play based on *Between Friends*, invite a professional director and costume designer to your class. Ask them to explain their jobs. Make a list of questions concerning your production which they can answer.

3. Create a late-night-show discussion of attitudes toward the handicapped.

4. Investigate great actors who have succeeded in spite of their handicaps.

5. Role-play Jill and DeDe in separate monologues. The characters speak about each other and their friendship.

Music:

1. Listen to a version of the *Nutcracker* and identify each particular section such as the "Dance of the Sugarplum Fairies."

2. View a videotape of a production of the *Nutcracker*.

3. Listen to a recording of "That's What Friends Are For" by Dionne Warwick and Stevie Wonder. Discuss how their song relates to Jill and DeDe's friendship.

4. What range of feelings was expressed in this book? List the various feelings. Find recordings of music that express them. See if your classmates can determine which character you are describing with music.

Social Studies:

1. Investigate the services available in the community for handicapped persons. Discover how volunteers help.

2. Learn more about education for the handicapped. Interview a teacher of retarded children. Ask questions that the class has prepared concerning the mentally handicapped's education.

3. Research the Special Olympics and what it involves. Present a mini-report to the class.

4. Have students do mini-reports on handicapped persons who have made great accomplishments.

Science:

1. Invite a pediatrician to your class to explain more about Down's syndrome—its causes and the research that is adding valuable information to understanding the condition.

2. Research to learn about spina bifida. What effect can prenatal care have on many preventable conditions?

3. Interview a physician or nurse to learn how the PKU test tells if a child has brain damage. Learn more about diets and if they can guard against brain damage.

4. Plant some seeds to see them grow and develop. Eliminate one element such as light or water and record the results.

Math:

1. Investigate the statistics of birth defects in various countries.

2. Compare the life expectancies of victims of Down's syndrome from 1950 to 1990.

Bulletin Board

<u>Between Friends</u>

Friendships are magic meetings. Demonstrate webbing an idea with "magic friendship" as the central theme. Each student writes a story of how a friendship has been magic in that it has led to new interests, new learning, and so on. Cut circles of colored paper for balloons attached to a bow of ribbons. Display student stories on balloons.

Where the Red Fern Grows

Wilson Rawls

Where the Red Fern Grows
by
Wilson Rawls
Doubleday, 1961

Billy, ten years old and growing up in the Ozark Mountains, wants a dog more than anything. But his parents can not afford to buy one.

In a sportsman's magazine that he found, Billy sees an ad for coonhound puppies. He is determined to have two of them for hunting. After two years of working and saving, Billy finally has enough money to order his dogs. Although he does not tell his parents that he has ordered them, he does confide in his grandfather, who helps him out.

Billy trains his dogs, Old Dan and Little Ann. After many weeks they are ready to coon hunt. The dogs and Billy explore the hills around Tahlequah, Oklahoma, and the river bottoms. The pair of dogs turn into an excellent team for coon hunting. Old Dan is tough and physical, whereas Little Ann is gentle but has the brains for hunting.

These first-class hounds live up to their reputation by winning the annual coon hunt contest, but in the effort Billy's grandfather is injured.

A confrontation with a mountain lion forces Billy to face a tragedy that calls for courage again and again.

This story has the warmth and love for animals that is universal.

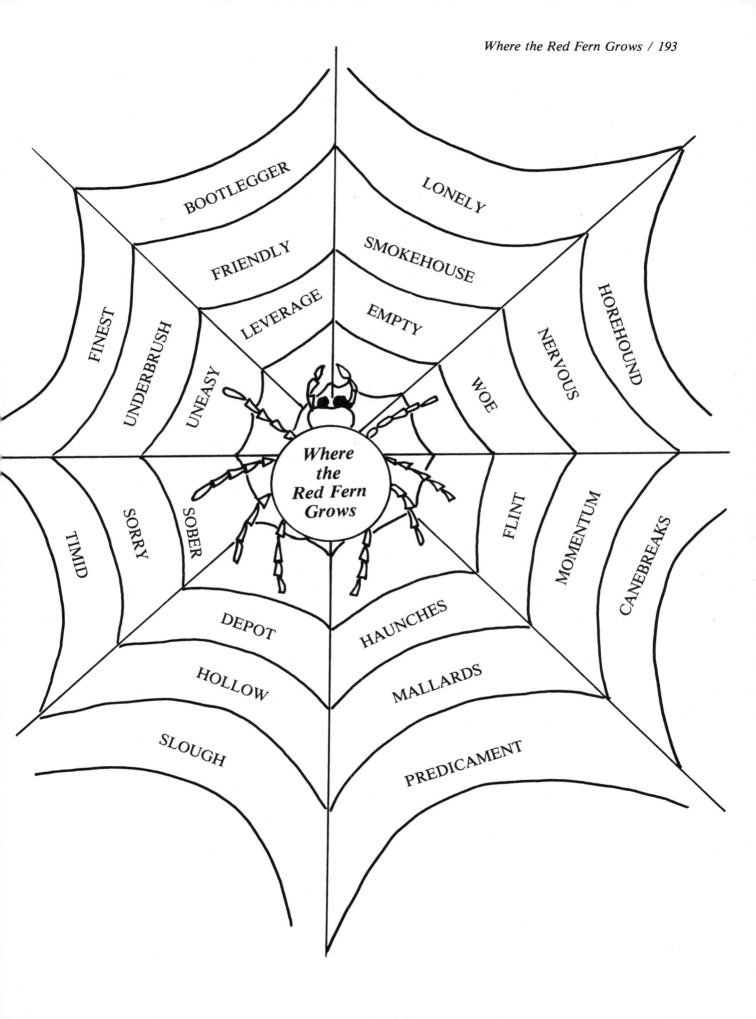

BOOTLEGGER

LONELY

FRIENDLY

SMOKEHOUSE

FINEST

UNDERBRUSH

LEVERAGE

EMPTY

HOREHOUND

NERVOUS

UNEASY

WOE

Where the Red Fern Grows

TIMID

SORRY

SOBER

FLINT

MOMENTUM

CANEBREAKS

DEPOT

HAUNCHES

HOLLOW

MALLARDS

SLOUGH

PREDICAMENT

Chapters 1 through 5

Literal Thinking:

1. Explain how Billy raised the $50 and how long it took him.

2. What animal was a potential danger during Billy's night in the cave?

3. Why did Billy think his two dogs would make a perfect team?

4. How old was Billy when his real story began?

5. What was the first unhappy resident of the traps?

6. Why was hunting season such a strain on Billy?

7. What was the one problem with getting the dogs?

8. What new thing did Billy try while in town?

Interpretive Thinking:

1. Why do you think Billy wanted the dogs so badly?

2. What reaction could Billy's grandfather have to face with his parents when they found out about the secret purchase of the hounds?

3. How would the personalities of Old Dan and Little Ann affect their performances during coon hunts?

4. If the family had the money, should the family spend it on Billy's coonhounds or a new mule? Debate.

5. How was Billy's comment "Every boy in the country had a good hound or two" typical of a child who really wants something? Explain to a partner.

6. What did his grandfather do that showed he appreciated the self-control and sacrifices Billy had made to collect his money?

7. Why do you think the townspeople had such a different attitude about dogs than the hill people such as Billy?

Creative Thinking:

1. Read aloud the most exciting part of chapters 1 through 5. You may make recorded sound effects or background music for your selection. Go to another class and encourage them to read *Where the Red Fern Grows* with your presentation.

2. Organize a book celebration where favorite books can be reviewed. Invite second- and third-grade students to encourage reading unfamiliar books.

3. Make a poster for your media center advertising *Where the Red Fern Grows* and *Summer of the Monkeys*, both by Wilson Rawls.

4. Using watercolors or markers recreate the scene of the Illinois River with all the various trees. Be sure to include the varieties mentioned in the story.

5. Using the description given in the book, draw a cartoon of Billy going to get his dogs.

Critical Thinking:

1. If Billy had had a lot of friends do you think he would still want the dogs? Why or why not?

2. Read and compare *Summer of the Monkeys* by Wilson Rawls to this book. Have a panel discussion to determine:

   - what makes the books appealing

   - their similarities and differences

   - what changes you would make to either story

   - whether you would recommend the books to other readers

3. Which character in chapters 1 through 5 seemed to understand Billy the best? Explain and support your opinion with examples from the book.

4. "Know yourself" is a famous truth. How did Billy show he already knew the essence of this truth as a very young boy?

5. Remember a time when you wanted something so much that you didn't think you could exist without it. What was your feeling after you had received it? Compare answers with a partner.

6. After Billy got his dogs did the people's attitude toward him improve? Analyze why they were so mean. Do you know of an incident in which someone behaved in a similar manner? Explain.

Chapters 6 through 10

Literal Thinking:

1. Why did Grandpa recommend tin to trap a raccoon?

2. Why did Billy think he should get the raccoon by himself?

3. Where did Billy get the names for the dogs?

4. Explain the *Ringtail Blues*.

5. How did Billy attempt to lighten the load of the puppies on the trip home?

6. What had Billy done with his extra money?

7. After getting his dogs, what was Billy's next want?

Interpretive Thinking:

1. Have you ever had an experience in which your determination to persevere against all odds brought you to your goal? Share your experience.

2. Which incidents in chapters 6 through 10 show the devotion that Old Dan felt for Little Ann?

3. How do you know that Grandpa was very proud of Billy?

4. What was Billy's attitude toward coon hunting?

5. Do you think it was right for Billy to let his grandfather explain his absence? Why or why not?

6. Can you think of other animals that might also be caught by their curiosity?

Creative Thinking:

1. Pretend you are Billy; write to a friend describing how you felt catching your first coon.

2. Read *Rascal* by Sterling North. Pretend you are a reporter for a sports magazine. Report on your findings of the intelligence and craftiness of raccoons for your editor.

3. Think up two different names for Old Dan and Little Ann.

4. Draw a portrait of Grandpa.

5. Out of cardboard, material, or paper create a collar especially for each dog.

6. Design a trap to catch but not kill a raccoon or other wild animal.

Critical Thinking:

1. What parts of chapters 6 through 10 were the most exciting? Read them aloud and tell why you chose your selection.

2. Sportsmen are known to tell stories that get bigger with each telling. Pretend you are Billy and through a series of interviews make your story of catching the coon the tallest tale. Have a contest with classmates; judge who has created the best story.

3. Explain the mystery of the wind's being only around the sycamore.

4. Billy's father thought there was a lot more to school than reading and writing. What do you think are the most important things you receive from school? Compare answers.

5. Everyone's first thought was that the male was going to be the best hunter. Little Ann actually proved them wrong. Cite a time when your first impression or instinct was wrong.

Chapters 11 through 15

Literal Thinking:

1. What two things happened on the journey to the big hunt that made Billy feel grown-up?

2. What is the superstition about a screech owl?

3. Who encouraged Billy to call Rubin's bet?

4. Which one of the dogs got into a serious predicament?

5. Name two things that were problems because of Annie's small size.

6. Which prayers did Billy's mom say had been answered?

7. Why do you think the Pritchard boys were afraid of Billy's grandfather? Explain to a partner.

8. List Billy's reasons for feeling he was the luckiest boy in the world.

Interpretive Thinking:

1. Why do you think Billy "whooped" when he started a hunt?

2. What was life like in the Pritchard home? Describe a typical day.

3. How did the Pritchard's outlook on life affect where they lived?

4. How could Rubin's death eventually change Rainey's life?

5. What do you feel was the reason Billy didn't want to kill the ghost coon?

6. How did Grandpa continually show his love and concern for his grandson?

7. How did Billy's mom show that she was sensitive to the needs and wants of both her husband and her son?

Creative Thinking:

1. Billy had a passion for coon hunting. Relate an activity for which you have a passion.

2. If Billy had given a speech after winning the silver cup, what would he have said? Practice with a partner before giving the speech to the class.

3. Create a beauty contest for the pets of your classmates. After either showing pictures or bringing pets to school, design awards or ribbons for each entry.

4. Old Dan and Little Ann were involved in many humorous and harrowing incidents in this story. Tell the funniest or most dangerous experience you have had with pets.

5. As Grandpa, create and fill in the entry form for the dogs. Be certain to list characteristics, special talents, and so on that they need in order to be included.

Critical Thinking:

1. Do you think that Billy should feel guilty about the accident? Explain.

2. What is your opinion of hunting for sport or for fur? Research by reading articles about the rights of fur-bearing animals. Write a dialogue between a furrier and a representative from the Society for the Prevention of Cruelty to Animals.

3. Which of these three events—(a) Little Ann's near drowning, (b) Little Ann's winning of the silver cup, or (c) the episode with the ghost coon—was the most exciting to you? List reasons why for a class discussion.

4. Rubin's mother's action with the flowers was a touching scene. What do you believe she was thinking then? Compare opinions.

5. Grandpa felt at fault for Rubin's death. Share with a partner an incident in which, against your better judgment or because of a strong emotional reaction, you agreed to something you would not have done otherwise.

6. What important lesson could most people learn from the devotion of the two dogs to each other?

Chapters 16 through 20

Literal Thinking:

1. What attacked the dogs?

2. Who was injured during the blizzard?

3. When the weather changed to sleet Billy predicted the coon would take what action?

4. How did they get the warmth to Grandpa's injured foot?

5. How did Billy stop Old Dan from bleeding to death?

6. Why didn't Billy's mother feel they should bring Little Ann back to the house?

Interpretive Thinking:

1. Why did Billy believe that a brewing storm was a good time to hunt?

2. Why does Little Ann give up?

3. Have you ever been in a competition in which you participated for someone else, as Billy did for Grandpa? Discuss with a partner.

4. How would you describe Grandpa's personality?

5. What, if anything, do you think could have influenced the intelligence of Billy's dogs?

6. Why do you think that Grandpa would not leave until Billy received the gold cup?

7. Why did the two oldest girls feel that they each had a right to the silver cup?

8. Why do you think Billy preferred doing the hard things, like burying Little Ann, all by himself? Explain your opinion.

Creative Thinking:

1. Imagine a dialogue between Little Ann and Old Dan about their impressions and feelings concerning all the adventures of the championship hunt.

2. Think of other ways that Billy could have attempted to save his dogs' lives. Discuss.

3. Draw your concept of the golden cup, complete with its new engraving.

4. Write a eulogy for the dogs emphasizing their strongest qualities.

5. Design a joint marker for the dogs.

Critical Thinking:

1. *Where the Red Fern Grows* relates how good can come out of the worst experiences. What parts of the story prove this truth most vividly?

2. What do you think were the most valuable lessons Billy learned from the various experiences with his dogs? Present reasons for your opinion.

3. Do you think Billy will ever want to own dogs again? Why or why not?

4. With all the pain, fear, and constant concern over your animals, would hunting with coon dogs be worth the aggravation? Discuss your opinion with a partner.

5. These dogs hunt and react by instinct. Do you feel that these instincts are positive or negative?

6. There have been many documented instances of animals pining away after losing their masters. Read the classic story of *Greyfriars Bobby* by Eleanor Atkinson and compare his loyalty to Little Ann's. Discuss.

7. Why do you think Billy felt he had buried part of himself with the dogs? Is that reasonable or not? Support your opinion.

Additional Activities

Visual Art:

1. Using burlap as a background, recreate a favorite scene from the book with various colors and sizes of yarn.

2. Create a family picture album of scenes that were turning points in the story. Pen and ink, watercolors, or colored markers may be used.

3. Create a word game based on the ghost coon chase. Make an award for the winner.

4. Draw an illustration that shows why the title of this book is *Where the Red Fern Grows.*

5. Illustrate the old home, barn, and surrounding fences as they would be after years of neglect. Include the various items Billy left behind.

Creative Writing:

1. Billy's entire life centered around his two coon dogs. Write a story about an experience you may have had in which you were very close to an animal or animals.

2. Invite a storyteller of Indian legends to your class. Create your own legends.

3. Create a folktale about these brave and loyal dogs similar to the legend of the ghost coon dog. Share with a partner.

4. Write a newspaper announcement after the loss of these two champion dogs. Interview people who knew them to add interest to your article.

5. Research another legend from the Ozarks. Share with the class.

Drama:

1. Read the story of *The Velveteen Rabbit* by Margie Bianco; create a dialogue between the velveteen rabbit and Old Dan concerning the meaning of love.

2. View the video production of *Where the Red Fern Grows.* Using a magazine or newspaper movie critique as an example, write your opinion of the production.

3. As Billy going to a new school in town, tell your classmates about winning two championship coon hunts.

4. Role-play Billy's sisters as adults recounting the story about their brother and his coon dogs.

Music:

1. Make up lyrics based on an Indian legend. Find recorded music for Indian dances and create a song.

2. "Ghost Coon" could be the title of original poems. Use appropriate mysterious-sounding music to be played in the background as the poems are read.

3. Research the sources of mountain music. The people often told true stories through songs. Listen to the rhythm and style and compare it to music commonly heard today. Discuss the differences.

4. Bluegrass is very popular and has been for nearly 200 years. Some of it extends back to old English folk songs. It mainly uses stringed instruments. Listen to examples of this old music form.

5. Have students look around the room or bring simple noisemakers from home to create a rhythm band to accompany music. Spoons are a very common utensil which can be used as a musical accompaniment.

Social Studies:

1. What types of entertainment did Billy have besides hunting as a child? Compare to entertainment alternatives of today.

2. Research the Trail of Tears march which culminated near Tahlequah, Oklahoma, and tell the story to your class.

3. Invite experts on mountain crafts to visit your class, perhaps a dulcimer designer or a quilt maker. Learn about cross-stitch to create a design about a favorite scene or symbol from the book.

4. Many animals have instinctively helped people and often have saved lives. Possible subjects for research might be the St. Bernards of the Alps, dolphins, and various acts of heroism by family pets.

Science:

1. Investigate animals that are being hunted to extinction. Was this a concern in Billy's time? Should it have been?

2. The red fern had a legend written about it. Research other mysterious plants like the Venus's-flytrap and black lily. Write an original legend about your selection.

3. Have a dog trainer visit the class to explain how to train animals. Concentrate on a certain area, such as hunting dogs.

4. Birds have been used to help human beings, from canaries used by miners to check that mines are free from poisonous gases to homing pigeons used to deliver messages during both peace and wartime. Research and present a report to the class on human-animal working partnerships.

5. Do a botany activity. Create a booklet either of native plants and trees mentioned in this story or of those indigenous to your area.

Bulletin Board

Where the Red Fern Grows

Surrounding a large gold cup, arrange students' writings with a blue ribbon attached. Each student relates the story of a meaningful achievement in his/her life.

The Bears' House

Marilyn Sachs

The Bears' House

by

Marilyn Sachs
Doubleday, 1971

Fran Ellen Smith and her family have been living in dire poverty since her father deserted them. Her mother has regressed to showing interest only in the possibility of receiving a letter from her absent husband.

The oldest son, Fletcher, has assumed the position of head of the household. They all are careful that outsiders should not learn about their true circumstances. Each of the four older children have special responsibilities; Fran Ellen's is to take care of her baby sister, Flora, who just happens to be her favorite person in the world.

At school Fran Ellen is either shunned or teased by the other children. She is a thumb sucker and possesses a rather distinctive odor.

Her teacher is planning to retire at the conclusion of the school year and offers at that time to present the most improved student with her treasured bears' house. This is a playhouse, made by her father, which she uses as a reward when a student completes work. Fran Ellen takes her math assignments home the night before they are assigned to be assured some time with the bear family. She has no need to touch the house; she merely sits down next to it, puts her thumb in her mouth, and fantasizes about living with the bear family and their love for her.

Through a set of trials and adjustments Fran Ellen is awarded the bears' house as the most improved student. The family finally must reveal its living situation when her teacher helps her bring home the prize.

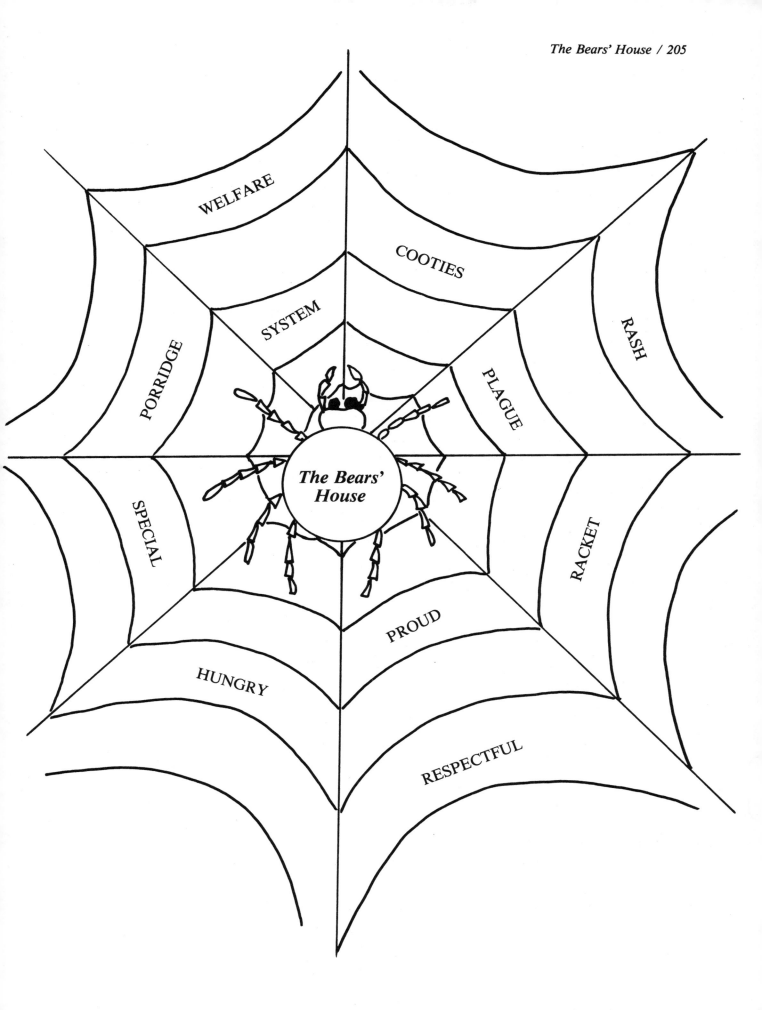

WELFARE

COOTIES

SYSTEM

RASH

PORRIDGE

PLAGUE

The Bears' House

SPECIAL

RACKET

PROUD

HUNGRY

RESPECTFUL

Chapters 1 and 2

Literal Thinking:

1. Describe the bears' house.

2. What is the official name of the bears' house?

3. How do students get to play with the bears' house?

4. How many are in Fran's family?

5. Where did they feel Fran's daddy might have gone?

6. Who built the bears' house for Miss Thompson?

7. What habit does Fran Ellen have that annoys her teacher and classmates?

8. Which of Fran Ellen's brothers and sisters is her favorite?

Interpretive Thinking:

1. Have you ever had a teacher or adult who was very special to you? Write a short speech about your favorite person and deliver it to your class. Remember posture and eye contact.

2. Fran Ellen longed for beauty and order, good manners and shared responsibilities. What in her background had probably influenced her thinking?

3. How will the bears' house go on being Fran's even though the teacher may give it to someone else?

4. Why does Fran never hit back?

5. Why did Fran feel she did not need to earn the right to touch the house anymore?

6. When did the general decline in the family begin?

7. What do you think may have happened to Fran's mother to make her behave in the way she does?

8. Which one of the children contributed the most help to the family; the least?

Creative Thinking:

1. Draw your concept of the bears' house.

2. As any one or all of the children, write a letter to the father which might be held by the uncle until he hears from him.

3. Create a drawing with a saying you would like to have as an embroidered picture in the bears' house.

4. Role-play a scene between Miss Thompson and the principal. What would Miss Thompson say about her puzzling student whose behavior she would like to see changed?

5. Invite a builder of miniature houses to your classroom. Prepare interviews to ask how the houses are constructed, where to buy furniture, and so on.

Critical Thinking:

1. Did the children choose correctly from the three alternatives to surviving as a family?

2. Which of the children is showing the most strength and leadership? Do you think this is natural or out of necessity? Compare opinions.

3. The act of sucking her thumb was comforting to Fran. As a young child, did you have a habit that was difficult to break?

4. Evaluate why Fran feels so close to Flora in comparison to the others.

Chapters 3 and 4

Literal Thinking:

1. What time of the school day did Fran dislike the very most?

2. Explain how the children goaded Fran to have an excuse to hit her.

3. In the bears' house, who does Fran target for her aggression?

4. When does Fran not suck her thumb?

5. What reason did Fran give her teacher that her mother could not visit?

6. What question does the mother always ask?

7. Why did Miss Thompson want Fran Ellen's mother to come for a conference?

Interpretive Thinking:

1. Fran Ellen could have become a famous writer. What does Fran Ellen do that is very important to writing?

2. Why was Fran Ellen becoming more frightened about her home situation as time went on?

3. Why doesn't Fran tell Fletcher about the note from Miss Thompson?

4. Why did the imaginary birthday party make Fran feel happy that she had gone to school that day?

5. What does it say about Fran that she keeps falling for the same ploy used by the two girls?

6. How has Mama Bear replaced Fran's own mother?

Creative Thinking:

1. Using scraps and whatever you can find, create a toy for Flora.

2. Create a monologue for Fran. Have her explain her life thus far.

3. Make a before-and-after picture. The first part shows how Fran Ellen's classmates viewed her. The second shows how Fran Ellen wished her classmates to view her.

4. How could a fairy godmother have helped Fran Ellen? Use the same characters and turn Fran Ellen's story into a fairy tale.

5. Create a dialogue between Fran and her brother telling him about the situation with the girls at school.

Critical Thinking:

1. Why do you think Miss Thompson is not more helpful to Fran?

2. What do you think Fran thinks of herself?

3. What is bravery? Was Fran Ellen brave in some situations, but not in others? Why? Analyze the reasons and discuss.

4. What would have been the most caring thing Fran Ellen's mother could have done for her family? Brainstorm.

5. What are the most important reasons Fran Ellen sucks her thumb? Make a list of reasons in order of importance.

6. The children are mean to Fran. Have a class discussion about reasons children can be so mean to others. How much is real dislike or peer cooperation? Judge the fairness of the behavior.

7. Why do you think Fran didn't just go to Miss Thompson and tell her what was going on with the girls?

Chapters 5 and 6

Literal Thinking:

1. If the class was in session when Fran got back from home, what excuse was Fran going to use about where she had been?

2. Why didn't Fran tell Miss Thompson right away where she lived?

3. How did the children solve the problem of having someone with Flora in the afternoon?

4. How did the teacher finally discover Fran had been leaving the school?

5. Which child is becoming ill because of neglect?

6. Which student received the bears' house?

7. Who discovered Flora's worsening condition?

8. Why is Fletcher so worried?

Interpretive Thinking:

1. What does Miss Thompson say that tells you that she understands the family situation?

2. What was probably Miss Thompson's most definite clue that something was very wrong in Fran Ellen's family?

3. How aware do you think Miss Thompson is of the family situation? Give reasons for your choices.

4. Why did taking Miss Thompson up to her apartment alter Fran's opinion of her teacher?

5. Why do you think Fran still did not tell Miss Thompson the truth about why she was leaving school? Why do you think she reverted to acting like Florence?

6. One positive result of the family's problems is that Fran stops sucking her thumb. Why do you believe she did that?

Creative Thinking:

1. Role-play the continuing confrontations between Susan, Jennifer, and Fran. Create a new solution for Fran.

2. Role-play Miss Thompson talking to the principal or a social worker about the Smith children.

3. Predict what will happen to the family.

4. Have you ever been unkind to someone like Fran? Do you now have a better understanding? Explain.

5. Create similes and metaphors for the main characters in the story. Example: Fran Ellen was as fanciful as a....

Critical Thinking:

1. Was Fletcher fair to accuse Fran Ellen of causing the crisis with Miss Thompson? Why or why not?

2. What part of Fran Ellen's fantasy best describes the depth of her love for Flora?

3. Do you think Fletcher and Fran were relieved after Miss Thompson took charge?

4. Fran just "felt scared" when she walked into school. Have you ever had a funny feeling about something without knowing why? Share with a partner.

5. Judge why their teachers underestimated the abilities of both Fletcher and Fran.

6. Evaluate why, after everyone made fun and urged Fran to stop sucking her thumb, they didn't notice when she finally did stop. Describe a time when you waited for someone to notice a change and the person did not. Share with a partner.

7. Fletcher was the one who made the big decisions, yet it was Fran who created the excuses for Miss Thompson. Evaluate why.

Additional Activities

Visual Art:

1. Draw a fine drawing of the outside of the bears' house, but make it large enough to use as a home for the Smiths.

2. Create a mosaic of words and pictures that relate to the bears' house.

3. Fran Ellen had many embarrassing times in the story. Each student shares with a partner an illustration of one of life's most embarrassing moments.

4. How did Flora view Fran Ellen? How did her classmates view Fran Ellen? Illustrate with cartoons. See if other classmates have the same opinion as you.

5. Design a congratulations card for Fran Ellen for the progress she has made despite great obstacles. Design a congratulations card for a classmate.

Creative Writing:

1. Have students bring baby pictures or family snapshots. Write humorous captions for each.

2. Brainstorm what might happen in the future after the family's problems are disclosed. Draw pictures for a family album that shows what happens to each child, and write captions for the pictures.

3. Create an imaginary place you would like to go to when you are troubled. Write a description of your place.

4. Write a summary of the story from Florence's viewpoint.

Drama:

1. Create a readers' theatre script, with each of the children exploring their feelings about the happenings in their lives. Keep in mind their given personalities.

2. Pretend that the bears' house is Fran Ellen's house. The bears and Goldilocks observe the problems of the family. Write a dialogue of their opinions and observations with problem-solving ideas.

3. Make a verbal chain story of what happened to Fran Ellen's family after the last chapter. Each student adds one or two sentences to create a chain of action describing the family's future.

4. Is guilt or innocence affected by point of view? Was Fran Ellen a runaway student or a responsible sister? Was Goldilocks trespassing? Were the bears irresponsible in not locking their doors? Role-play as an investigative reporter to explore the truth.

Music:

1. Listen to folk songs and notice how the lyrics tell a story. In small groups, create lyrics for a song that tells the story of Fran Ellen and *The Bears' House*. Adapt the lyrics to a well-known melody.

2. Listen to a recording of "My Favorite Things." What would be Fran Ellen's favorite things if the lyrics were changed? What are your favorite things?

3. Locate a piece of music that best illustrates each personality (e.g., something very excitable for Florence). Create movement to coordinate with each.

4. Create a rap song expressing Fran's feelings.

Social Studies:

1. Investigate the welfare services. Discover whom they help and how.

2. Collect news articles on poverty and the homeless problem. Share as a class your findings.

3. Ask someone who runs a shelter for homeless people to come and discuss the plight of the homeless in your area. Compose questions for the speaker.

4. Research famous archeological digs. Archeological digs tell the story of a culture. Fran Ellen's family was not unusual, living in a crowded, ill-equipped dwelling as is found in many metropolitan areas today. What might future archeologists find that would tell the story of such conditions in our culture?

Science:

1. There is said to be a pecking order among chickens. Find out more about this behavior. How does it relate to Fran Ellen and the way her classmates treated her?

2. Scientific studies tell us that touching is very important to human development. What was Fran Ellen doing that was extremely important to Flora's development?

3. Scientific studies show that behavior that is reinforced with positive results will be repeated. How did Miss Thompson use this method to help Fran Ellen?

4. Have a discussion on proper nutrition and what you need for a balanced diet. Take into consideration the ones who receive a free lunch. Discuss the limits and possible long-range side effects of such diets.

5. Investigate how stress affects relationships and health.

Bulletin Board

The Bears' House

Flora was closest to her sister Fran. Each student writes a story about a favorite person and the reasons for the choice. The title may be "My Favorite Person" or "The Person I Most Respect." Arrange them around a large paper Teddy Bear. Fold the paper in half and cut the shape, accenting the facial features with black marker. A paper vest and tie can also be cut.

Crossword

The Bears' House

Across

1. Fran Ellen's teacher.
5. Red eruption on body.
6. She lived in The Bears' House with the bears.
11. Name of only boy in family.
12. Agency that checks on the needy.
13. The house where Fran Ellen felt happy and secure.
14. Baby sister's name.
16. Where their mother had worked before she became ill.
17. This person deserted the family.

Down

2. To go forward in spite of hardships.
3. To be absent from school without permission.
4. Where the Smiths were from.
7. Miss Thompson was going to give The Bears' House to the student who was the most _____.
8. Thumb sucking was Fran Ellen's _____.
9. Mother looked for this daily.
10. Flora's favorite drink.
11. The type of special lunches the oldest children received at school.
15. Time when Fran Ellen snuck home.

Words: The Bears' House

ALABAMA	FREE	PERSEVERE
BAKERY	GOLDILOCKS	RASH
BEARS	HOOKY	RECESS
FATHER	IMPROVED	SECURITY
FLETCHER	KOOL-AID	THOMPSON
FLORA	LETTER	WELFARE

Puzzle Answers: The Bears' House

ADDITIONAL BOOKS
ON RELATIONSHIPS

1. *Aaron's Door.* Miska Miles. Little, Brown, 1977.

   After his parents' divorce, Aaron distrusts even the couple who adopts him. Not until he feels secure with a place at the table does the boy begin to trust again.

2. *A Gift for Mama.* Esther Hautzig. Viking Press, 1981.

   Sara's family always treasured homemade gifts. Sara saves money for slippers. Her mother is disappointed with the gift until learning of the diligence that went into the effort.

3. *Carnival and Kopeck and More about Hannah.* Mindy Skolsky. Harper & Row, 1979.

   Hannah and her grandmother go to the carnival. After Hannah misbehaves and has her first argument with her grandmother, Hannah internalizes her anger until the grandmother teaches her that even people who love each other become angry.

4. *Grandmother Didn't Wave Back.* Rose Blue. Watts, 1972.

   Grandma frequently forgets and has little interest in life. This is about the experiences and loving care a family gives to an Alzheimer's patient.

5. *Like Jake and Me.* Mavis Jukes. Knopf, 1984.

   This is the story of a blended family, their individual differences, and compromises.

6. *Living in Two Worlds.* Maxine B. Rosenberg. Lothrop, 1986.

   This nonfiction focuses on bi-racial families, their relationships, and how cultural differences affect family units.

7. *Seven Kisses in a Row.* Patricia MacLachlan. Harper & Row, 1983.

   Emma and Zachary have always had seven kisses in a row from their parents. Staying with their uncle and aunt is the opposite of their more flexible household. The children teach valuable lessons in parenting.

8. *Somebody Else's Child.* Roberta Silman. Warne, 1976.

   Peter is a friend of the bus driver who is teased about being adopted. Consequently, Peter questions his own adoption. Through their combined efforts in finding a lost pet, the two become even closer. They realize that the essence of family is loving and nurturing relationships.

9. *We Don't Look like Our Mom and Dad.* Harriett Sobol. Coward, 1984.

   Two Korean children are active in their school and home. Although adopted, their parents remind them and reinforce the pride of their Korean heritage.

10. *What's Drunk Mama?* Al-Anon Family Headquarters, Inc., 1977.

    Christy's home is in constant turmoil due to her father's constant drinking problem. Through Al-Anon, the family begins a gradual recovery program.

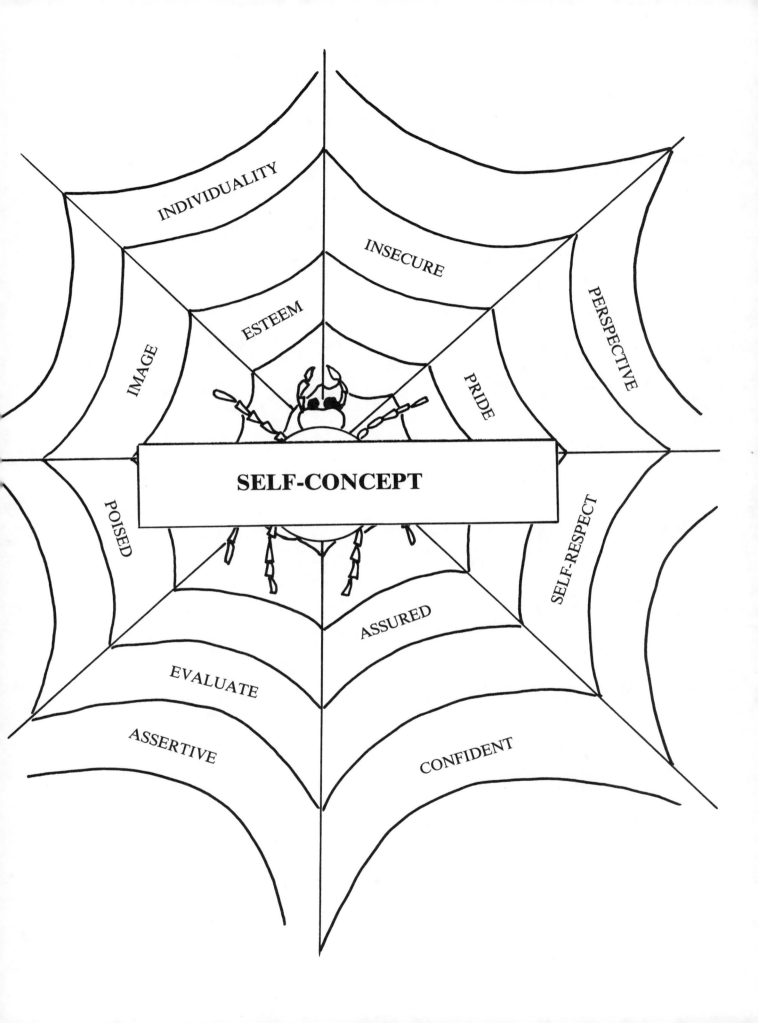

Edith Herself

Ellen Howard

Edith Herself

by

Ellen Howard
Atheneum Macmillan, 1987

Edith is a small child whose mother and father are dead. It is necessary for her to live with her older sister Alena's family since she is the youngest child.

The new home is different and Edith misses her parents and things at home. Alena is loving, but her husband John and his mother are very cold toward Edith. John's father is kind and makes Edith feel more at home. Alena's and John's son Vernon teases her and will not share the friendship of his dog.

During all of these adjustments, Edith receives some more bad news when she begins to have seizures. John's mother adds to her misery by insinuating that it is Edith's fault. When Edith suffers a second seizure she makes a bargain that she will put up her treasures to please God and then be well.

More than anything, Edith wants to attend school and learn to read stories. After having a seizure at school Edith is devastated and tempted to stay under Alena's protection. However, statements from John, her best friend, and, of all people, Vernon, give her the support she needs to pursue her life.

This story, set in a time before people and science understood epilepsy, concerns the great courage of a little girl.

BULLIES

COWARDS

TEARS

INDIGNATION

WHISPER

WHISPERS

FRIEND

SKEPTICAL

PAIN

TAUNT

Edith Herself

EXPULSION

DESECRATE

CONSCIOUSNESS

VEXED

FIT

VERMIN

BENEVOLENT

SHIRK

SYMPATHY

IDIOT

TENTATIVE

Chapters 1 through 5

Literal Thinking:

1. Why was Edith under the back steps?

2. What happened to the mice Edith found in the barn?

3. Where did Edith, at first, think her mother might have gone?

4. Explain the relationship of John and Alena to Edith.

5. What did Edith miss the very most from her old home?

6. Why was the gift from the ladies of the Missionary Society so special to Edith?

Interpretive Thinking:

1. Have you ever felt left out of a group as Edith did? What did you do about the situation? Explore your feelings in a journal entry.

2. Tell about Edith's arrival from Vernon's point of view.

3. What was worrying Edith about going to live with Alena and John?

4. By observing the illustrations and story, guess what the time setting for the story is.

5. Do you feel Alena and John have a marriage in which the partners are equal? Why or why not?

6. Why didn't anything belong to Edith in her new house?

7. Why do you think Edith needed to find a place of her own?

Creative Thinking:

1. Edith thought of the asters as part of the sky and moon. How else could she have described the flowers? Think of other metaphors and similes.

2. List what people say to you similar to "Go play," "Can't you see I'm busy," or "Not now, later."

3. What are "some things" that belong to you and no one else?

4. Write a short conversation between Helen Keller and Edith, both as adults. They can compare their feelings of rejection, attempts at communication, and ultimate triumph.

5. Edith missed her "treasures." Draw an example of one of your special treasures and share it with the class.

6. Draw a picture of Pansy Violet Rosebud.

7. Predict what will happen in the relationship between Vernon and Edith.

Critical Thinking:

1. Why is Edith so worried that she might be sick?

2. What do you think Edith learned from the experience with John?

3. Were John and Vernon unfeeling toward Edith? Examine their point of view versus Edith's observation.

4. Edith missed having her own things and feeling a part of her surroundings. Think of a time when you were new to a situation, perhaps a new school or neighborhood. Explain your feelings and share with a partner.

5. Brother John was certainly wrong in his method of eliminating the nest of mice. Discuss whether they should have been allowed to live.

Chapters 6 through 10

Literal Thinking:

1. Why was the Chinese basket so important to Edith?

2. What part of the story of Cinderella upset Edith?

3. Why was Alena so angry with John?

4. Why couldn't Edith manage to eat dinner?

5. What was the one thing that gave Edith comfort?

Interpretive Thinking:

1. Why did John's statment about "a child of my family" have meaning for Edith?

2. Why would John, a teacher, not want stories told in his house?

3. Why does Grandma Malcolm seem to thrive on conflict?

4. What leads you to think Vernon's attitude toward Edith is changing?

5. What was Edith's attitude about going to school?

6. Explain why Edith felt that she spoiled her sister's visit.

Creative Thinking:

1. Role-play a lesson of a classroom at the time of the story.

2. Tell a new version of the story of Cinderella. The stepsisters have the personalities of John and Grandma Malcolm. Edith is to be Cinderella.

3. Look at Grant Wood's painting *American Gothic*. Draw an illustration of Grandma and Grandpa Malcolm accentuating their personalities through their facial expressions.

4. Write a short script for a morning in John's classroom. How would he respond to various students: shy students, noisy students, creative students? How would he respond to change in the classroom?

5. Create a doll, possibly out of old pieces of material or a paper bag.

6. Cat's Cradle was a game played by children of the early settlers; Vernon plays it in this story. Bring in some string and have one of the students teach their variations to the rest of the class.

Critical Thinking:

1. Explain the difference between a lie and a story.

2. Does there seem to be a pattern to Edith's seizures? Discuss.

3. Do you think Edith's decision to put away the Chinese basket and her doll was wise? Why or why not?

4. Evaluate how John's attitude and feelings about things would affect him as a teacher.

Chapters 11 through 15

Literal Thinking:

1. What happened that embarrassed Vernon?

2. Why did Edith lie to Rosa about owning a doll?

3. Who helped Edith get rid of the jeering boys?

4. What secret did Vernon and Edith share?

5. What embarrassing experience did Edith have at school?

6. What did John think was the most important reason Edith should return to school?

7. Explain how Edith showed her worth as a friend and a person when Vernon needed it.

Interpretive Thinking:

1. Why would Vernon loudly announce to Edith's classmates that she had fits?

2. Why is something that is forbidden, such as Edith's doll, often more desirable?

3. How did Edith prove that when a person overcomes a difficulty he/she is often stronger?

4. Why does Edith want to go to school?

5. The idea of being a good Samaritan can sometimes backfire. Explain how this is true in the current situation.

Creative Thinking:

1. Give an example of having a grin "feel like a hug."

2. Create a paper stitchery of a saying Edith might want in the house.

3. Draw a family portrait gallery with the object that best exemplifies each member's personality. For example, John might be shown with a ruler.

4. Create a recipe with the illustrations for a magic day for Edith. The ingredients will be the things she loves the most.

5. Using black construction paper or poster board and chalk, make your own slate.

6. Make a flip book of approximately fifteen to thirty pages. On each succeeding page you alter the position of your subjects just a small amount. Once that is complete, staple the pages in order and flip them from front to back. It will give you the illusion of movement. Use an action filled scene such as the one where the cow chases Edith.

Critical Thinking:

1. Why did John not interfere with the students who were taunting Edith?

2. Is it true that the older person is always wiser? Analyze the characters and write about the wisest one.

3. John displayed both negative and positive actions. Make a list of his positive actions for chapters 11 through 15. How were these actions of the greatest benefit to Edith?

4. Why is *Edith Herself* a fitting title for this book? Brainstorm other possible titles.

5. Of John or Alena, which one was really anxious for Edith to mature and learn to handle herself? Debate.

6. How does Edith's handling of the children outside the school reveal her increasing maturity?

Additional Activities

Visual Art:

1. Invite a folk artist to teach your class how to make apple dolls. Display your doll around a copy of *Edith Herself* in your media center.

2. Early settlers used what was nearby to beautify their lives. They even created pictures using hair trimmings. Find a common object and create a picture with it or around it.

3. Create a visual box with your most treasured things in it. Think of unique ways to decorate and display your box.

4. Children often created their own entertainment. Make up an outside or inside children's game they might have been able to play.

Creative Writing:

1. Write a story for Edith to read to the baby. Put it in a booklet with illustrations.

2. Write a paragraph on how your feelings for the handicapped have changed since reading this book.

3. As Edith, write a letter to Grandma, John, and the jeering children. Tell each how you felt about their behavior.

4. As Edith, write a letter to Rosa about their friendship. Have a partner write Rosa's reply.

Drama:

1. Videotape (a) the most exciting, (b) the saddest, and (c) funniest scenes from *Edith Herself*.

2. Role-play a family conference among the older members deciding, after the mother's death, the placement of the children. Give reasons for their opinions.

3. Role-play Edith and Vernon at the end of the book having a discussion about their first feelings toward each other and sharing the reasons behind those feelings.

4. As a grown-up Edith, pretend to speak to a group of epileptic children concerning her experiences and problems with her condition. Have a roundtable discussion.

Music:

1. Invite an expert on the playing and building of dulcimers to your class.

2. Listen to a country song. The lyrics tell the story. Tell about Edith's stay with similar lyrics or a rap.

3. Create a game Edith and her classmates would have played. Incorporate music into it in a manner similar to Musical Chairs.

4. Tchaikovsky was an epileptic. Listen to some examples of his music such as *Swan Lake* or the *Nutcracker Suite* and discuss.

5. Square dancing was very popular in rural areas. Learn how to perform one, as well as the two-step, and try each as a class.

Social Studies:

1. Survey classmates on their knowledge of epilepsy. Design a survey with at least four questions.

2. Investigate famous persons who have been successful in spite of having epilepsy. Some examples are Julius Caesar and Vincent Van Gogh.

3. Do handicapped people have more rights now than in the past? Cite examples to support your opinion.

4. Do most modern senior citizens reside with their children as Grandma and Grandpa Malcolm did? Research to find reasons for changes in the care of senior citizens.

5. Research the one-room schoolhouse and, if possible, interview someone who attended one. Look to your relatives, people from church, or people in nursing homes. Report to the class.

6. Research social activities common to this era and location, such as hoedowns, church socials, and barn raisings. Compare to the social activities we have today and discuss as a class.

Science:

1. Who was Hippocrates? Find out why he is still important in medicine today.

2. What is the scientific method? Why is it necessary to follow it in finding cures for diseases such as epilepsy? Research and share the information with your class.

3. Contact your local Epilepsy Foundation for information regarding the disease. Invite a speaker to come to the class.

4. Interview a neurologist about the physical implications of epilepsy and the latest scientific advancement regarding its causes, control, and possible cures.

Search-a-Word

Edith Herself

```
N U D H C L O A K R O O M O S G Y L A R E N U F D L A U R M
T D A G J M Z Q Z I N T G V B E X E D B J K Y O C J T J S N
O Y X B U H F M M I H R N G O S I S P C D X T M X X X F Q J
R S F Z X G L M Y R J E H R X J M Z U K Y P K Z G T P B J J
I T Q S M F G I F A U A F U U W T F U O A B I N T F S K U C
G U P V O S M A O G J S Q E L O S N Q R A C S O R Y O C H U
F A M I L Y T R B M N U V C I X M H T W E R U N O T T J K T
J V C T E N T L D V L R H I W I D N K W T S J R S K X S W X
C J Z Z G A I Q S N R E Z M A N U B Y Q F V M E A Q R Z H Z
X P D O A X U C J V S S P H J E Q A Q V R I D V X E H C A N
E V S C Y L Y R T B M O O Q L J X C G I Z K Z E K T W F L J
B U R F R W Q O M O O T Q V R S X L S S O F O C C X F I Z H
U I E B S Z Y O J C Q C N A H M W T A R B I I D D X R S S L
H O T I L P T K Z N H Q Y E D I T H D E S N I L S G B R I I
C I S I S T I E W R W D T S M R X S I A S G L A N T O P J E
O I I H E Y U D X O E S C O C U F K B P I R A I Q D Q C W Z
O I S K E W E   P C M U F J K R G B Z W W I C O Y M T T A H
R H S O S F I H A W X I D S C L A R C E Y E L T Z K D T A A
B A C G G R K O K I G A X X H T A G A I O F N F U U W H K J
B R I Z D S K R P Y M M D P H J T D E A T H M F O G S R L U
C X T N L G U N W V S U S C H O O L M A S T E R Y G J T P Q
E K Y B K X U H E P P D O L L A H X I R G P G K B O S I L G
O A F Y O L Y E A I R U E X L M E B W U L I N Z O Y J E W U
Q R F F R I R Y H C D A D G V X S H G N Q I O R C H A R D D
K R P R L O C S Q M I P T W D L G C W Z V O Y S P E L I P E
P O T H F I D O S Z F N T E A F P W K C B Z W V Z K O Y S O
D Z L A A N U F U D L L D T E C J S J T P A I P S I V S U Z
A D N S E N J O I V K Q E E Y A V V U D P I N E I S H I J C
H I N I J H Y L N I Q B E W R H Q I T L X F P A G Y C Y R R
P U R R P A H Q Y J X C R Q E E D B W C E V B Y L E H W O P
F F R I Y R W F P H D M F V T Y L X N H S X X E C R I R R F
A L K O P L U H S L H W D E Z K U L O Q L T Y F F R N A H P
B F A Q Y F R X N B E D T P R O Z X A W L F I I O U A P V T
K T B E Z R W F L Z O H M Y Y Q O O L Q O S D D W S I F V J
W N A R J T H U Y F C H P U X M X Y T K U S K K F L S J N Z
```

Words

EDITH	EPILEPSY	DOLL
MOURN	TREASURES	ORPHAN
VERNON	SEIZURES	PINAFOREE
BASKET	SISTERS	ROSA
FRIENDSHIP	MICE	CLOAKROOM
ORCHARD	SNICKER	DEATH
FAMILY	SCHOOLMASTER	QUILT
CINDERELLA	CORNCOB	BROOCH
GRIEF	FUNERAL	ARGUMENT
SLATE	CROOKED HORN	SURREY
SABBATH	CHINA	

Edith Herself—Puzzle Answers

```
. . . . C L O A K R O O M . S . . L A R E N U F . . . . . .
. . . . . . . . . T . . . E . . . . . . . . . . . . . .
. . . . . . . . . R N . . . I . . . . . . . . . . . . .
. . . . . . . . . E . R . . . Z . . . . . . . . . . . .
. . . . . . . . . A . . U . . . U . . . . N . . . . . .
. . . . . . . . . . S . E . O . . . R . . . O R . . . .
F A M I L Y . . . . . U . C . . M . . . E . . N O . . .
. . . . . . . . . . R . I . . . . . . . . S . R S . . .
. . . . . . . . . . E . M . . . . . . . . . E A . R . .
. . . . . . C . . . S . . . . . . . . . . . V . E . .
. . S . . . R . B . . . . . . . . . . . . K . . .
. . R . . . O . O . T . . . . . . . . . C . . .
. . E . . . O . C . . N . . . . . . . I . . .
H . T . . . K . N . . . E D I T H . . S N . . .
C . S . . T . E . R . . . M . . . . A S G . . .
O . I . E . . D . O . . . . U . . B . . R . . .
O . S K . . . . C . . . . . G B . . . I . . .
R . S . . . H . . . . . . A R . . . E . . .
B A . . . . O . . . . . T . . A . F . . .
B . . . . . R . . . . . H . T D E A T H . . . .
. . . . . . N . . . S C H O O L M A S T E R . . . .
. . . . . . E . P D O L L . . . I . . . .
O . . . . . E . I . . . . . . U . . .
. R . . . R . H C . . . . . S . . Q . O R C H A R D .
. . P . . O . S . . I . . . L . . . . Y S P E L I P E
. . . H F . D . . . . N . . A . . . . . . .
. . . A A N . . . . . . D T . . . . .
. . N . E N . . . . . E E . . . . .
. . I . I . . . . . . R . . . Y C . . .
P . R . . . . . . . . E . . . . E H . . .
. F . . . . . . . L . . . R I . . .
. . . . . . . . L . . . R N . . .
. . . . . . . . . A . . . U A . . .
. . . . . . . . . . . . S . . .
```

Bulletin Board

Edith Herself

Cover the background of the bulletin board in checked or calico fabric. Make a banner with *Edith Herself* accentuated. Around the banner, each child writes a story with his/her name and herself or himself in the title. The stories tell why the student is unique, special, and worthy of praise. Small triangles of black paper may be attached to corners for an antique look.

From the Mixed-up Files of Mrs. Basil E. Frankweiler

E. L. Konigsburg

From the Mixed-up Files of Mrs. Basil E. Frankweiler

by

E. L. Konigsburg
Atheneum Macmillan, 1967

This is the story of Claudia, who decides she is going to run away from home. Claudia is not your usual child.

Her leaving home is carefully planned, since she decided she needed to run to a wonderfully interesting and beautiful place—the Metropolitan Museum of Art in New York City. She includes one of her younger brothers, Jamie, who could be counted on to keep both a secret and his money. They come to the museum and, through ingenuity and more than a little luck, manage to hide among the exhibits. During the day they blend with the visitors to the museum; at night they manage to find wonderful places to sleep, such as a wonderfully ornate sixteenth-century bed.

They become involved in proving that one of Claudia's favorite statues was sculpted by Michelangelo. Thus they get involved with Mrs. Basil E. Frankweiler, an eccentric and reclusive contributor to the museum. The three of them work together to validate the statue. Claudia's life is changed forever by her association with Mrs. Basil E. Frankweiler.

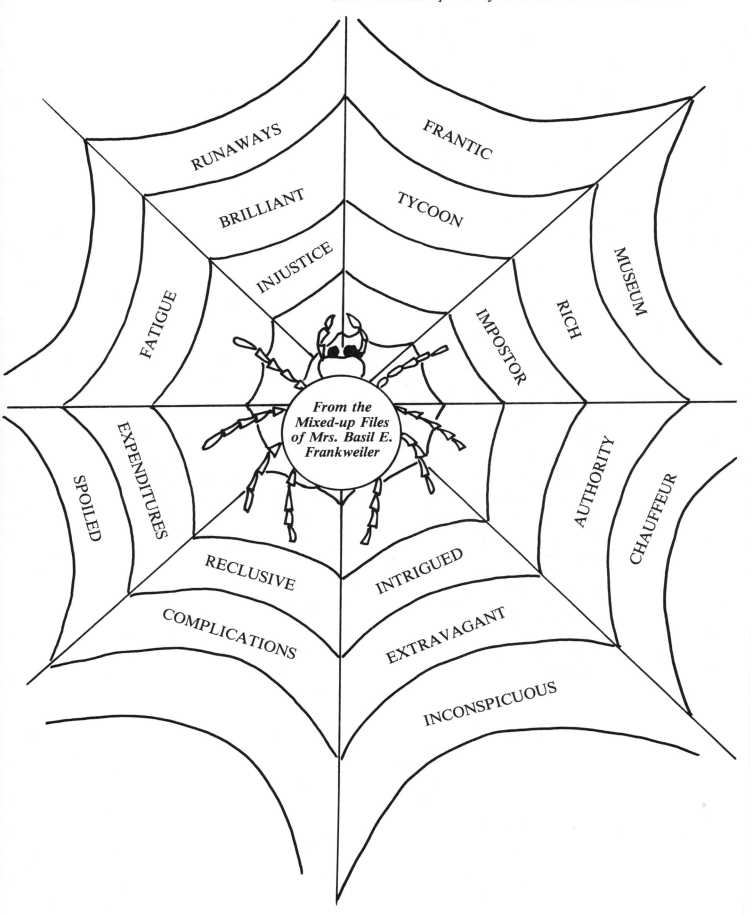

Chapters 1 and 2

Literal Thinking:

1. How did Claudia and Jamie hide from the guards after closing?

2. What was the unusual object that Jamie took on their adventure?

3. Why did Jamie feel chosen instead of picked on by Claudia?

4. List all of Claudia's reasons for running away.

5. What did Claudia consider an invitation to leave on her adventure?

6. Why did Jamie wish he had taken up the bass fiddle instead of the trombone?

Interpretive Thinking:

1. Discuss some of Claudia's plans that show her to be an organized individual who thinks things through.

2. Evaluate the wisdom of Mrs. Richter's statement that her son would "come home lost." Think of other commonly used phrases that make an equal amount of sense.

3. What makes you feel that Claudia is very dramatic and has some acting talent?

4. Was the Metropolitan Museum of Art an unusual place to run to?

5. What would be your destination, mode of transportation, and plan for finances if you had planned the trip instead of Claudia?

6. What kind of books do you think Claudia has read? What are some of the titles?

7. Why did Claudia choose the museum for their adventure?

8. Does Jamie have faith in Claudia's ability to take care and provide for them?

Creative Thinking:

1. Design a travel ticket for your special adventure. Include a place of origin, destination, mode of transportation, and cost.

2. Role-play the way Jamie and his friend Bruce entertained themselves on the bus. Keep in mind their ages and the seriousness of their commitment. Continue through Claudia pulling him away to inform him of their upcoming adventure. Include her enthusiasm for the escapade and his anger an annoyance with her.

3. Draw a caricature of Jamie as a business tycoon.

4. Claudia considers herself to be a group leader. Draw a caricature of her as a group leader.

5. Write a letter to the director of the Metropolitan Museum of Art. Ask for information about class tours.

6. What if a *lost children* bulletin had come over the loudspeaker of the train? Write an additional chapter describing the children's reaction.

7. Draw an illustration of Jamie and his teeth after disposing of the secret instruction sheet.

Critical Thinking:

1. Do you think children should have experience in assuming more responsibility for themselves as Claudia and Jamie did? Why or why not?

2. In what careers would Claudia be very successful?

3. Decide what would have happened if Jamie had forgotten his money, or Jamie had told his parents about the plan, or Claudia had decided upon another city. Brainstorm solutions.

4. Evaluate why Claudia is very mothering to Jamie. Have you ever encountered a peer who had a tendency to mother you? Tell about it and how you felt about that person at the beginning of the relationship as well as after a period of time.

5. Most children consider running away from home at least once. Share your feelings about this with a friend.

Chapters 3 and 4

Literal Thinking:

1. Where did Jamie and Claudia sleep the first night? How did it help conceal them?

2. Who owned the statue before the museum purchased it?

3. Who might have sculpted the statue of the angel?

4. What was Jamie's first decision as treasurer?

5. Why did Jamie always win when he played cards with Bruce? What was his reason for doing it?

6. What was the most dangerous time for them?

7. What is an approximate number of artworks housed at the Metropolitan?

Interpretive Thinking:

1. Why do Jamie and Claudia feel that New York is a good place to hide?

2. At what point did Claudia and Jamie become investigators?

3. What did Claudia do that showed concern for her parents' feelings?

4. List all the things that were becoming big problems for the children.

5. Have you ever felt unimportant until you discovered what you considered your treasure? Write a poem about your treasure—a friend, a thought, an object, or a feeling.

Creative Thinking:

1. Draw a picture of the statue, your interpretation of how it would look.

2. Design a picture postcard depicting a famous New York landmark.

3. Write the New York City Tourist Bureau and request information regarding tourist sights.

4. Role-play a scene between the janitor and Jamie after he found Jamie that first morning. Make the janitor not so accepting of Jamie's answer.

Critical Thinking:

1. The children felt that they had become a team. Read the author's description on page 39. When have you felt such a oneness with someone else? Share with a partner and include the inward feelings it produced.

2. Compare the personalities of Claudia and Jamie. How did their different natures balance each other? Support your point of view.

3. Evaluate why Claudia was upset with her parents and others because they didn't make her running away easier for her. Do you agree or disagree with her reasoning?

4. What do you think Claudia and Jamie would have done if they had read the article about their disappearance?

5. Should the children think about how worried their family might be?

6. The author states that the elusive search can often be more exciting than reaching the goal. How does this apply to you? Discuss.

7. What are the most important reasons people are continually interested in the lives of kings and queens?

8. Which reaction in the story resembles how you would have reacted in the same situation?

Chapters 5 and 6

Literal Thinking:

1. Why did the children write to the head of the museum?

2. What important discovery did Claudia and Jamie make in the velvet drape?

3. Where did Jamie and Claudia go to do research on Michelangelo?

4. What is the clue to the artist that Jamie and Claudia discovered?

5. What was the mark the children discovered?

6. What part of their daily routine still wasn't comfortable for Jamie?

7. Why did they decide homesickness really wasn't an issue for them?

Interpretive Thinking:

1. Given Claudia's personality, why would the idea of a mystery be so attractive to her? Share your ideas with a friend.

2. The painting *Mona Lisa* by Leonardo da Vinci has always created a controversy. Look at a print of it and discuss what the circumstances might have been.

3. What happened when they were almost caught that illustrated they felt like a team and were intuitive of each other?

4. What motivated Jamie to go along with Claudia's plan to investigate the statue?

5. Why do you think Jamie and Claudia use the names Sir James and Lady Claude?

6. Have you ever felt you wanted to make a difference in the world, like Claudia? Share your view.

7. From whose point of view are chapters 5 and 6 written?

Creative Thinking:

1. What might have happened to the way Claudia thought of herself had she not discovered the angel and made it her special mystery?

2. Suppose Claudia had told her family she didn't feel special. Write a new ending for the story based upon this change.

3. Imagine you are the night watchman in the museum and you find Claudia and James in the fountain. What would you do?

4. If you were living in the museum, which section would interest you most?

5. Create a limited invitation to a private viewing of the angel statue.

6. Make a drawing of the fountain and Jamie's great discovery.

Critical Thinking:

1. The description of Michelangelo on page 72 was rather unusual. Debate whether Claudia's evaluation would have been the same were he not considered a "master." Relate your feeling to children you know. Share your opinions.

2. Debate the statement "A nation's history is reflected in its art." Using the principles of debate, pick two or three points to validate your position.

3. Do you think Jamie has a good sense of humor?

4. Why is it important to study the past through history? Think of a specific action in history that, if pondered, would change current world attitudes.

5. Determine why research to solve something that you personally think is mysterious will be longer remembered. Research a mystery you have wondered about.

6. When the head of the museum receives the children's letter, what will his reaction be?

7. Why is there more likelihood of making a difference in the world when you pursue an intense interest? Explain.

Chapters 7 and 8

Literal Thinking:

1. What happened to make them feel the "mountain had come to Mohammed"?

2. What was Michelangelo's last name?

3. What did Michelangelo's biographers, who knew him personally, say about the little angel? According to records, did Michelangelo himself ever refer to it?

4. Why did Claudia decide to tour the United Nations building?

5. What information was in the letter from the museum?

Interpretive Thinking:

1. If you had been Jamie, what would you have said when the girl selling tickets asked why he was out of school?

2. Claudia and Jamie eventually have to tell their parents about their decision to go to Farmington. Can you think of a positive way to tell them?

3. What would you have done if you had received the friendly rejection from the museum? Discuss.

4. Why do you think Jamie chose the name he did for box rental?

5. Explain why Claudia felt she might be the discoverer of great truths.

6. Why does Claudia refuse to go home until she accomplishes something?

7. What evidence do you have that Claudia likes to learn about things?

8. Why do you think Jamie did not inquire about the price of train tickets to Farmington?

9. What did Claudia mean when she said that the man at the U.N. building looked as if he belonged there but didn't act like it?

Creative Thinking:

1. Write a letter to Jamie and Claudia giving them advice on what they should do.

2. Pretend the book is a movie. Make a larger poster to advertise it.

3. Interview classmates to find what makes them feel special. Write and illustrate a how-to booklet for children like Claudia telling ways to feel special.

4. Create a code that Claudia and Jamie could use for communication. Using the code, write a message to a partner about hiding in the museum or about the angel.

5. Create a model of a mastaba using cardboard, clay, or papier-mâché.

6. Research Egyptian words dealing with ancient Egypt, such as *pharaoh, pyramid, heir, mastaba*, and *cartouche*. Create a search-a-word or crossword puzzle. Have them duplicated and distribute them to the class.

Critical Thinking:

1. The expression about the mountain coming to Mohammed is used fairly often. Research its origin and analyze its usual meaning. Relate it to a time in your life when it would have been appropriate.

2. Various people throughout history have been known by only one name. Brainstorm and research to compile a list of these people. Chart your results and the area of their fame.

3. The children talk about the uniqueness of Claudia's acting on a hunch rather than planning something out. Jamie also listened to a hunch and kept from being discovered. Have you ever had a hunch that proved to be important? Have a class discussion.

4. Do you think being the oldest child has anything to do with how Claudia feels about herself?

5. What if Claudia and Jamie had chosen the library for their adventure? How would it have changed the story?

Chapters 9 and 10

Literal Thinking:

1. In what file did the children find the history of the angel?

2. Who disclosed to Mrs. Frankweiler where they had been?

3. Describe Mrs. Frankweiler's house.

4. Who drove the children home?

5. What message did the children send Mrs. Frankweiler that made her decide to see them?

6. Why did Mrs. Frankweiler feel that her house was "thickened by time"?

7. List ways in which the children tried to get Mrs. Frankweiler's attention. What was easiest for her to ignore?

8. Why were the children's pictures used in the newspaper so outdated?

Interpretive Thinking:

1. Write a letter to E. L. Konigsburg. Ask if she knew someone like Mrs. Frankweiler or why she was interested in Michelangelo.

2. What would you have done as Mrs. Frankweiler to ensure that the secret of the angel would never be discovered?

3. Explain why Claudia didn't feel comfortable with their imaginary royal identities anymore.

4. How did Jamie make Mrs. Frankweiler reevaluate herself?

5. Explain how their secret gave the children and Mrs. Frankweiler an instant rapport with each other.

6. What does Mrs. Frankweiler mean when she says that she never looks past her eyes and that way she is always pretty?

7. Will Mrs. Frankweiler be a good grandmother? Why or why not?

Creative Thinking:

1. Develop a scavenger hunt through your school. Treat it as a mystery and develop clues that carry you from place to place. Work in teams.

2. Draw an illustration of Mrs. Frankweiler as she looked when the children first saw her.

3. What if Mrs. Frankweiler had captured the children for ransom? Write an additional mystery chapter.

4. Create a trial scene for Jamie and Claudia as trespassers. Determine their guilt or innocence with a trial by jury complete with judge, attorneys, and witnesses.

5. Interview Claudia as an adult and the new head of the Metropolitan Museum of Art. Ask her about her experiences—as a child, in the museum, with Mrs. Frankweiler—and her choice of career.

Critical Thinking:

1. Recreate the piece of paper validating the statue.

2. Is it good advice that five minutes of planning is worth fifteen minutes of looking?

3. What part of living away from home would you like most? What part would you like least?

4. Would you like having Claudia for a sister? Why or why not?

Additional Activities

Visual Art:

1. Evaluate the illustrations in the book and give suggestions for improvement.

2. Mosaics are found in many museums. Create a mosaic of an object, such as the angel, that was important in the story.

3. Research the ancient Egyptian game of Senet. Learn the rules of the game. Construct your own game board from poster board.

4. Using *Drawing on the Right Side of the Brain* by Betty Edwards have a drawing lesson with the class. Evaluate the validity of the techniques.

5. Choose an impressionist master such as Monet and bring in a print for the class to see. Discuss technique, characteristics, and so on. Create impressionist paintings with watercolors using the print as a guide.

Creative Writing:

1. Write a newspaper article about the children who lived in the Metropolitan Museum. Base it on an interview with them and include anecdotes.

2. Write about a place you would like to hide in for a few days.

3. Write a critique of the book.

4. Create a travel brochure of the museum.

Drama:

1. Watch the video production of this book. Be a drama critic: (a) Was the choice of actors appropriate? (b) Does the film version carefully follow the plot? and (c) Would you make any changes in costumes or sets?

2. Goldilocks also trespassed in a fairy tale. As a school counselor, interview both Claudia and Goldilocks. Find out the reasons behind their actions and help them find other outlets for their adventurous minds.

3. Create a readers' theatre of *From the Mixed-up Files of Mrs. Basil E. Frankweiler*.

4. Role-play an art curator. Show classmates prints of famous artists.

5. Develop a radio broadcast about the missing children including an interview with their parents.

6. Role-play the section in which Jamie finally is tired of Claudia's never being satisfied and stands up to her.

7. Go into one of the exhibit areas such as Colonial America, Marie Antoinette, or Ancient Egypt and make up a role-play about that particular era.

Music:

1. Listen to a recording of Mussorgsky's *Pictures at an Exhibition*. Share the mental images it creates.

2. Get a recording of Don McLean's song "Vincent" ("Starry, Starry Night") which deals with the life of Vincent van Gogh. Listen to the lyrics and compare your opinions and assumptions.

3. Using the previously mentioned music obtain some slides of the artist's works and create a slide show coordinating the lyrics with the pictures.

4. Listen to a recording of baroque music. Find pictures of art and architecture of the period. Contrast the style with modern art and music. How does each reflect the lives of the people in that era?

5. Woven tapestries are displayed in many museums. Listen to music such as *Danse Macabre* by Saint-Saens. Determine how a central melody runs through the music like a thread in a tapestry.

Social Studies:

1. Have a class committee plan a field trip. Choose those students who are talented in planning.

2. Runaways are a problem in the United States today. Research some information from the police and other public agencies regarding this problem. Report to the class.

3. Research the artworks of the Vatican with particular emphasis on the Sistine Chapel. Include the unique way it was painted.

4. Research the Metropolitan Museum from its beginnings through current times. Include little known but interesting pieces of information regarding some of their acquisitions. Which items are the oldest; which are worth the greatest money?

Science:

1. Discover what great inventions were made during the fourteenth century.

2. Investigate how artifacts are preserved.

3. Pretend that you are living 100 years from now. Design an art museum. Write a paragraph on how artifacts will be preserved and what security will consist of.

4. Investigate what was used in paints during the Renaissance.

5. Leonardo da Vinci was not only a master painter, but a prolific inventor. He developed prototypes of the airplane, submarine, and many other items. Research his scientific efforts and report to the class.

6. Michelangelo carved statues from marble. Find out (a) how marble is formed, (b) the various types of marble, and (c) the most valuable marble and why.

7. Invite an expert on rocks and gems to your class. Interview to find how certain rocks are formed.

Museum Activities:

Pictured is a hypothetical floor plan for a small museum. Using this plan, complete one of the following activities.

1. Become the primary architect for the museum and design a second floor. Their request is for additional exhibits, a garden area and a section designed especially for children.

2. Create a puzzle. Correlate written clues and a maze through the rooms of the museum.

3. Develop a board game in which you move through the museum by correctly answering a question based on either the book or art.

Museum Floor Plan

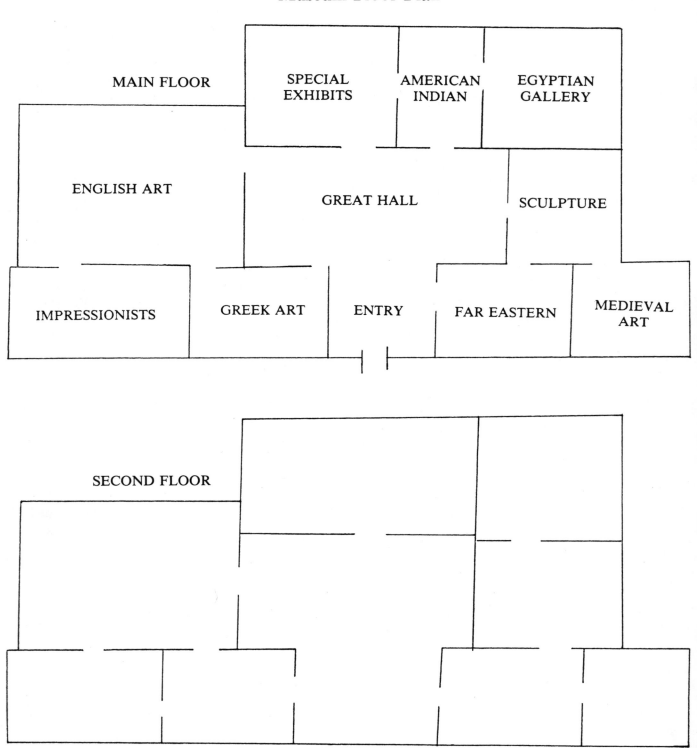

Bulletin Board

From the Mixed-up Files of Mrs. Basil E. Frankweiler

NEW *and* DIFFERENT

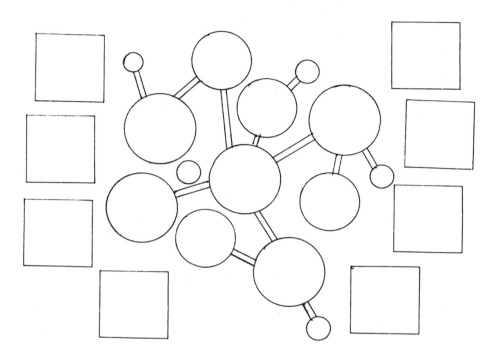

INVENTIONS

Use painted styrofoam balls cut in half and connected with drinking straws to form a molecular model. Apply to bulletin board with double-stick tape. Students create "wacky" inventions for ordinary needs. Place each design with its purpose and instructions on paper beside the model.

Call It Courage

Armstrong Sperry

Call It Courage
by
Armstrong Sperry
Macmillan, 1940

Mafatu, a young Polynesian boy, was afraid of the sea after an incident in which he and his mother were caught in a storm. His mother died while he was saved.

Mafatu was considered inferior by the others in the tribe except by one boy, Kana. Mafatu's best friends were Kivi, an albatross, and Uri, a dog. One day, Mafatu heard his only human friend, Kana, tell the others he agreed with them about Mafatu.

Feeling totally rejected, he and Uri leave in a canoe to travel to another island. The story deals with his adventures and trials until his eventual triumphant return to his own tribe.

DESOLATION

MILL RACE

SHOAL

INDIFFERENCE

INHABITED

VICTORY

WAILING

THWART

COURAGE

BUOYANCY

TERROR

Call It Courage

FEAR

JIBES

SCORN

PREMONITION

CHAOS

COWARD

ATOLL

BRAVERY

PREOCCUPIED

TREMBLING

Chapters 1 and 2

Literal Thinking:

1. Why was Mafatu such a disappointment to himself and his father?

2. What did the people of Hikueru worship?

3. Who were Mafatu's friends?

4. Why did Mafatu feel he had to leave the island of his ancestors?

5. Which youth on the island was friendly to Mafatu?

6. What island was considered to be the golden island?

Interpretive Thinking:

1. Why does the author feel that the Polynesians are no longer great in numbers and fierce of heart?

2. Why was Kana's rejection of Mafatu so important to him?

3. In what ways is Mafatu different from the others in the tribe?

4. Why do you think Kana befriended Mafatu?

5. Describe in your own words the night at sea, using words that convey sound and feeling.

6. In what ways was Mafatu's concept of the world becoming larger?

7. Relate a situation when you felt that you had to face fear in order to prove your abilities to yourself and others.

Creative Thinking:

1. Tell the story of Mafatu's sea voyage from Uri's point of view.

2. Define what courage means to you.

3. Form an outrigger from hollowed-out clay or soft balsa wood.

4. Create a vocabulary book of all the Polynesian words included in the book with English translations.

Critical Thinking:

1. What is the difference between realistic fear and cowardice?

2. A will to live carried Mafatu forward. Evaluate if this involves instinct, stubbornness, reflex action, or a conscious decision.

3. How do you think Mafatu's sea voyage will change the way he thinks of himself?

4. Why did Mafatu feel so empathetic toward Kivi and Uri?

5. Debate the idea of Mafatu's cowardice. Were the reasons for it due to his past experiences or his current views of himself?

Chapters 3 and 4

Literal Thinking:

1. Which god did Mafatu feel had helped carry him across the ocean?

2. How did Mafatu know that the island was formed from a volcano?

3. How did the boy know that people had recently been on the island?

4. What was the importance of the boar-tooth necklace?

5. What continually robbed Mafatu's bamboo trap?

6. What gave Mafatu the strength to kill the hammerhead?

Interpretive Thinking:

1. Why was Mafatu's relationship with Uri becoming more important all the time?

2. Mafatu was grateful for his skills in fashioning tools. Relate a skill of yours that could be used in an emergency or crisis.

3. When was the first time Mafatu realized he was not afraid?

4. How did conquering one enemy give Mafatu more incentive to challenge the next?

Creative Thinking:

1. Using clay, form your own version of the ancient idol.

2. Using watercolors, illustrate the distinctive features of the hammerhead shark.

3. Create a facsimile of Grandfather Ruau's necklace. Use a salt, flour, and water combination for the dough sculpture. Color with tempera paints.

4. Draw the strange picture described in chapter 4.

Critical Thinking:

1. Explain how various bits of information learned over the years helped Mafatu now.

2. Analyze why what others think of you affects how you think of yourself. Predict whether Mafatu's new-found confidence will continue on his own island.

3. What leads us to act with courage when we would, ordinarily, be fearful?

4. What evidence does the author give that Mafatu was a creative thinker?

5. Why was taking the spear a turning point in Mafatu's life? Write a paragraph about a time when facing a fear was a turning point in your life.

6. View a video production of a Jacques Cousteau ocean exploration. How are his adventures like Mafatu's? List the similarities and differences.

7. Which challenge in chapters 3 and 4 took the most courage for Mafatu to face? Debate with classmates.

Chapter 5

Literal Thinking:

1. What saved Mafatu from the black canoes full of savages?

2. What played on Mafatu's nerves as he neared his island home?

3. Explain the causes of a lagoon fire.

4. What showed Mafatu he was near Hikueru?

Interpretive Thinking:

1. Why is a book about courage and facing fear timeless?

2. Have you ever felt especially good about yourself after facing a difficult task and completing it? Share your experiences with a partner.

3. Predict what Mafatu's role in the tribal village will be after his return.

4. Will Mafatu have his intense fear of the sea again? Discuss.

Creative Thinking:

1. Illustrate the war canoe and the natives complete with painted faces and ironwood war clubs.

2. Darken the classroom, using a candle to simulate a camp fire. As Mafatu, tell the villagers stories of your adventures.

3. Imagine yourself on a raft day after day. Brainstorm ways to break the monotony.

4. Experiment with various Polynesian dishes. Find a Polynesian cookbook and prepare a special dish for the class.

5. Write a journal entry for five days by Moana, the sea god. Explore his point of view concerning Mafatu's voyage.

6. Create a panel discussion of characters from other books such as Harriet from *Harriet the Spy* by Louise Fitzhugh, Billy from *Where the Red Fern Grows* by Wilson Rawls, and others of your choice. Mafatu leads the panel discussion about the challenges each character faced and how each conquered his/her fears.

7. Write to or visit a travel agent to ask questions about island vacations. Plan a magical vacation to one of your choice.

Critical Thinking:

1. It is said that the better one feels about one's self, the better one generally treats others. Debate with classmates whether you feel this is true. Give examples to prove your point of view.

2. What do you consider the most important lesson to be learned from *Call It Courage*?

3. Analyze why Mafatu felt the gods were against him when he was challenged.

4. In what ways were Mafatu and Moana alike? Different?

Additional Activities

Visual Art:

1. Create a *missing* bulletin about the boy who disappeared from the island.

2. Find out about the artist Paul Gauguin, who painted the people and islands of Tahiti.

3. Mafatu was determined to face his fears and find his own identity. Fingerprints are unique to each individual. Using fingerprints and thumbprints, create a design. Fine-line markers can define your design.

4. Find various colors of aquarium rocks. Draw an object from *Call It Courage*. Place glue on paper in the area to be filled with the rocks, then sprinkle them on. Allow to dry.

5. Mafatu used natural materials to make his clothing. Find commercial dyes to tie and dye T-shirts simulating island designs.

6. Create a folded picture in three parts depicting Mafatu at the beginning, middle, and end of the story.

Creative Writing:

1. As Mafatu on the raft, write a letter to your father.

2. Mafatu had a problem facing his fears. As an author, what would be your leading character's problems and how would he/she solve them? Share the original stories in class.

3. What if the man-eaters had captured Mafatu? Write a script of a trial in which Mafatu's fate is decided.

4. Think of a folktale in which a character who lacks courage may be included. Write a new chapter including the character facing his/her fears.

5. Create a limerick about Kivi or Uri.

Drama:

1. Role-play a scene between Uri and Mafatu.

2. As a newscaster, interview Mafatu about the most perilous parts of the journey.

3. Focus on facial expression. Mime the emotions of important turning points in the story. As partners, one person reads the selection as the other mimes the action.

4. As a class, conduct a survey of books such as *Call It Courage* that deal with courage or change of self-concept because of bravery. Present a series of mini-scenes from these books for videotaping or for a visiting class.

5. Write a dramatized sequel to *Call It Courage* to explore the next year of Mafatu's life on his island home.

Music:

1. Find a recording of *La Mer* by Debussy. Listen to the sounds of the sea in its changing moods. Compare your interpretations with those of classmates.

2. Find the vocal collection of songs from *Free to Be You and Me* by Marlo Thomas and others. Learn how they apply to Mafatu and you.

3. Find a traditional Hawaiian song that tells of a local superstition. Listen to it as a class.

4. Island songs used drums for communication. Explore drumming patterns that could convey a call to war, danger, and so on.

Social Studies:

1. Investigate real-life experiences of people traveling long distances on a raft and surviving.

2. Research the history of the Hawaiian Islands from their long period of internal warfare between island chieftains to the coming of King Kamehameha and subsequent unification.

3. Research some of the unique tourist attractions in Hawaii from the black and green beaches to the little people of Kauai.

4. Compare the menehunes to the Irish leprechauns. Compare stories and deeds attributed to each.

5. Learn more about different cultures to find out unusual facts. Consult sources such as encyclopedias. Create a board game based on the facts.

6. Mafatu was isolated from his tribe because he was different. Find examples of national problems in newspapers and magazines based on differences. Share with the class.

Science:

1. Research the various leaves and trees mentioned in this book. Make an illustration of each. Give short descriptions along with any possible medicinal uses.

2. Build a volcano of chicken wire and papier-mâché. Leave an opening in the center. Place baking soda in the crater with vinegar to produce a foaming eruption.

3. Mafatu observed dolphins ready to consume flying fish. Find out what predators attack dolphins, and the defenses of the dolphins.

4. Invite a scuba diver to your class. Interview to find out about training, experiences, and rules of safety.

5. Research work being done to study sharks. Learn about newly developed defenses against them such as bags and repellants.

Math:

1. Shells were often used as money in tribal societies. Create a store selling island products such as bananas. Determine the number of shells needed for a purchase. Make posters telling how many shells will buy a bargain!

Bulletin Board

Call It Courage

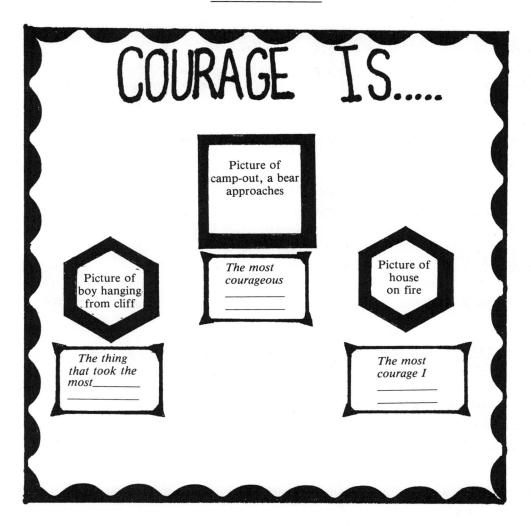

Each student writes about a courageous experience in his/her own life or another person's. These accounts of courage may be located in books, magazines, and newspapers. Draw a picture of the experience with crayons. Apply the crayons heavily. Brush over the entire picture, lightly, with black tempera.

ADDITIONAL BOOKS ON SELF-CONCEPT

1. *A Matter of Pride*. Emily Crofford. Carolrhoda, 1981.

   Meg's mother can't adjust to her move to a plantation; she is afraid of anything new. Meg's concept of courage and of her mother is changed when her mother confronts Mr. Bowers.

2. *Dumb Old Casey Is a Fat Tree*. Barbara Bottner. Harper & Row, 1979.

   Rita is embarrassed about her weight. Through encouragement and sacrifice, she loses weight and gains a new perspective.

3. *Jamie's Turn*. Jamie DeWitt. Raintree, 1984.

   Jamie's stepfather is injured on a tractor and must be hospitalized. Although Jamie has learning problems, he has the responsibility of the farm. Jamie's self-concept is changed by his experience.

4. *Katy Did It*. Victoria Boutis. Greenwillow, 1982.

   Katy feels her backpacking attempts are laughable, but goes backpacking with her father. The achievement of climbing to the top of the mountain changes the girl's self-concept.

5. *Marinka, Katinka, and Me (Susie)*. Winifred Madison. Pantheon, 1975.

   Three girls have become inseparable friends until Marinka and Katinka quarrel. Their friendship is strained leaving Susie feeling disloyal. A final talk restores the friendship.

6. *My War with Mrs. Galloway*. Doris Orgel. Viking/Penguin, 1985.

   Rebecca declares war on her baby-sitter. Rebecca is left feeling angry and aggressive owing to Mrs. Galloway's angry words. The final battle resolves into new understanding, friendship, and maturity for Rebecca.

7. *Not Just Any Ring*. Danita R. Haller. Knopf, 1982.

   Grandfather is injured in a truck accident. Jessie must fight her own fears to find help. Jessie learns what courage and wisdom are.

8. *Shoeshine Girl*. Clyde Robert Bulla. Thomas Y. Crowell Co., 1977.

   Sarah Ida has a poor concept of herself when she is sent away to her aunt's home. Here she learns to take responsibility of Al's Shoeshine stand. She learns the value of friendship and how a caring relationship improves self-esteem.

9. *The Pinballs*. Betsy Byars. Harper & Row, 1977.

   Three foster children feel like pinballs without control of their lives. Through wise and loving care by their foster parents, they learn to appreciate their own individuality.

10. *Tramp*. Malcolm Carrick. Harper & Row, 1977.

    A shy boy hides from other children. In his refuge, he meets a tramp who befriends him. Through their relationship, the boy gains the courage to make new friends.

STORYTELLING AND READING ALOUD

Storytelling

Teachers traditionally have been storytellers, retelling bits and pieces of history or traditions throughout time. This long-used technique is returning to the classroom to help students refine their creative thinking skills, imagination, listening skills, and expression of their inner feelings.

Storytelling—in the form of reading directly from a book, using a felt board, or merely using the voice—is a very good way to reach the inner selves of children. It nurtures their compassionate nature and thus aids in learning about the emotions and needs of others. It also can provide skills needed to help either themselves or others with their problems.

A good story might reveal the joy and difficulties that are all part of the human experience. Beginning with fables is often very effective. Those of Aesop or Arnold Lobel are excellent for younger children, as James Thurber may prove to be more appropriate for older children.

The following are some guidelines for implementing storytelling in the classroom:

1. Locate a story that is correct for you and your personality as a storyteller as well as appropriate for the age group.

2. Develop a comfortable environment and give thought to the feeling of the story.

3. Do not memorize the story. Telling it in your own words is much more effective.

4. Characterizations need to be developed in a way comfortable to you as the storyteller, whether gestures or descriptive language.

5. Speak slowly but clearly, loudly enough for the audience to easily hear. Try to maintain some type of eye contact.

6. Use various media to promote interest. Mime, dance, music, sound effects, puppets, creative drama, or video photography can all be effective.

Your enjoyment of the story will communicate itself to the children in turn, promoting their interest and imagination. Children learn from discussions and various activities. This is a shared moment of experiences and thought with literature between storyteller and child.

Reading Aloud

The shared experience of reading aloud provides unity for students in the classroom. Stories that are experienced together provide a basis for emotional interaction within a group.

When children hear stories read aloud, they are encouraged to read for themselves. Finding independent reading adaptable to personal interests and needs, they may improve the quality and quantity of their reading. In addition to providing an emotional stimulus for individual reading, hearing stories read provides a basis to meet and respond to the beauty of the written word.

Reading aloud can broaden children's interests in bibliotherapy. Much of this literature will address students' deepest needs and feelings, helping to put problems into perspective. When children hear selected literature read aloud, their feelings can be deepened by the revealing of characters' inner motives and thoughts.

A major goal of education is to stimulate lifelong learning. The dramatic elements in books that highlight children's problems relate to problem solving in life. Selected literature, read aloud, provides a practical way to approach this goal.

A Taste of Blackberries

Doris B. Smith

A Taste of Blackberries
by
Doris B. Smith
Thomas Y. Crowell Co., 1973

A Taste of Blackberries tells of two young boys who were best friends. One was rather aggressive and somewhat of a show-off, but still they were very close.

One day, while helping a neighbor clear her grapevine, one of the boys was stung by a swarm of bees. He was allergic and subsequently died.

The remainder of the story deals with his friend's coping with and ultimate acceptance of his death.

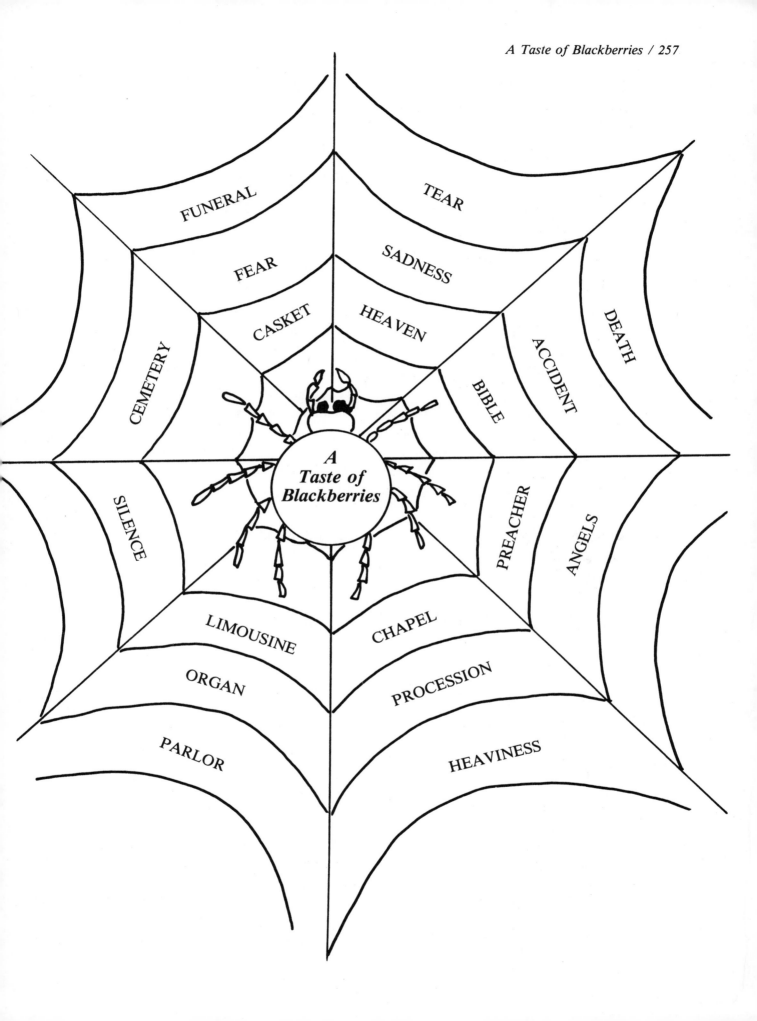

Chapters 1 through 4

Literal Thinking:

1. What caused Jamie's death?
2. What did Jamie do that showed he was a caring child?
3. Why did Jamie feel that helping Mrs. Houser might be fun after all?
4. How did Jamie provoke the bees?
5. How did the boys communicate at night?

Interpretive Thinking:

1. How would you have felt if you had been Mrs. Houser? Create a web design with Mrs. Houser's name in the center. Web the different emotions she must have felt.
2. Have you ever been involved in a life-and-death situation? Share your experiences with a partner.
3. What would you have done if you had seen Jamie writhing on the ground? Describe your plan.
4. How did the boys figure out a simple solution to running the string into place? Explain why their Morse code was more effective than the first method they tried.

Creative Thinking:

1. Draw an illustration of how your heart could "beat paradiddles."
2. Create a necklace or card for a person to wear showing his/her sensitivity to bee stings.
3. The creek was their "secret faraway" area. Draw what you would consider to be a perfect secret haven.
4. Draw a small treasure chest. Fill it with accounts of events or illustrations of objects associated with the boys' friendship.
5. Do you think Jamie's death will change his friend's life? How? Draw a before-and-after picture showing the transformation that will occur.
6. Have you ever experienced an unexpected death in your family? Write about your feelings in your journal.

Critical Thinking:

1. How could Jamie's friend's mother have been more gentle in telling of Jamie's death? Discuss.
2. What element of Jamie's personality will probably be missed the most by his friends? Why?
3. What emotions does the author make the reader feel upon reading of Jamie's death? Which is the most pronounced?
4. Debate the advisability of either being a hitchhiker or picking one up. Did the circumstances the children found themselves in alter your opinion?
5. What do you know about Jamie's personality from reading chapters 1 through 4? What object would typify his personality?

Chapters 5 through 8

Literal Thinking:

1. Whose garden was a sanctuary for Jamie's friend?
2. What finally triggered the tears for Jamie's friend?
3. Which were the only flowers that appeared to be sad about Jamie's death? What was the real reason for this?
4. Why was Jamie's friend so hesitant about seeing Jamie's mother?

Interpretive Thinking:

1. What statement did Jamie's friend make that showed that he is initially denying his friend's death?
2. Which words and actions of Miss Mullins showed that she is a wise person?
3. Why did Jamie's friend finally decide he needed to attend the funeral?
4. Explain why Miss Mullins had stone benches placed around her garden.

Creative Thinking:

1. Write a journal entry as if you were Jamie's friend. Express your feelings while in the garden.
2. Compose a haiku about silence.
3. Draw a basket of blackberries like the one Jamie's friend delivered. Enclose a card expressing your feelings of sympathy for his mother.
4. Write a letter to Doris B. Smith telling her your impression of *A Taste of Blackberries.*

Critical Thinking:

1. Did Jamie's friend feel better after he delivered the blackberries to Jamie's mother? Was compassion important in his healing? Discuss.
2. Was the author successful in giving the reader a candid look at the process of grieving? What was the most difficult stage for Jamie's friend?
3. What was the most empathetic and nurturing aspect of Mrs. Mullins's conversation with Jamie's friend?
4. Explain why Jamie's friend wasn't crying for Jamie but for himself. Do you agree or disagree? Explain your opinion.
5. Analyze the statement "I could almost hear the colors in my ears."
6. Discuss the statement that one of the hardest things we have to learn is that some questions do not have answers.

Additional Activities

Visual Art:

1. Create a watercolor interpretation of Jamie's friend's sky. Include houses, lamps, and floppy-eared dogs.
2. Create your own butterfly, colored in distinctive patterns. Cut out and display it.

3. Look at the cover of the book. Draw illustrations of what happened before and after the picture.

4. Make a paper wreath for Jamie from his friend. Perhaps paper blackberries could be included.

5. Construct a mobile with objects that celebrate Jamie's and his friend's relationship.

Creative Writing:

1. Write a postcard to a friend or acquaintance who has moved from your area.

2. Read the Greek myth about Daedalus and Icarus. How does Icarus remind you of Jamie? Write a role-play of Icarus and Jamie telling their parents about the lessons they have learned.

3. Has a friend, relative, or someone else ever given you valuable advice during a personal crisis? Write about the special moment someone like Mrs. Mullins helped you turn a negative situation into a positive one.

4. This story points to the fact that life can be unexpectedly short. Write about your ultimate dream or experience for the future. Include your proposed plans for achieving that dream.

5. At times, Jamie seemed to take too many risks. As an investigative reporter, interview Jamie's family to learn the underlying causes. After the interview, write a news story about the need for balance between risk-taking and caution in learning situations.

6. Discuss the importance of conflict in creative writing. Bring an example of conflict from literature to share with the class. Suppose Jamie's mother had blamed his friend for her son's death, for example. Brainstorm other possible conflicts. Write dialogue expressing creative problem solving.

7. Does guilt make a person grow? Write in your journal about a time when you felt guilty. What action did you take to resolve the situation? What was the most important thing you learned from the experience?

Drama:

1. What were the most touching emotional moments in the story? Role-play them.

2. Role-play and subsequently videotape an action scene before Jamie died. After viewing the scene, analyze each character's motivation for his/her actions.

3. Perform a soliloquy of Jamie's friend picking blackberries: the running conversation with himself, the blackberries, and Jamie relating memories of a wonderful friendship.

4. Write a letter to Jamie's mother expressing the feelings and wishes that were difficult to communicate. Read the letter aloud, as Jamie's friend.

5. Perform a scene as Jamie registering what happened to him and his reactions to what all the others are experiencing. Remember, if he attempts to talk to them, they will not be able to see or hear him.

Music:

1. Locate a song that you feel would be expressive of Jamie or his friend. Analyze why the choices are appropriate.

2. Videotape various insects in motion from a nature show. Set their actions and movements to recorded music.

Social Studies:

1. Research the changing role of the funeral in modern life. Is it becoming more personal and less directed or the opposite? Discuss the reasons for changes, or whether there is a need for additional changes.

2. Why and how were the pyramids built? What was the Egyptian mummification process? Research a pharaoh of your choice to find out.

3. Research why some European wines are actually produced from American vines. Write to the California Winery Association for more information.

4. Funeral customs have differed throughout history. Research a Viking, American Indian, East Indian, or Mayan funeral, or the Japanese custom of floating candles on the water.

Science:

1. Why were the flowers very symbolic in the story? Tell the life story of a flower from its point of view. Emphasize the gradual process of life and death. The exalted orchid's story would be much different from that of the sunflower.

2. Why do some plants like blackberries have thorns? What are some unusual protective devices of plants? Create a contest between plants such as Venus's-flytraps. Each plant describes its outstanding protective qualities. Award the most unusual plant.

3. Jamie and his friend appreciated nature. What is a mystery of nature you would like to explore? Research to find your answers.

4. Learn more about bee-sting allergies. How do people discover whether they have this particular allergy? What precautions do these people have to take?

5. Research four or five varieties of moths or butterflies. Draw each as both a caterpillar and an adult. Make a booklet describing each variety including habitat and migratory path.

Bulletin Board

A Taste of Blackberries

Many times, friends or family move away or are deceased. Bring photographs of the friends or members of the family who are departed. Each child writes about the memories of the happiest times he/she can remember involving these people.

The Big Wave

Pearl S. Buck

The Big Wave

by

Pearl S. Buck
Curtis Publishing Co., 1948

This story is about Japan and its traditional life-styles. It centers on a village bounded by a potentially active volcano and the unpredictable sea. The characters depict the fatalism of their lives, tending to center not on *if* something will occur, but *when*.

A tidal wave destroys the village homes and takes many lives. Jiya is a young boy who loses his entire family. He must choose between living with a well-to-do Old Gentleman or the family of his best friend.

Jiya goes through the steps of mourning to emerge as an accepting, mature adult.

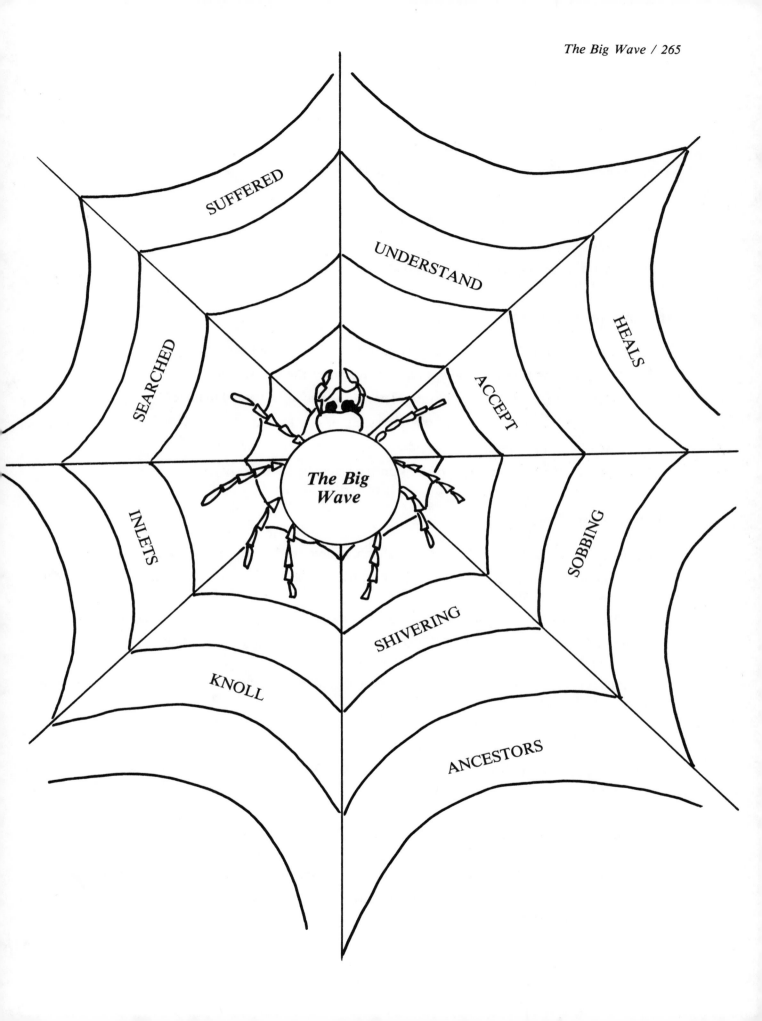

Part 1

Literal Thinking:

1. To whom did the island belong?

2. What was Kino's father afraid of on land?

3. Who were responsible for building the stone walls?

4. Who did they consider their enemy?

5. What caused the wave?

6. What did the Old Gentleman do to save the people?

Interpretive Thinking:

1. How can you tell that Kino's family is very responsible and caring?

2. Why was it better that Jiya was unconscious after the big wave?

3. Explain the meaning of the phrase "That is the way of a good Japanese"?

4. Compare the boy's attitude to the harvesting of rice to that of harvesting fish.

5. Why didn't the villagers have windows facing the sea in their homes?

6. Why was Jiya never willing to sleep on the island?

Creative Thinking:

1. Draw an illustration of the Old Gentleman as described by Kino and Jiya.

2. Imagine you are a rock that has spent centuries being buffeted and worn smooth by the ocean. Describe your experience.

3. Create a news broadcast about the villagers awaiting what they consider to be a certainty.

4. Kino's father remained relatively calm throughout the disaster. How would you have reacted in the face of overwhelming disaster? Explain.

5. Pick one saying of Kino's father that you especially believe and write a brief essay supporting it.

Critical Thinking:

1. Why did Kino's father state that "Every day of life is more valuable now than it was before the storm"?

2. Was it wise for Kino's parents to take Jiya in as their son?

3. Discuss and evaluate the phrase "Must we always be afraid of something?" Refer this both to the story concept and real life.

4. Evaluate the aura of fatalism expressed by the elders' resignation to fates deeded to them.

5. Analyze and list the signs of a pending earthquake.

6. Why did Mr. Kino tell his son that life overcomes death?

Part 2

Literal Thinking:

1. What is Kino's father's definition of *death*?

2. Tell why Jiya wanted to marry Setsu.

3. Where did Jiya build his new home?

4. What did the red flag signify?

5. Relate the interest the Old Gentleman took in the orphans of the waves.

6. How did Jiya prepare for the big wave?

Interpretive Thinking:

1. Why did Jiya feel compelled to build his home on the beach?

2. Have you ever felt compelled to face a personal fear? Explain.

3. Why did Jiya choose not to be the Old Gentleman's son?

4. Explain how, as long as Jiya is alive, his family still exists.

5. Relate why people divided time into *before* and *after* the big wave.

Creative Thinking:

1. Create a news story about the massive destruction caused by the wave.

2. Illustrate your story with a before-and-after drawing.

3. The red flag and the tolling bell alerted the villagers to the impending danger. If you were confronted with a potential disaster, how would you warn people quickly?

4. Change the story, telling of Jiya's life had he gone to live with the Old Gentleman.

5. Retell the story of the island swim as a mystery. The Old Gentleman kidnaps the boys.

6. Describe the most frightening weather phenomenon you have ever experienced.

7. Describe what you would like about living either on the land or on the beach in Japan.

Critical Thinking:

1. List three sentences that prove the wisdom of Kino's father.

2. Which character in *The Big Wave* would you most like to meet? Why?

3. Would you have moved back to the beach as Jiya and Setsu did?

4. Evaluate the wisdom of Jiya's acceptance of the ocean.

5. Research the life of Pearl S. Buck and the reason for her lifelong interest in Asiatic cultures.

Additional Activities

Visual Art:

1. Research the Japanese artists Hokusai and Hiroshige. Compare their subjects, styles, and composition.

2. Select a character and draw items that would be most symbolic of that person. Discuss your choices.

3. Make carp banners to celebrate Kino's and Jiya's lives. Suspend the banners around a copy of *The Big Wave* in your media center.

4. Write a haiku about experiences in facing a crisis with courage. Illustrate your poems with watercolors on rice paper.

5. Make a mural of terraces going up a mountain, with the sea at the bottom.

Creative Writing:

1. Setsu wanted to give Jiya her pet duck to comfort him. Write and illustrate a story about something you derived comfort from during a stressful situation.

2. Write a letter as Jiya. Tell about the catastrophe that happened to his family and his emergence through grieving to acceptance.

3. Write a legend about how the ocean became angry and created the big wave.

4. Write a tall tale about *The Big Wave*. Use the volcanic eruption and tidal wave as integral parts of the story.

5. Create a poem about the earthquake and tidal wave.

6. Summarize *The Big Wave*, emphasizing how Jiya and Kino grew in their understanding of life.

Drama:

1. Find turning points in the story. Create Kabuki masks. Dramatize the scenes with accompanying drums and cymbals.

2. Compile information on the Kabuki theatre and its importance throughout centuries. Include the reasoning behind the exclusion of females in male theatres and vice versa.

3. Find folk legends of Japan. Learn more about Bunraku, a Japanese puppet theatre. Create a Japanese puppet show using a script based on folk legend.

4. For the Kabuki presentation of *The Big Wave*, learn theatrical terms. Make a poster explaining *stage left, stage right, center stage, upstage, downstage*, and others.

5. Role-play Jiya and Kino as grown men discussing the big wave.

Music:

1. Listen to recordings of oriental music. Play some as background music as you tell parts of the story for your class.

2. The Japanese celebrate nature in many ways. Write rhymed and unrhymed poetry about nature. Turn your poem into lyrics for a song celebrating nature.

3. Listen to recordings of the sea and surf. Act out a pantomime between Jiya and Kino telling of earthquakes and tidal waves.

4. Research Japanese music and dance. Choose an example of a traditional dance, and its accompanying music, that illustrates a belief or custom; for example, The Lion Dance.

5. Research traditional Japanese instruments. Create an example of one.

Social Studies:

1. Research Japanese customs and superstitions regarding the ocean. Include such customs as two rocks that were next to each other for centuries being joined by a marriage rope, and the yearly ritual to renew their commitment.

2. Research Pompeii and Herculaneum and the destruction caused by the eruption of Mt. Vesuvius.

3. Study a modern-day volcanic eruption and the ramifications of its destruction. For example, Mount St. Helens and the resultant atmospheric dust.

4. Research man-made accidents that have had far-reaching effects; for example, Chernobyl.

5. Compare and contrast Japanese culture and your culture.

6. Research Japanese festivals. Focus on *Tonge-no Sekku* (boy's festival) and *Hina-Matsuri* (doll festival). Create banners and display dolls to celebrate the festivals in your classroom.

7. Write to Kyoto, the ancient city filled with Japanese artifacts. Ask for information to share with your class.

Science:

1. What is most important in caring for a trauma victim? Invite a resource person from a trauma center to speak to your class. Make a list of questions for an interview.

2. Create a *bonsai* or miniature garden for your classroom. Invite a designer of the gardens to your class.

3. Research to find out about the progress made in robotics and about other technological advances in Japan. Report to your class.

4. What islands have been created by volcanic activity? Choose an island group to research. Report to your class.

5. Research volcanoes and the differences between them; for example, the results produced by slowly versus quickly moving lava.

6. Research the dependence of the Japanese on fishing. Include their stance on the international limits on territorial waters and the killing of whales. Debate the pros and cons.

7. Using a world map, locate islands created by volcanic activity.

8. Set up an experiment on the effect of rapidly moving water on a stationary object. Create four or five various structures; for example, glue and toothpicks, stones, and notched ice-cream sticks. Gauge the effect of varied amounts of water on them (e.g., 8 ounces of water poured on each, or 16 ounces on each). Do the same experiment with arm action depicting wind involvement. Record and tabulate the results.

Bulletin Board

The Big Wave

Setsu wanted to give her pet duck to Jiya to comfort him. Each student writes and illustrates a story about something comforting to him/her during a stressful time. Cut a duck shape from paper with nests of paper or real straw. Display story and illustration on each nest.

Sarah, Plain and Tall

Patricia MacLachlan

Sarah, Plain and Tall
by
Patricia MacLachlan
Harper & Row, 1985

On the day after he was born, Caleb's mother died; now, everyday, he asks his sister Anna about his mother and how she would sing.

Caleb's and Anna's papa put an advertisement in the paper for a wife. The reply is from Sarah Elisabeth Wheaton, who writes that she is plain and tall.

When Sarah arrives for a month-long visit, the children are afraid that the prairie is too different from her home in Maine. Because they do not want her to leave, they try to point out similarities of the prairie to the sea.

One day, Sarah goes to town in the wagon and the children know she must be getting a ticket to take a train back to Maine.

Sarah returns with something from the sea and the assurance that she will stay on the prairie. There will soon be a wedding, and the children feel happy and secure.

WRETCHED

EERIE

DIED

SMILING

HELP

REMEMBERING

RASCAL

SQUALL

Sarah,
Plain and
Tall

FEISTY

LAUGHED

HARSHLY

PESKY

ENERGETIC

RUMBLE

PUNGENT

GRINNING

ROAM

Chapters 1 through 4

Literal Thinking:

1. Where did Papa advertise for a new wife?

2. What gifts did Sarah bring to remind the children of the sea?

3. Why did Caleb want Anna to remember the songs his mother used to sing?

4. Which members of the family first cared for Sarah?

5. How old was Caleb when his mother died?

6. What was the reason Caleb's father gave for not singing?

Interpretive Thinking:

1. Analyze the statement in the letter, "Tell them I sing."

2. Why was it important for Sarah to share parts of her life with the family?

3. Explain the unusual thing Sarah did with the cut hair and why she did it.

4. Discuss the feelings of the children as they waited for their father to return with Sarah.

5. Analyze why Sarah always made certain they understood she was "plain and tall."

6. What is significant about the look on Sarah's face when she listened to the conch shell?

Creative Thinking:

1. Suppose Sarah had been a lady who wore silk dresses and fancy shoes and didn't like the prairie? How would the story have changed? Role-play it.

2. If you were writing to Sarah, what questions would you want answered? Role-play with a partner the roles of Caleb and Sarah. Compose a list of questions for your partner to answer.

3. What would you say to Sarah to convince her to stay on the prairie?

4. Create a watercolor of your impression of the "middle of a foghorn sea."

5. You are Papa. Write an advertisement in the newspaper for a new wife.

Critical Thinking:

1. Was it fair for the father to advertise for a new mother without asking Caleb and Anna? Explain.

2. List the reasons why Caleb thinks Sarah will stay. Do you think he is right?

3. Judge whether the children's father made a good decision in advertising for a wife.

4. Discuss the most positive aspects and serious concerns of the children about having a new mother.

5. Determine why Caleb is so anxious to have memories about his mother told to him over and over.

6. Discuss how Sarah's presence has enriched the children's lives.

Chapters 5 through 9

Literal Thinking:

1. Relate the first time the children felt that Sarah was beginning to really feel at home.

2. What caused the children to realize the chicken would not be used for food?

3. Where did Sarah teach the children to swim?

4. What caused Sarah to cry?

5. What was the dune made of that Papa created for Sarah?

6. How did Sarah bring the sea to the family?

Interpretive Thinking:

1. Why was it important for Sarah to learn such skills as plowing?

2. What leads you to think Sarah loves wild creatures?

3. Why was having a friend who had also moved to the prairie important to Sarah?

4. Analyze the meaning of "There are always things to miss ... no matter where you are."

5. Why do you believe Sarah felt that she had to leave her home in Maine?

Creative Thinking:

1. List all the things that are common to the prairie and to the sea. Write a poem using these common words.

2. Draw your interpretation of the sky as depicted at the beginning of chapter 8.

3. As Sarah, write a short description of how the prairie reminds you of the sea.

4. Draw your impression of Sarah's home in Maine. Include the seals, whales, ocean, sand dunes, and her home. Use watercolors, colored markers, or tempera.

5. Choose of the drawings Sarah makes of the family and recreate it.

Critical Thinking:

1. What gift from Maggie showed her empathy for Sarah?

2. Why was Caleb extremely uncomfortable about Sarah's going to town alone?

3. Why would Caleb's solutions for keeping Sarah not work?

4. What connection was drawn between the sea and the morning after the storm?

5. What was the most surprising thing Sarah did in chapters 5 through 9?

6. Sarah said she was plain and tall. Was her personality plain and tall? Discuss.

Additional Activities

Visual Art:

1. Create a mural including the sea and the prairie. Use pastel chalk with a spray fixative.

2. Using colored paper, create what you think Sarah's yellow bonnet looked like.

3. Make a paper patchwork quilt showing favorite scenes from the story.

4. Create a black-and-white drawing of the prairie with windmills and sheep as Sarah did.

5. Draw two pictures of Sarah: the first picture as she thought of herself, plain and tall; the second as others saw her, vibrant and beautiful.

6. Use *American Gothic* by Grant Wood as a prototype. Draw a similar picture of the new family.

7. Seal's footprints were mentioned in the story. Create a cartoon about Sarah using your thumbprints.

8. Create an illustration of the neighbor, Maggie, with her hair the color of a turnip.

Creative Writing:

1. Look in the *personals* column in the newspaper. How do people describe themselves? Advertise for a friend: Write an ad describing your best qualities of friendship.

2. As the children, design a thank-you card to Sarah for the wonderful things she has brought to your lives.

3. Write the story from Seal's viewpoint. Tell of his perceptions of his new home and family.

4. Using a contest format, write responses to Papa's original letter. Papa will interview each applicant to choose the most congenial companion.

5. Write scripts for radio shows. With sound effects, recreate the dune slide or other action scenes.

Drama:

1. Write a script for role-play based on "what-ifs," such as Caleb and Anna come to dislike Sarah, or Caleb secretly advertised for a new mother. Brainstorm additional new endings to the story for role-play.

2. Create a skit with children acting the parts of some of the animals described in the story. Each gives an opinion about their strange humans and happenings around the farm.

3. Perform a soliloquy of Sarah discussing her involvement with the family from the first letter.

4. Explore the readers' theatre format. Create a readers' theatre presentation based on *Sarah, Plain and Tall*.

5. Role-play a telephone conversation between Sarah and her family in Maine. As Sarah, share your impressions of the new home.

6. Create a comic Wild West melodrama. When Sarah goes to town, a bandit is robbing the local bank. What does Sarah do? Role-play it.

Music:

1. As Caleb and Anna, write a rap song for Sarah about Bride's Bonnet similar to the one for Wooly Rag-wort.

2. Locate songs about pioneers and/or folk songs of the plains. Note the courage and determination depicted in the songs. Choose a favorite to learn as a class.

3. Listen to a recording of *The King and I*. How was Sarah much like Anna? Discuss.

4. Create lyrics for a song that describes the prairie as a sea. Sing to a familiar tune.

5. Locate a recording of the sounds of the sea. As Sarah, create a dance that expresses your longing for the sea.

6. In isolated areas, musical instruments often are not available. Create your own instruments, using items found in most homes.

Social Studies:

1. Write to the tourism board in Maine. Ask for information about the state's topography. Share the information with your class.

2. Locate books such as the prairie series by Laura Ingalls Wilder. Analyze the similarities and differences in pioneer settlement between these stories and *Sarah, Plain and Tall*.

3. Find out why farmers such as Anna's and Caleb's father was in conflict with cowboys and ranchers during the western settlement.

4. Find current newspaper articles telling why farming is becoming very difficult in parts of the United States today.

5. Research the invention of barbed wire. What dramatic changes did it introduce to western settlement?

6. Learn more about famous male and female bandits of the Old West. Report your findings by being interviewed by your classmates.

Science:

1. Learn about the habits of seals. Research seal hunting. Are there international laws protecting seals? Discuss.

2. Research the following: marsh hawks, moon snails, sea stone, and Indian paintbrush. Present mini-reports to your class.

3. Find wildflowers in your area. Using the same techniques as Sarah, press and dry the flowers. Glue to paper, laminate, and cut into shapes for bookmarks.

4. Are all whales dangerous? Is whale hunting still permitted? Make a report based upon your research. As an introduction, read aloud an excerpt from *Moby Dick* by Herman Melville, describing early whale hunts.

5. Invite a meteorologist to your class to discuss severe weather conditions typical to your area. Interview to find out more about safety precautions.

6. Find out what mica is and what effect its presence has on a sand dune.

7. Locate a book about folk medicine. What plants or herbs did pioneers use to promote healing? Make a chart showing interesting and unusual facts.

Bulletin Board

Sarah, Plain and Tall

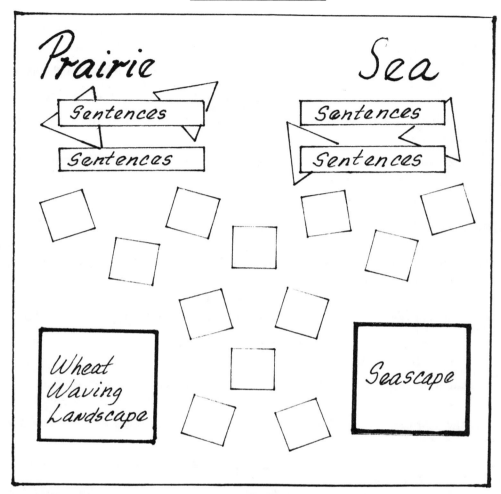

Using this book or other pieces of literature, students write sentences using similes and metaphors comparing the prairie to the sea (e.g., The prairie grass was like the waves of the sea).

ADDITIONAL BOOKS FOR STORYTELLING AND READING ALOUD

1. *The Bad Times of Irma Baumlein.* Carol Ryrie Brink. Macmillan, 1974.

   New in the school, Irma works very hard at trying to impress her classmates. This turns into a disaster and gets completely out of control. This book has humor and wonderful lessons concerning truth, relationships with friends, and the pressure of peers.

2. *Burnish Me Bright.* Julia Cunningham. Dell, 1980.

   A famous pantomimist, now living in poverty, meets an orphan boy who wants to learn the art of mime. The sharing between them relieves the loneliness that has clouded their lives. The book explores love, friendship, and courage.

3. *Family Secrets, Five Important Stories.* Susan Shreve. Knopf, 1979.

   Here are five stories about a boy and his family as they encounter the death of a pet, the suicide of a neighbor, the care of an elderly grandparent, a divorce in the family, and cheating in class. The five episodes in a child's life were written with sensitivity and hopefulness.

4. *Free to Be You and Me.* Edited by Carole Hart, Leroy C. Pogrelin, Mary Rodgers, and Marlo Thomas. McGraw-Hill, 1974.

   This collection of stories, songs, poems, and photos aims to inspire children to their highest potential, regardless of sex or race. A recording of songs in the book is also available.

5. *If I Were in Charge of the World and Other Worries.* Judith Viorst. Atheneum, 1984.

   This is a collection of forty-one poems that give perspective to both children and parents on the feelings and fears that are experienced while growing up.

6. *Listen, Children.* Edited by Dorothy Strickland. Bantam, 1982.

   This is a collection of Afro-American literature—poetry, myths, folklore, and biographies. It includes stories from the lives of Rosa Parks, Wilma Rudolph, and Stevie Wonder.

7. *Sara Crewe.* Francis Hodgson Burnett. Putnam, 1981.

   Sara Crewe attends an exclusive London boarding school. After becoming orphaned and penniless, she lives as a servant under a cruel headmistress. Sara keeps her courage and holds onto her hopes. After she finds a friend, the relationship helps her to realize her dreams.

8. *The Secret Garden.* Frances Hodgson Burnett. Lippincott, 1962.

   This children's classic is about an orphan who comes from India to live with a depressed uncle in his mansion on the moors of England. While trying to amuse herself on the grounds, she discovers a wonderful secret garden, a new friendship with one of the village boys, and a love for an invalid in the old manor. This story is about growth and relationships. It is appropriate for the more experienced listener.

9. *Sing Down the Moon.* Scott O'Dell. Houghton Mifflin, 1979.

   This is a story of the plight of a Navajo Indian girl in 1864, when all of the Navajos were forced from their Arizona home and marched 300 miles to New Mexico. In Fort Sumner, they were prisoners for four years. The story, told by a fourteen-year-old, relates the injustices and great courage that the Navajos showed during this time of oppression by the U.S. government.

10. *Womenfolk and Fairy Tales.* Rosemary Minard. Houghton Mifflin, 1975.

These traditional stories about strong women are suitable for storytelling or reading aloud. The female characters are courageous, clever, and intelligent.

Index

About the Authors

From left to right: Dorothy Nixon, Shirley Vickers,
and Carolyn Mohr.

Carolyn Mohr is a teacher in the Tulakes Gifted Resource Center, Putnam City, Oklahoma, and co-director of "Counterpoint," a summer arts program for talented students. Dorothy Nixon is also a teacher in the Tulakes Gifted Resource Center and is well-known for her workshops on left/right brain activities and implementing whole language programs in the curriculum. Dr. Shirley Vickers is coordinator, Gifted/Talented Programs, Putnam City Schools, and is president, Oklahoma Council for Special Education and president, Oklahomans for Gifted/Talented. She is also a member of the advisory board of the Oklahoma State Department of Education for Gifted Endorsement.

These three women are also the authors of *Thinking Activities for Books Children Love*, published by Libraries Unlimited in 1988.